P9-DWT-665

Complete

GARDEN GUIDE

to the

NATIVE SHRUBS

of

CALIFORNIA

GLENN KEATOR

CHRONICLE BOOKS
SAN FRANCISCO

Copyright © 1994 by Glenn Keator.

All rights reserved. No part of this book
may be reproduced without written permission
from the Publisher.

Printed in the United States of America.

Cover illustration by Kate Thomssen

Illustrations in this book are from
The Manual of Flowering Plants of California
by Willis Linn Jepson, 1925.

Design by Christine Taylor
Typesetting by Wilsted & Taylor

Library of Congress
Cataloging-in-Publication Data available.

ISBN: 0-8118-0402-X

Distributed in Canada by Raincoast Books,
112 East Third Avenue, Vancouver, B.C. V5T 1C8
10 9 8 7 6 5 4 3 2 1
Chronicle Books
275 Fifth Street, San Francisco, California 94103

ACKNOWLEDGEMENT

I offer my sincerest thanks to the Jepson Herbarium.
Illustrations in this book are from
A MANUAL OF THE FLOWERING PLANTS OF CALIFORNIA
by Willis Linn Jepson, 1925.
Permission was granted by the Jepson Herbarium,
University of California at Berkeley.

CONTENTS

PART TWO
ENCYCLOPEDIA *of* NATIVE SHRUBS

PART THREE
APPENDICES

INTRODUCTION

This book deals with the woody plants of California: native shrubs. It has been written to complement the book *Complete Garden Guide to the Native Perennials of California*. Although several books already deal with native shrubs, they address mainly the modest shrub selection carried by even most natives nurseries, with emphasis on the wild lilacs in the genus *Ceanothus* and the manzanitas of the genus *Arctostaphylos*. Here instead are many little-known genera and species, with some unavoidable redundancy in shrubs that are also listed in other books.

The book is organized similarly to *Native Perennials*, beginning with habitats and conditions under which native shrubs grow naturally, then moving on to their needs in the garden, methods of propagation, and suggested landscape uses. The second half is an encyclopedia, organized alphabetically by scientific name. (If you don't know a plant's genus, check the "Cross-References of Common to Scientific Names," p. 70.) For each, encapsulated information directly under each name is followed by a discussion of merits and uses, differentiating species.

Although the book covers a large number of entries, this is only a beginning, for California is particularly rich in diverse shrubs from diverse habitats, and many still await garden trial.

As with the perennials book, I have written the present book based on knowledge of how some shrubs have behaved in my garden, but with educated guesswork and the experience of other gardens for the remainder. I hope the realm of native shrubs will provide an exciting adventure in your garden.

Glenn Keator

PART ONE

COLLECTING, GROWING, *and*

DESIGNING LANDSCAPES

with NATIVE SHRUBS

THE HABITATS OF NATIVE SHRUBS

The gardener's first question when contemplating a new native shrub for the garden should be: "Where does it come from?" This simple question leads to an understanding of the climate, topography, soil, and biological setting for each species. Let's explore each element in turn.

CLIMATE

Climate is the mix of precipitation patterns and temperature fluctuations. Together, precipitation and temperature tell a great deal about the parameters to which any species is adapted. Although these parameters are seldom absolute, they guide an understanding of what plants will or won't flourish in a given garden setting. California's native shrubs come from four basic climates:

1. *Mediterranean.* Mild winters (with relatively few nights of freezing temperatures), rain from winter through spring, and dry, hot summers and falls. This climate is typical of most of coastal California through the foothill region, excluding the immediate coast. Large portions of the gardening public live in this area, so shrubs from a Mediterranean climate are appropriate for large numbers of gardeners.

2. *Modified Mediterranean.* Mild winters (never or seldom freezing), rain from winter through spring, with cool, foggy summers. Fog drip adds extra summer water. This climate is typical of the immediate coastline, especially from Point Conception north in a broadening belt. Many climates are intermediate between true Mediterranean and modified Mediterranean. Shrubs from such climates require a measure of summer water when they're away from the fog belt, and may require cooler summer temperatures and/or shade. A smaller but significant portion of the gardening public lives in this climate or some variation of it.

3. *Desert.* Mild to very cold winters (depending upon elevation), scattered and scant rains in winter and spring, and sometimes flash floods in summer. Very hot summers. The major factor affecting this climate is the low rainfall—frequently less than ten inches per year. In southern California, the population living in or close to a desert climate is increasing.

3

4. *Montane.* Cold to very cold winters (depending upon elevation), with freezing temperatures over several months, snow in winter and spring, and scattered summer thunderstorms. This severely limits the active growing period. Summer temperatures are moderately warm into early fall. Two factors to reckon with are short growing seasons and very cold winters, which keep shrubs dormant. In addition, shrubs from this climate require some summer water. On the plus side of the ledger are the favorable long-day summer months with moderate temperatures, which favor rapid growth. Only a minority of the gardening public lives here.

TOPOGRAPHY

Although California's topography is rugged and varied, its most important elements are not in the ruggedness per se but the drainage and temperatures related to it. The steeper the slope, the better its drainage, which is a major consideration for the gardener. Temperature gradients also relate to topographic features: shrubs from the tops of hills have experienced less cold air than shrubs from hill bottoms. In winter temperatures, for example, the difference between a hilltop and valley bottom can be several degrees, enough to determine a different level of hardiness.

SOILS

Factors relating to soils naturally fall into three broad categories:

1. Soil texture   **2.** Soil pH   **3.** Soil profile

SOIL TEXTURE

Soils are classified by texture as sands, silts, or clays. Sands are coarsest, with relatively large particles and ample air spaces between. Sandy soils drain rapidly and easily and offer good oxygenation to roots, an important factor in maintaining root health. They are relatively low in exchangeable nutrients, however.

Clay soils, at the opposite end of the spectrum, consist of very fine particles with minimal air spaces between. Clay soils retain water well but become hard and cementlike when fully dry. They are poor at allowing proper oxygenation but offer an abundance of exchangeable nutrients. Silts are intermediate, in particle size and density, and so also in their properties' utility for gardening.

Ideal garden soils are called loams, and these offer the best mixture of the properties of sands and clays: good water retention, ample oxygenation between particles, and efficient exchangeability of nutrients. Garden soils are created and continually enhanced by abundant additions of organic material. Original, naturally occurring soils vary widely. Their evolution as garden soil is therefore a continuing creative process, and they improve with the years when properly tended.

Much of California's foothills and valley bottoms have clays, although floodplains of permanent watercourses may have sands or silts, or both. Coastal sand dunes, beaches, and many desert areas offer sandy soils, as does decomposed granite in the high mountains.

SOIL pH

Soil pH is the measure of acidity or alkalinity of soils, literally the proportion of exchangeable hydroxyl to hydrogen ions. An even balance gives a neutral pH (7), while an excess of hydroxyl ions results in alkalinity and an excess of hydrogen ions in acidity. It is important to learn the approximate pH of soils to which each shrub is adapted and then find the corresponding pH in your own garden. Large differences indicate a strong chance of incompatibility. In general, cool, damp coastal climates—particularly under conifer forests—result in acid to very acid soils. Dry, hot areas with scant rainfall often yield soils that are decidedly alkaline. Other areas vary according to climate, the parent rock, and the rock's history as it gradually becomes soil.

Few shrubs are adapted to strongly alkaline soils, but those that are, are useful where there is salt spray from the ocean, or salt crust deposits, and in desert climates. The goosefoot family, Chenopodiaceae, is the best overall source of shrubs adapted to alkaline soils.

Several shrubs are acid lovers. Especially acid loving are shrubs from redwood and pine (or other conifer) forests, and specifically most members of the heather family, Ericaceae.

The pH of garden soil can be changed according to these simple guidelines:

· Test the soil first with a simple pH kit. (Litmus paper will give a very rough idea of relative pH.)

· If soils are too acid, add lime.

· If soils are too alkaline, or need acidification, add ferrous sulfate or plenty of conifer needles.

Soil Profile

A soil's profile tells a great deal about it; a profile is a cross section from the soil's surface down to the underlying bedrock. The O horizon is the organic material that accumulates on soil surfaces; the A layer is the true top soil; and the B layer is the less well developed soil below that, often extending down to bedrock. A thick A layer is typical of soils from river valleys and other bottomlands, while a thin A layer is common in rugged new terrain, where soils have a brief history of development. The O layer varies from practically nil in deserts, where little litter is wasted and recycling is rapid, to a thick thatch in cool montane and coastal forests, where pine needles and other leaf litter decompose slowly. The gardener can enhance any soil by increasing the O layer through mulching, although shrubs that originate in areas where the O layer is minimal may need more direct contact between the air and the top soil.

Finally, there are special kinds of soils that have developed from unique kinds of rocks, such as serpentine, lava, or limestone. Most of these soils drain rapidly and have special pH values (acid for serpentine; alkaline for limestone). They also often have peculiar quirks in their nutrient composition. This is particularly true for serpentine, which is low in calcium but high in magnesium. Shrubs adapted to such soils might be expected to need special nutrient mixes in the garden, but this is seldom the case (as is discussed further, pp. 13–16). Generally, a well-balanced garden soil will give better performance than the original natural soil. The key is to remember pH and drainage, producing what a shrub from a special soil needs on just these two counts.

BIOLOGICAL SETTING

"Biological setting" is just another way of citing the communities in which all plants grow and in which all vegetative components interact. Although animal interactions too may be important, they can generally be ignored unless the same animals play a role in both the garden and the original settings. In particular, deer are important "pruners" in the wilds through their browsing, and in the garden can have the same role, making the difference between vigorous growth and death. Resistance to deer is seldom consistent; in one area the deer may leave a particular species alone in preference to another, but in a different area the same shrub may suffer considerable damage. To avoid depending on trial and error, protect young shrubs through screening or protect the whole garden with tall fences, a double fence being best.

Shrubs are found in two basic types of plant communities: forested and open. Those from forested places obviously need some shade; the amount of shade varies from periodic and partial shading, as at the forest edge, to the full shade of a mature forest's understory, and from the partial shade of an open forest (such as an oak wood-land) to the more solid shade of a fully closed canopy (such as a virgin redwood forest).

Shrubs from open plant communities are usually the dominants there (that is, the most obvious as well as tallest plants), and so need full light. Botanists who deal with such communities—particularly of low-growing or widely spaced shrubs—refer to them as "scrub." Scrub communities are generally much more drought tolerant than others and are amenable to sunny, often summer-hot settings.

Here is a breakdown of plant communities with the important factors to bear in mind for each:

- *Chaparral*. Open shrubland adapted to rocky, often steep slopes with hot, dry summers. Shrubs from here need little or no summer water but plenty of light and good drainage. Chaparral-edge shrubs are short-lived opportunists that grow quickly but don't live long.

- *Montane Chaparral*. Open shrubland similar to regular chaparral but occur-ring from middle to subalpine zones in the mountains; it thus experiences cold to very cold winters with some snow, and summers with occasional water. Shrubs from here are adapted to cold winter temperatures and may need some winter dormancy in the garden. They require excellent drainage but minimal summer water.

- *North Coastal Scrub*. Open shrubland adapted to rocky slopes near the central and northern coasts, where summer fogs prevail. Shrubs from here need occasional summer water to look best, and may need very light shade inland as protection against the hot summer sun.

- *Coastal Sage Scrub*. Open shrubland adapted to sandy to rocky slopes near the coast in southern California. Shrubs from here may survive without summer water but look better with occasional deep watering. Many of these shrubs are tender in areas with cold, freezing winters. Also, many lose leaves when summers are particularly hot and dry.

- *Sagebrush Scrub*. Open shrubland of scattered, well-spaced plants in sandy, sometimes alkaline soils, in high deserts. Shrubs from here show tolerance for alkaline soils, need little water, and survive very cold winters, but they are not likely to do well with cool or foggy summers.

- *Creosote Bush Scrub*. Open shrubland of scattered, well-spaced plants in stony or sandy soils, in low deserts. Shrubs from here have tolerance for slightly alkaline soils, need little or no water, and survive very hot summer tempera-tures. They are not so tolerant of cold winters, and many are quite frost tender. They are also unlikely to adapt to cool or foggy summers.

- *Closed-Cone Pine, North Coastal Coniferous, and Redwood Forests.* All three communities have cool, foggy summers, moderate to abundant winter rains, and acid soils. Notice particularly whether shrubs from here live along the relatively light forest edge or directly under the dense canopy. These shrubs need acid soils, cool summers, light to deep shade, and some summer water. Inland gardens may not duplicate these characteristics, but extra shade and summer water will help.

- *Mixed-Evergreen and Mixed-Coniferous Forests.* These forests, like the three immediately above, also provide dense shade directly underneath, but they have neutral to slightly acid soils, warm to hot summers (some coniferous forests have occasional summer rain), and cool to cold winters (according to elevation). Shrubs from here tolerate hot summers and are winter hardy.

- *Subalpine and Other High-Elevation Forests.* Subalpine forests do not generally produce dense shade. They have very cold winters with relatively little total precipitation, and they have short summer growing seasons punctuated by thunderstorms. Soils are slightly acid. Shrubs from these forests are poor at adapting to most lowland gardens.

- *Riparian Woodlands.* These are river or permanent-stream "corridor" forests, closely following watercourses. Since riparian woodlands occur throughout the state, from the immediate coast to timberline in the mountains and from the far north to the hot southern deserts, there is great variation in temperature tolerances in shrubs from these forests. All need constant moisture, little winter shade (since most trees here are deciduous), and light to heavy shade in summer (when tree crowns are fully leafed out).

- *Oak and Foothill Woodlands.* These are open woodlands with spaces between tree crowns. They experience cool winters with relatively low rainfall and hot, dry summers. Shrubs from here require shade according to their position in the woodland, without summer water and with little winter chill. Many are excellent candidates for the summer dry garden.

TECHNIQUES FOR NATIVE SHRUB
PLANTING AND CARE

TRANSPLANTING

Plant shrubs in their permanent positions after careful planning, which should include details of their placement and design within a pleasing, integrated landscape. Also carefully prepare the site beforehand.

Move shrubs into the garden from one- to five-gallon containers; larger sizes may not move successfully nor adjust to their new home as quickly. Follow this sequence of steps after you've dug one exploratory hole and filled it with water to check for prompt drainage:

1. Mark the site in the garden carefully, taking into account the position of neighboring shrubs and other plantings. If you're planting under a tree, check that the hole you dig won't disturb already established tree roots.

2. Measure the depth of the container, then dig a hole equally deep. Extra depth may be needed where drainage is poor. The diameter of the hole should be twice that of the container.

3. Place a one- to two-inch layer of potting soil or friable loam in the bottom of the hole, and work it into your garden soil. Where drainage is a problem because of heavy soil, increase the bottom layer to several inches of fine gravel below the potting soil. At the same time, mix the soil you've removed from the hole with a good measure of potting soil.

4. Rap the container sharply against a hard surface and slip out the shrub's root ball. The soil should be slightly moist (but not soggy) to aid this process. Inspect the root ball carefully for roots wound around the outside of the ball, and loosen or prune off the worst offenders. Minimize exposure of the root ball to dry air; if you must leave it temporarily, wrap it in wet moss or with a soggy burlap bag.

5. When all is ready, place your new shrub on its layer of potting soil in the prepared hole. Now you can carefully back fill around the root ball with the ammended soil from the hole. Tamp soil carefully around and into the roots without applying excessive pressure. (Too much pressure will destroy delicate feeder roots and compact the soil, thereby eliminating all breathing pores.) Make sure soil completely surrounds all parts of the root system to prevent drying air pockets. Fill in soil to one or two inches from the top of the hole. If you've positioned your plant properly, soil should extend to just below the top of the root crown.

6. Water immediately and thoroughly, until water fills the hole to the rim. Note how swiftly the water disappears into the soil; you may need to flood the hole more than once for complete penetration of water if your soil is dry or porous. Try digging with your finger to determine how deeply the water has soaked. By contrast if water sits for several minutes before soaking in, you've got a major drainage problem and need to start over.

7. Now it's a good idea to do some judicious tip pruning, especially of new growth. New growth is extra vulnerable to drying out and wilting. Roots need to recover from the shock and damage of transplanting before the shrub can resume normal growth. Shrubs should not be transplanted while flowering or fruiting. If they are in this condition, remove all flowers, flower buds, or fruits, or the shrub will continue putting its energy into their development instead of healing and developing new roots.

8. New shrubs may need temporary shading if the air is warm. When air is exceptionally cold or there are overnight frosts, protect shrubs by heavy mulching around the base (at the root crown) or by protective enclosures, since they're vulnerable until well established.

9. For the first few months, check carefully for adequate soil moisture around roots. New growth signals that roots have recovered, and at that point watering becomes less critical. Nonetheless deep, fully established roots take time; new shrubs benefit even in summer from *occasional*, *deep* watering.

MITIGATING MICROCLIMATES' EFFECTS

In addition to an understanding of broad climatic requirements, you need a strong familiarity with the concept of the microclimate, and with the characteristics of the microclimates in your own garden. Most gardens of ordinary size contain these pockets, which differ in temperature, moisture, and sunniness as compared to other parts of the garden. Some of the most dramatic differences are in temperature, at both ends of its range.

Here are some factors of microclimates by which to recognize them or mitigate their effects:

· South and west sides of buildings retain heat best in winter; they also receive the greatest heat in summer.

· Conversely, north and east sides of buildings are coldest in winter; they remain cooler in summer.

- Overhangs, patios, and other extensions from buildings help protect from frost damage and summer heat.

- Low valleys, gulches, and ravines collect cold air in winter; cold air drains from high places into low, where it settles.

- Deciduous trees allow sun to come through in winter, whereas evergreen trees create shade all year.

- The denser the foliage and branch pattern of trees, the heavier the shade they create.

- Tall trees with high limbs (the lower limbs missing) create high shade, allowing the sun to reach what's underneath when its angle is near the horizon.

- Plants that are under trees gain some protection from frost; those fully exposed do not.

- Ponds create cooling local microclimates in summer and may help moderate winter chill.

- Shade can shift patterns according to season and time of day to greatly varying effects.

- The color of the soil or of mulch or other dressing helps determine the temperature of the soil surface; dark soils absorb heat and can become unbearably hot in full sun.

- Soils in shade dry out much less rapidly than those in full sun. Allow for the fact that the trees creating the shade do have thirsty roots.

- Shallowly rooted trees create much drier conditions for shrubs than deeply rooted trees.

- Mulched surfaces lose moisture much less rapidly than fully exposed soils.

PRUNING

Pruning encourages the development of side branches from dormant buds below the point of the cut stem. Pruning may be used to achieve the following results:

- Remove dead stems and branches that would otherwise create a fire hazard and eyesore. Dead branches often occur below living branches and are brittle and leafless.

- Encourage bushier shape or more branching in a horizontal direction.

- Create multiple trunks where one formerly existed. (In order to do this effectively, you need to prune the main trunk early in the shrub's life.)

- Remove the previous year's growth to encourage a new framework of branches. This is often necessary with woody vines such as wild grapes and vine honey-suckle, and with such subshrubs as Matilija poppy. Old growth simply gets in the way of the new, so that new growth is not as vigorous or healthy as it otherwise would be.

- Encourage more primary growth. This is often especially effective in cases where flowers appear on new growth rather than old. Keep careful notes on where flowers are initiated for each kind of shrub—on new growth only, old growth only, or both.

- Reshape the shrub. Sometimes drastic pruning can serve as a sort of surgery (for example, on an overly tall, spindly shrub, to create a dense, rounded crown).

- Maintain formal shapes, such as those for closely spaced hedges. Pruning should be frequent.

- Open up the framework of the shrub. Too great denseness, especially toward the middle of the shrub where little light penetrates, results in a maze of ugly overlapping, unhealthy branches. Opening the middle and interior creates a spacious, airy feel, improves overall health and vigor, and is visually pleasing. This is particularly important if you want to display the beautiful bark colors and textures of such dramatic shrubs as manzanitas, ironwood, and red shanks. (The exception to openness being an advantage is with hedges and barrier plantings.)

Ordinary lopping shears should work for 80 percent of pruning chores; if branches are so thick they can't be removed this way, the shrub has been neglected much too long. Pruning saws will take care of very thick trunks and branches.

The degree and frequency of pruning needed vary according to the kind of shrub and time of year. Generally, it's easier to shape a shrub during its dormant period—in summer for many chaparral shrubs and in winter for many deciduous shrubs—but watch closely for fungal infections in cuts made during sieges of wet weather.

Finally, remember that shrubs may lose their ability to regenerate if you prune too far back on old growth; usually you can determine if this vulnerability exists by noting whether buds are still visible. For example, junipers keep dormant buds for a few years, then lose them and the ability to resprout. Pruning back too far on such shrubs causes slow death of the branch, or sometimes the entire plant. In general, the faster-growing shrubs can be pruned harder and more completely than the slower-growing kinds.

MANAGEMENT OF SOIL AND WATER

No other factors are so important to successful cultivation of shrubs than soil and water. Probably more shrubs have been killed by improper management of these two factors than by any other factor. Yet despite these failures, the basics of soil and watering are straightforward: soils should be loose, friable, well draining, and amended with organic materials; watering should temporarily saturate soil to its full depth, then be repeated only when the upper surface is thoroughly dry. If these rules are adhered to, few problems result for the majority of plants. Of course, there are always exceptional plants whose roots need to be in constantly moist soil, but even then some movement of water is necessary to maintain health.

Soils that never drain and are finely textured with few pores are to be avoided. If you have soil such as heavy clay with an underlying hardpan, you must either improve the soil in some way or water with extreme caution. It is always best to change the soil condition to a more favorable one than to try to compensate by not watering much. Let's look at these two factors in more detail.

SOILS

The ideal garden soil is one whose texture (due to the pores between soil particles) is loose and crumbly, but not so coarse or porous that water moves right through. Sandy soils are too coarse and have major problems with proper water retention; clay or adobe soils are too fine and have little pore space for the needed oxygen exchange between roots and air. They also drain too slowly. The ideal soil is therefore a loam with intermediate properties. Another consideration is that the upper topsoil layer have some organic material in it. This allows better pore structure while helping retain water, and adds minor amounts of needed minerals.

In California you are likely to have either a sand- or clay-type soil. In some ways, sandy soils are the most difficult: although they drain well, they dry out rapidly and are hard to rewet after drying. Also, most sandy soils are low in organic matter. Consequently, the only effective way to improve sandy soils is to add lots of vegetable matter—a compost pile is a handy source, or use peat moss, leaf mold, or shredded bark.

One caution should be observed with regard to adding organic matter: some types of leaves and twigs break down to create an uncommonly high acidity (especially pine and other conifer needles). These are best used for plants whose original habitats have acid soil (for example, rhododendrons, azaleas, and huckleberries from redwood forests). Homemade compost, if properly heated, should be relatively safe in this respect. Many available books detail the ways to make a workable compost pile.

Strangely enough, the way to improve a clay soil as well is to add lots of organic matter. You can also add sand or various other amendments such as perlite or vermiculite, but the quantities needed and the general loss of them through the soil makes this costly and wasteful. Adding organic matter year after year finally results in an airy, crumbly soil.

For both sandy and clay soils, there is another solution that is swift and effective: build your garden with good soil on top of the original soil. This has two advantages: it raises the overall level of soil to give improved drainage, since the beds are now raised, and it introduces soil whose structure is better suited to plant growth right from the start. For this method, consider three factors:

1. Raised beds help only with smaller shrubs; large shrubs, of a height greater than four feet or so, have more deeply delving roots that require more than a foot of amended soil.

2. Mixing the new and old soils at their interface, so there is a gradual transition from old to new, prevents water from accumulating or running off there.

3. The depth of a new soil layer that will allow plenty of root room is a minimum of about a foot.

The ideal way to utilize this concept is to create raised beds bordered by wood planks or rocks so that the beds are totally independent of the original soil cover.

For truly large shrubs, the best solution is to plant on a slope. Provide ample room around the original root ball for amended soil, work it partly into the native soil, and exercise great care not to overwater.

One final alternative to the poor-soil syndrome is to garden in containers. If you have a deck or lawn around which to place planters, this may be the ideal solution. You can fill containers with the best possible soil—a potting mix that has already been sterilized. As in raised beds, truly large shrubs may not always lend themselves to container culture, although many can be trained in the manner of bonsai by periodic careful clipping of the root ball, removal of extra branches, and application of balanced fertilizer. It is beyond the scope of this book to go into bonsai techniques; there are many other books on the subject.

Questions frequently raised about soil for native shrubs are:

· Do shrubs require special soils when they have grown on unusual soils in nature (for example, serpentine)?

· How often do they need fertilizer?

The answer to the first question is a resounding "no." Shrubs grow naturally on special soils—dolomite, limestone, serpentine, lava—not because they need those soils but because they avoid competition there, since these soils provide unfavorable growing conditions for the majority of plants. Some kinds of shrubs also grow on these special soils only in stunted form; in these cases, the stunted quality disappears when they're moved to ordinary fertile soils. With serpentine shrubs in particular, experiments have shown that many actually perform better when planted in ordinary garden soil, as long as they don't have to compete with other plants.

Two additional factors in the performance of shrubs from special soil are drainage and soil pH. Shrubs from rocky soils need sharp drainage; shrubs from acid soils seldom grow well in neutral or alkaline soils. Litmus paper can be used to get a rough idea of pH conditions. Remember that soils from conifer forests and, in general, from damp cool climates are acid, and soils from hot desert areas range toward alkalinity. Lime (calcium carbonate) will sweeten an acid soil; pine duff and leaching help to correct alkalinity. The process of leaching involves passing water through the soil to remove excessive salts; it would be successful only where drainage is excellent.

With respect to fertilizer, the general rule is not to worry about it. Few native shrubs are used to highly rich soils. Thus, for most species, a light fertilizing is all that is needed for ordinary growth, and that is sometimes unnecessary. In general, soils low in organic matter and sandy soils need nutrient supplements more than other soils. Also in general, woodland shrubs may need extra fertilizing because of hungry nearby tree roots. Excess fertilizer is likely to be harmful to most shrubs, particularly fertilizers rich in nitrogen, since this makes growth unnaturally prolific. When shrubs grow faster or for longer periods without rest than they would in nature, their growth may become spindly or they may burn themselves out, thus shortening their usual life spans. The best fertilizers are those with slow release of nutrients: for containerized shrubs, Osmacote; for bedded shrubs, an organic source such as manure that has been well rotted beforehand. Garden conditions may shorten natives' life cycles through their nutrient richness; one does not need to compound this by adding rich fertilizers. However, when seedlings or newly rooted cuttings are just starting out, it is beneficial to boost vigorous new growth with a dressing of Osmacote pellets.

MULCHES FOR SOIL

One final word about soils is a word much in favor today: mulch. Mulches are top dressings of soil other than the soil itself; they vary almost as widely as do soils. The several sound reasons for mulching are as follows:

- Most mulches gradually release trace nutrients to the topsoil.

- Most mulches gradually break down into smaller bits of organic matter, which help improve upper soil texture and maintain crumbliness.

- Mulches often improve the appearance of beds, giving them a tidier look.

- Mulches smother and suppress growth of weed seedlings.

- Mulches help retain soil moisture so that much less water is lost.

The last two reasons are perhaps the most important and persuasive. Mulches are applied everywhere but on the shrubs, thus keeping weed-pulling chores low. And because a mulch helps cover vulnerable top soil, loose particles are not carried away by winds, nor are they dried rapidly by heat and winds as they otherwise would be. In gardens where water is minimized to begin with, mulches make extra summer water even less necessary.

What materials can be used for mulching? The list is a long one, and even inorganic materials are used (though they are less desirable). Here are some possibilities: black plastic (strictly for keeping weeds down; does not amend soils), ordinary leaf duff or mold (pine and other conifer needles help create acid soils), compost (please—well rotted only), grass trimmings, cocoa hulls, pressings from grapes, coarsely ground bark (again, conifer bark helps maintain acidity), and pea gravel. The thicker the mulch, the more effective it is for reducing evaporation and weeds. But remember, mulch that is to have benefit beyond just inhibiting weeds must be coarse enough to allow plenty of air channels, to keep oxygen flowing into the soil for healthy roots.

WATERING

If your soil is loose and friable and your drainage good, sufficient watering is much easier to gauge. Remember, the advantage of many native shrubs is that they seldom need to be watered. Their cycles are geared to the climate you live in—namely late-fall, winter, and spring rains and a dry period in summer and early fall. But note that there are many important exceptions to this rule. Here are the outstanding ones:

· All shrub seedlings and cuttings need constant moisture.

· Most shrubs, even if planted during the rainy season, need some summer water their first year to establish deep roots.

· Many shrubs look better if they receive occasional, thorough summer water.

· Shrubs from bog and wet meadow margins must have summer water.

· Shrubs from the higher mountains need summer water.

· Shrubs from redwood forests and other coastal forests need some summer water.

· Shrubs planted in sandy soils may require some summer water.

· Shrubs from coastal situations need summer water when planted inland.

The biggest worry about watering shrubs in summer (other than that extra time is needed to do so) is that some are actually killed this way. Water molds and other soil fungi (such as oak root fungus) grow rapidly in summer, when conditions are both wet and warm. They grow so slowly or poorly in winter that wetness is seldom a problem. The only way to learn about which shrubs are sensitive to these fungi is through trial. Many chaparral shrubs are sensitive, as are native oaks. Any native oak in your garden may be weakly infected with this fungus pathogen, which may then pass from the oak roots to adjacent roots of shrubs, so extreme caution is needed.

A few rules about how water is applied will help assure success:

· Water in the early morning, if possible. Evening watering may encourage mildew; watering during the warm hours of the day promotes leaf burn and wastes water through evaporation.

· Water thoroughly. Each situation differs in time required for a thorough soaking, but remember it is always better to water thoroughly a few times than to water skimpily many times. Water needs to penetrate to the bottom layers of soil in order to encourage roots to reach deep. Deeply penetrating roots carry the plant over dry periods much better than shallow roots. In general, sandy soils need to be watered longer than loams; clay soils require the shortest time. You can determine how thoroughly the soil is wetted by digging down into it.

· The frequency of watering should depend upon soil type, the original environment of the plant (as outlined above), the amount of organic material in the soil, the angle of slope, and the season. Remember that organic matter helps retain water, making frequent watering less necessary. The steeper the slope, the more poorly it retains water. And, of course, on hot summer days soils dry much faster than they do on cool winter days. Another condition to watch for is wind: wind can evaporate water from leaf surfaces just as rapidly as hot sun.

- It is best to apply water as a slow seepage, with a soaker hose or from emitters of a drip system. Drip systems work well where large shrubs form a foundation or barrier-type planting, or where single shrubs stand apart from smaller plants. There are sophisticated computerized timer systems that unify drip systems for the entire garden.

SOURCES OF NATIVE SHRUBS

COMMERCIAL OUTLETS

One of the most important questions for the gardener is where to obtain a particular shrub. The answer must be qualified and expanded when it comes to natives because commercial sources are all limited, and the wilds as a source offers its own set of restrictions. The range of native shrubs available from nurseries is often standardized, even from those dealing exclusively in natives. This would seem contradictory were it not for the economic realities of business: most native nurseries are small and depend upon each item selling well enough to make carrying it worthwhile; only the shrubs that are already well known sell. It's a sort of catch-22 in which new material has no existing place, so it is seldom introduced. There are, however, quite a number of native nurseries; see the list in Appendix A.

Some commercial outlets do offer the more unusual natives, and these outlets also help support a number of nonprofit organizations whose specialty is plants: the various botanical gardens, arboreta, and plant societies. Most such sales occur only annually, so it is important to find out the dates. An especially fine source of material is the local chapter sales of the California Native Plant Society. The society is instrumental in helping preserve and teach the value of natives, and membership is quite reasonable. Also see Appendix A for a list of the society and other organizations.

There are several advantages to obtaining material from propagators:

- Material is usually accurately named.

- The more decorative cultivars are offered.

- Material is grown under garden conditions; root systems may be more vigorous than otherwise is possible.

· At reputable firms, material is propagated from already established garden stock rather than depleting wild populations.

One of the biggest problems with nursery material is that the time at which it looks best may be the worst time to plant it. If yours is a garden with little summer water, do not plant shrubs in the late spring or summer. Instead, wait until late fall or even winter before planting. Such a plan follows nature's cycles better, allowing the natural rains to do the watering and inducing the least amount of shock in the plant at transplanting time because of its semidormancy.

A third commercial source for shrubs is seed houses (also listed in Appendix A), although there are several disadvantages in their use:

· Shrubs from seed take considerably longer to reach maturity, and they do so with less uniformity (cultivars do not come true from seed).

· Some seed outlets do not have accurate identification of their material.

· Some seed outlets do not check the fertility of their seed, with the result that some batches may have low viability. (This is partly because some seed is gathered directly from the wild.)

· Germination of native shrubs is often much trickier than propagation from cuttings.

Aside from these drawbacks, seeds give a considerably broader range of available material than do other means of propagation, and they are interesting because of the variation found in the offspring. This is the way a new and desirable form may appear.

CONSIDERATIONS IN TAKING SHRUBS
FROM THE WILDS

If you cannot find the species you desire from commercial outlets, there is only one other way to go: natives from their own homes in the wilds. Before embarking on this route, however, consider the reasons for *not* using this source. Problems include: accurate identification of the plant, finding the plant at the right stage (especially for mature seeds), doing the removal legally (there are laws with fines covering removal), establishing a vigorous plant in the garden, serious depletion of plants in the wilds—disturbing the population and its breeding potential, and risking the high probability of killing a plant that is unable to adapt to garden conditions. If you feel you can deal with these problems reasonably, then read on—there are ways of obtaining shrubs from the wild with minimal impact and high chances for success.

Accurate Identification

The means of identifying your shrub may be available at a local university. However, don't rely on experts to identify large numbers of plants; they don't have the time. A better way is to have access to a library of books covering various parts of the state, unless you're already an expert and can use the technical manuals, such as Munz's *A California Flora*. You're apt to need many books for cross-referencing and for the sake of completeness; no one book covers everything unless it's a technical book, written at the level of advanced students. The use of line drawings, photographs, and flower color guides is helpful but is only a beginning. One of the best bets is to take plant identification courses from your local university extension or community college, so you know the important traits to look for and how to use an identification key. Appendix B lists some identification guides.

Finding the Shrub at the Right Stage for Propagation

The right stage depends on the method of propagation used. If, for example, you take cuttings from a shrub, you need to know the seasonal cycle of wood formation, and whether you need softwood, semisoft wood, or hardwood. If the shrub is not in flower it may be much harder to identify. And seeds, if they are your goal, usually ripen after the flowers have passed. Many shrubs may be hard to find when out of flower or fruit, so learn the plants in a given area, and when they flower, tag them so that you can identify them later.

Removing Parts of a Plant Legally

For legal removal you need a state collecting permit or permission from owners of private land. Many ranchers are glad to learn about plants on their land and, once they understand what you intend, are generous. Finally, *if* there is a new housing development or new road in an area formerly covered with mature vegetation, rescue work is not only legitimate, it's a way of saving some of the gene pool that would otherwise be lost. Large shrubs are unlikely to make the move successfully, so even in newly developing areas, transplanting should be limited to young shrublets in their first or second year.

Establishing a Vigorous Plant

Establishing plants is a problem we'll devote considerable attention to in the next chapter. Remember that timing is all important, and that for a rooted plant to adapt to a new home it must be removed when growth has slowed or halted during the rainy season. Another rule is that the greater the difference in climate between the plant's home and yours, the less likely rooted portions will move successfully. When the difference is considerable, plants should be started from cuttings or from seed.

HOW TO TAKE WILD PLANT MATERIALS

Now, consider a few of the rationales behind *not* taking shrubs from their environment. After all, many species and varieties are threatened in various ways: they are already rare, they are in a sensitive habitat that is being threatened, they have been sought by too many other collectors, or they have been wiped out by agricultural or other development. A list of rare and endangered plants is available from the California Native Plant Society; any plant on the list should be left alone in the wild and obtained only from already existing sources. What is the impact of taking shrubs, if they are not threatened or endangered in any way? It depends upon the method used.

Collecting Seeds

This is one of the most appropriate ways of taking shrubs. Consider that shrubs live several to many years, and so have many chances to make new seeds before they die. Seeds are needed in quantity in the wild to maintain genetic diversity and to overcome the pitfalls that await them—pests and diseases, consumption by animals and birds, and landing in the wrong place or at the wrong time. For this reason, don't collect large quantities of seeds at any one spot. You have better chances for more interesting variation, too, if you collect seeds from different plants in different locales.

Taking Cuttings

This is the best—least harmful—way of removing material, as long as you don't deplete any single plant of too many branches. Cuttings may actually stimulate the original plant to grow more vigorously, just as though you were pruning it. Be sure to observe the methods discussed in the next chapter to minimize any injury to the plant. Be aware that improper pruning can lead to wounds vulnerable to attack by insects and fungi.

DIGGING ENTIRE PLANTS

Shrubs should never be dug from the wild unless they are in imminent danger of being destroyed by development or road construction. Few mature shrubs make the move from one place to another, and the problem is compounded from the natural site to the garden. Shrub rescue transplanting should be limited to only young plants where a full root ball can be secured.

PROPAGATION OF NATIVE SHRUBS

Shrubs are propagated by seeds, cuttings, layering, suckers, and pups. Assume that you have already obtained shrubs, or you simply want to increase what you already have in the garden. What is involved with each kind of propagation?

SEEDS

The handling of seeds can be broken into component parts: seed storage, cleaning, pretreatment, planting, and seedling establishment.

SEED STORAGE

Seeds should be stored in airtight containers, away from heat and humidity. Glass jars are good containers, although cardboard boxes and paper bags may suffice. Not only do seeds need careful storage, it's best to plant them as soon as possible in order to realize maximum viability (fertility), although some shrub seeds are capable of remaining in a viable dormant state for several years. Those of chaparral shrubs adapted to fire are a prime example. Generally, the smaller the seed the less food reserve is available to carry the embryo through long dormant periods. In order for their life cycles to be in sync, plant seeds in late fall or early winter after rains have begun.

SEED CLEANING

It is not always necessary to clean pods or other chaff from seeds meticulously, but the more chaff is present, the greater the chance of contamination by fungal spores. This in turn leads to fungal infection and the demise of seedlings. Some seeds separate readily from their containers, and it is merely a matter of dumping them out to separate the chaff. Other pods become brittle, flaking off as seeds are prodded from them; in still other cases, the seeds are firmly enveloped by their containers, which must be broken open to release them. Where there is lots of chaff, gentle blowing may suffice to remove the lighter chaff, leaving the heavier seeds behind. Sometimes a little mechanical help eases the task. Various sizes of screens are available that will retain the seeds while allowing the chaff to pass through.

For seeds contained inside a tough ovary wall, methods are used according to size: the larger nuts (oak acorns, for example) are best handled by being individually cracked to remove the seed inside, or by being planted intact. Smaller hard fruits, such as the achenes of composites and roses or the nutlets of mints, are handled by crushing the achenes inside a paper bag, then winnowing away the chaff. In many cases, the achenes are so tiny (in the wild buckwheats, for example) that the whole achene is planted as though it were the seed.

Finally, a number of seeds are embedded in fleshy fruits. Often, a useful method here is to soak the seeds thoroughly, then force the pulp through a sieve that holds back the seeds. Fruits may also be left to ferment or rot, to make the removal of the flesh easier. This rotting process promotes softening of the seed coat, a necessary step for many since the fruits normally pass through the digestive tracts of animals before germination.

If seeds are contaminated with extraneous material or you suspect that fungal spores are present, rinse the seeds in a weak solution of bleach, which oxidizes and kills foreign matter. Be sure the solution does not penetrate the seeds, and that it is not strong enough to remove the seed coat. Gauge this by starting with a 10 percent solution of bleach to water as a trial on a few seeds; if rinsing removes the seed coat, bleach is penetrating the seed.

SEED PRETREATMENT

Shrub seeds are quite unpredictable in their readiness to germinate. Usually, the right combination of moisture (wet soils), day length (short days), and temperature (cool to cold nights) is necessary for germination, but even then many seeds steadfastly refuse to germinate, or do so only after months or years. Such seeds need pretreatment to break dormancy. Here are general guidelines (to which there are always exceptions) to determine whether seeds need pretreatment.

- *High-mountain shrubs* most often require stratification (described below). Stratification can be tried for one month, six weeks, two months, or even more, to determine the optimal time for each species.

- *High-desert shrubs* also require stratification.

- *Fleshy-fruited shrubs* frequently produce seeds with hard coats, which need partial removal or softening. Removal may be accomplished by filing the coat or by passing the seeds across sandpaper (scarifying); softening is done by placing them in a weak acid solution for a few minutes, then rinsing. Sometimes the act of soaking the seeds is sufficient; you can tell by noting whether the seeds swell, an indication that water has been taken in through the coat.

- *Chaparral shrubs* often are sensitive to fire. Such seeds may require the fire pretreatment (also described below) in order to germinate. Stratification may be substituted with more even results for some species.

- *Any seed with a very tough or hard coat* should be treated as you would fleshy-fruited shrubs.

- *If germination is poor without pretreatment,* try stratification. It is always best to retain some seeds for future trials.

Stratification is a cold treatment often needed by shrubs that are subjected to freezing winters, in order to trigger germination. To stratify, put seeds into damp perlite or sphagnum moss in a plastic bag, and put the bag into the refrigerator. Usually the regular cold compartment is sufficient, but certain seeds do better in the freezer. Some seeds even germinate while in the refrigerator; hence the advantage of using plastic bags to check progress. Plant immediately if you see signs of roots or leaves.

The special fire (also called burn) pretreatment is to plant seeds in the soil, then place pine needles or excelsior paper on top and set them on fire. Experimentation will determine how deep to plant seeds and how thick to make the fuel. The idea is to let the heat of the fire crack the seed coats but not destroy the embryos inside.

SEED PLANTING

This is a surprisingly simple task, given a little common sense. Seeds may be started in shallow flats, in separate plastic pots, or in peat pots. Each has its advantage: flats hold greater numbers of seeds; plastic pots are cheap and each may hold only one kind of seed; peat pots are directly plantable in the garden without disturbing the seedlings, though they tend to dry out quickly. The only soil to use is well-known commercial potting mixes. This cannot be overstated; potting soil has the advantages of good aeration and lack of disease pathogens and pests. An additional precaution is to water with a pan-drench-type fungicide. Damping-off and other fungal diseases are the worst foes of newly germinated seeds.

Two other points to consider are planting depth and thickness of sowing. Planting depth should be roughly once to twice the diameter of the seed; very fine seeds may be sprinkled on top of the soil and secured with a sprinkling of fine sand or fine sphagnum. How thickly you sow the seeds is determined by whether you intend to thin seedlings soon or leave them in place for some time. Sow thickly if you feel mortality of seedlings is likely to be high, or if you intend to thin quickly. To broadcast seeds more sparsely, mix them with fine sand beforehand.

Seeds need frequent watering; soil should remain damp but *not* soggy. It is especially important to have a soil mix that drains quickly. Extra-coarse sand may be added for plants that live in habitats with soils of grit or gravel. Seed beds should never dry out and should not be in direct sun. Special attention is needed with peat pots, because they dry so quickly—a saucer of water can be put under the pots or the pots plunged into a tray of moist soil, but capillary action may form a salt crust on the soil surface this way. The best way to water seeds is with a fine misting attachment so that soil is not disturbed in the process. Otherwise, seeds may be washed from their secure holes or clumped together.

Seed beds also need extra protection from snails, slugs, and birds. Snail bait takes care of the first two; mesh or netting above the seed bed should keep birds out. Otherwise, birds peck out seeds before they sprout, and later cut off tender seedlings.

Seedling Establishment

Much failure occurs at this critical step. At some point, the new seedlings need to be transplanted into their permanent environment, unless that environment is to remain a pot. Certain seedlings move poorly (for example, some taprooted shrubs) and should be started in deep pots and left there for several seasons, until adult plants are ready for moving. Most plants, however, can be moved into the garden in two or three stages. When seedlings have their first or second set of *true* leaves (as opposed to cotyledons), they are ready for thinning and transplanting. If there is an excess of plants at this stage, the weaker seedlings may be discarded. Seedlings generally need to be moved into deeper flats or small pots as an intermediate stage. These can then be gradually placed in ever stronger light to toughen the seedlings, and to allow maximum growth until they have reached gallon-can size. It is difficult to generalize about this size. Seedlings should be vigorous and have several sets of leaves before they are ready for the cans. When they have finally developed vigorous root systems throughout the cans, they are ready for the garden.

When seedlings are moved into their permanent position in the garden, they should be watched for at least two months. If seedlings have not reached a transplantable size by early spring, they should be carried over in the cans until the next rainy season for easiest establishment. Seedlings transplanted in late spring would otherwise have to be watched diligently and watered often. Even if seedlings are transplanted by early spring, they need to be checked for signs of wilting, and may require watering between rains. Some seedlings—even drought-tolerant species—do not establish deep roots fast enough to carry them through their first summer. Attention is needed to assure survival for that first critical dry period. By the second dry season, plants should be on their own.

CUTTINGS

Some subshrubs cannot be started from cuttings, since their stems are simply too soft to strike root before rotting. Fortunately, most of these can be readily propagated by seeds, and this is an easier way to go. Cuttings are most successful in shrubs with semi-woody to woody tissue in their branches or twigs. There are three categories of cuttings:

1. *Herbaceous Cuttings.* These are useful for a few species, such as certain penstemons and diplacuses that produce a minimum of woody tissue.

2. *Half-Woody Cuttings.* These are taken from small shrubs that develop woody tissue toward the base of the plant. Half-woody tissues occur when growth has halfway hardened, and this, in turn, depends upon the growth cycle. For example, shrubs that begin to grow in spring won't develop half-woody tissue until early summer, while those that commence growth in summer won't develop it until the summer's end. Half-woody cuttings are often the easiest way to increase subshrubs such as various salvias, solanums, and artemisias.

3. *Ripe-Wood (or Fully Woody) Cuttings.* These are taken after a full year's growth has occurred, because in shrubs the secondary growth that produces bark and wood doesn't get into full swing until a given branch has aged a year or more. Sometimes it won't be obvious whether a given shrub should be started from half-ripe or fully ripe wood; in these cases, both methods should be tried.

Obviously, then, to make successful cuttings some experimentation is necessary. Most important is the timing of taking the cuttings, and this can only be determined after getting acquainted with a particular species' growth cycle.

The process for cutting itself involves these safeguards:

1. Never take so many cuttings from a shrub that no primary branches are left. The bigger the original shrub, the more cuttings it will yield.

2. Always make cuts with a clean, sharp knife or pruning shears. To be meticulously clean, dip the shears in bleach before using.

3. Take cuttings of no longer than three or four inches.

4. Remove the lowest leaves of a cutting from the nodes, and rub or scratch the nodes to stimulate root growth (new roots develop from them). Incidentally, there's some controversy over whether rubbing the node is beneficial.

5. Remove flowers or fruits from the cutting. (Otherwise all the reserve food will go toward completing their development.)

6. Nip back the upper leaves so that only part of each is left for photosynthesis; this reduces the surface area exposed to air and consequent wilting.

7. Rinse the cuttings, or if there's reason to suspect fungal contamination, dip them in a fungicide or in bleach.

8. Dip the tips of cuttings in a rooting hormone (this speeds up the rooting process, but it will not cause roots to form if they would not otherwise) and shake off the excess.

Cuttings normally shouldn't go into ordinary garden soil, although some shrubs seem to root easily no matter what you do. For best results, set up a special cutting bed with the following considerations in mind:

· The bed should be in a shallow tray so that cuttings can be moved around to different sites as needed.

· Drainage holes in the tray are of utmost importance. Equally important is the medium used in the tray; ordinary garden soil should never be used. The ideal medium allows rapid drainage (to prevent rot) and good aeration. Most propagators use perlite, vermiculite, sand, or a combination. Some like to add chopped sphagnum moss or peat for better water retention.

· Cuttings should be inserted into the medium up to the intact leaves.

· Cuttings should be watered frequently, since they have no roots by which to absorb water.

· The rooting process can often be speeded by a special cable placed under the propagation bed to provide bottom heat. Cables for this purpose are available at many nurseries. The ideal temperature is around 70 degrees F. You could alternately rig a number of incandescent lights below the starting bed, but be sure to eliminate any risk of electrical shock from water. Check the soil temperature with a soil thermometer; elevated temperatures will cook cuttings.

· The cutting bed should be placed out of bright or direct light, since this only increases wilting and water loss. Commercial growers use glasshouses whose windows are heavily glazed or whitewashed.

· Covering the cutting bed with plastic or frequent misting helps reduce wilting, but care is needed to provide ventilation, or the cuttings will certainly rot. Automatic misters are available for those with the money and inclination.

Cuttings vary greatly in the speed with which they form roots; most take one to two or three months, so don't give up if roots don't form right away. You may gently loosen the cutting from the medium to check progress; if the lower stem feels mushy, the cutting has rotted; if the lower stem ends in a swelling (callus), root formation may soon begin. Be careful not to overdo your probing; too much disturbance is bound to retard root formation. Sometimes you can trim off the rotted portion of a cutting before it's gone too far and try again.

Cuttings should have several roots each, the roots an inch or more long, before they are ready to be moved. As with seedlings, don't move a rooted cutting directly into the garden; move it into a small pot, which you carefully watch. Gradually expose pots with rooted cuttings to more sun until the new plants are hardened off. If you started the cuttings in a glasshouse, also gradually habituate them to fluctuating temperatures. Again as with seedlings, it pays to move your new plant from a small pot to a gallon can before making the final move into the garden. You will know when plants are ready to be moved by checking to see if the roots protrude through the bottom drainage hole. Exercise care that the plant does not become root bound in its pot; this condition is obvious when you tamp the plant from its pot and see a series of roots wound tightly around the edge of the exposed root ball.

LAYERING

Layering is a variation on making cuttings; it involves a newly rooted section that is still attached to its parent plant. Layering is used where a branch can be bent to the ground and held there by a pin, or held simply by the weight of soil placed over it. Bury the section of stem after partially breaking it, removing leaves from the nodes in that area, and rubbing the nodes. Layering may take several months, but it has the advantage that the newly rooted plantlet is nourished and watered by the parent plant. When vigorous roots have formed, the new plant can be severed from the parent with a sharp knife.

Another kind of layering uses an upright branch. Remove leaves from and irritate a node at which you wish to have roots form, then wrap it in moistened sphagnum moss in a plastic cover. Many house plants are layered in this manner.

Many shrubs with low, pliable branches are amenable to rooting by layering; these include azaleas, spicebush, carpenteria, currants, and several others noted in the Encyclopedia section that follows.

SUCKERS

Suckers are stump sprouts, produced at the base of shrubs or from their sometimes wandering roots. Propagation by suckers is straightforward: cut off each sucker with a clean, sharp knife, and include as many attached roots as possible. Treat these suckers as you would a newly divided perennial or newly rooted cutting.

PUPS

Pups are the young plantlets encircling a mother plant and connected to the mother plant by underground stems. You find pups most often with rosette-forming succulents, including agaves and yuccas. Each pup may be severed from the parent by cutting the connection carefully with a sharp, clean knife. Be sure you miss the roots of the pup during this process. Treat each pup as you would a newly rooted cutting.

SIGNIFICANT FEATURES OF SHRUBS IN THE GARDEN

There are a number of shrub traits that merit serious consideration before you choose among shrubs for the garden. This section details the most important:

- shape and habit
- height
- leaves: deciduous or evergreen, dense pattern or thin; also leaf color and texture
- bark: color, pattern, and texture
- flowers: time of flowering, showiness, and flower color
- fruits: time of fruiting, showiness, and shape and color
- fragrance: fragrant leaves, bark, or flowers
- speed of growth

Any choice of shrub should rest on knowledge of these traits.

SHAPE AND HABIT

This characteristic is the first to make an impression, and the primary one with which you'll live from day to day. "Habit" is the word describing the overall aspect of a plant: its shape, actually, but implying as well the future shape that its growth patterns suggest. Bear in mind both points:

- *Overall shape.* Is the shrub pyramidal, conical, squat, rounded, globular, or some other shape? Tall, narrow shapes emphasize the vertical elements in the garden, with the reverse true for low, squat shapes. Startling contrasts may be created by planting shrubs of widely differing shapes side by side, but indiscriminate use of this technique will result in an unattractive hodgepodge. Similarity of shapes in neighboring shrubs helps harmonize plantings.

- *Ultimate shape.* The original shape of any shrub when first installed in the garden is not its final shape. In addition, the original shrub may spread by underground roots or suckers to create a hedge row or dense amalgamation of additional shrubs. Thus, the ultimate shape and visual effect of a shrub may differ greatly from the original. If these differences are not accommodated, expect to constantly do battle against the shrub's wanderlust.

HEIGHT

This characteristic is so obvious, it is sometimes overlooked. So many elements affect ultimate height, it isn't necessarily predictable. Genetics is the prime determinant. It gives each shrub a certain ultimate potential. But within the potential range of height the appropriateness of the habitat (including soil fertility, watering regime, and shading) determines the outcome. Also consider the time required for a shrub to attain its mature size. With slow-growing shrubs the changing aspect may be more easily accommodated than with rapid-growing shrubs.

Take into account as well how the shrub's likely height will influence the effect desired (to screen, form a backdrop, create a border), and how its height might impinge on all other plantings. Though it seems obvious that low shrubs go in front of tall shrubs, the obviousness can come to mind sometimes only in retrospect.

LEAVES

Leaf Patterns. How do leaves change from one season to another? Do they always remain in the same proportion on branches, or do they vary from season to season? The major seasonal changes relate to whether a shrub is deciduous or evergreen.

Evergreen shrubs should be used where an unchanging pattern is wanted, such as for screening, hedges, foundation plantings, or dramatic backdrops. Such shrubs can be thought of as immutable elements of the landscape, except for their flowering and fruiting.

Deciduous shrubs, in contrast, present possibilities for drama and change all year. They provide special focal points, perhaps as containerized plantings, as specimens separate from other shrubs, or for a background, where seasonal drama is important. Deciduous shrubs may delight the eye with arrestingly colored new spring growth, vivid green summer foliage, and dramatic color changes in fall. Since such shrubs are bare-twigged in winter they also should be selected for how they present themselves then, with interesting twig patterns, perhaps, or attractive bark patterns and colors. Finally, deciduous shrubs often necessitate extra clean up in autumn. In natural gardens, of course, the fallen leaves provide a ready-made mulch, and they lend a beauty to the soil beneath the shrub for seasonal interest.

Leaf Color and Texture

Leaf color and texture are primary in how well a given shrub fits into the landscape most of the year. Just as with habit, these aspects must be lived with day in and day out.

Shrubs display a wide range of leaf colors from the most delicate pale greens to deepest emerald. The range of greens not only is astounding but changes with the season, for even evergreen shrubs make a flush of new leaves in the spring. Shrubs whose leaves evince seasonal change from earliest spring through fall should be planted in a place of honor where they can be appreciated close at hand, particularly as separate specimen plants.

Not only are new leaves a lighter green than the last year's, setting them off nicely, but a number of shrubs also show new leaves in a flush of red to bronze before they turn green. Examples are common in the heather family: evergreen huckleberry (*Vaccinium ovatum*), summer holly (*Comarostaphylis diversifolia*), some manzanitas, and holly grapes of the genus *Mahonia* in the barberry family.

Other shrubs are reliable for fall color, which is particularly enhanced in environments where chilly fall nights alternate with warm days. The following are examples of fine foliage color:

- western azalea (*Rhododendron occidentale*), with bronze to flame-orange leaves

- vine maple (*Acer circinatum*), with reddish to scarlet leaves

- hazelnut (*Corylus cornuta californica*), with pale golden leaves

- water birch (*Betula occidentalis*), with yellow leaves

- thimbleberry (*Rubus parviflorus*), with palest yellow-green leaves

- willows (*Salix* spp.), with yellow leaves (followed by brown to orangish twigs)

- dogwoods (*Cornus* spp.), with purple, pink, or orange leaves

- gooseberries (*Ribes* spp.), with dark red leaves

- California grape (*Vitis californica*), with mauve to red leaves

Finally, California has a wide range of gray-leafed shrubs in shades varying from silvery and near-white to bluish gray. A composition of several gray-leafed shrubs in a rock garden setting or among culinary herbs creates wonderful droughty colors. Gray-leafed shrubs also create sensational contrasts with green-leafed kinds. However, a mixture of too many different shades results in chaos; a few bold grays among an otherwise green background enhances drama.

Some of the best gray-leafed shrubs are:

- saltbushes (*Atriplex* spp.), particularly desert holly (these are salt-tolerant as well)

- sagebrushes (*Artemisia* spp.), with leaves ranging from the bluish gray of California sagebrush to the soft wooly silver of dune sagebrush

- sages (*Salvia* spp.), with wrinkled leaves from dull green in Sonoma sage to whitish gray in purple sage

- southern hummingbird fuchsia (*Zauschneria cana*), with narrow whitish gray leaves

- bush mallows (*Malacothamnus* spp.), with felted maplelike leaves from dull green to velvety gray

- holly grapes (*Mahonia* spp.), with the drought-tolerant kinds ranging from dull bluish gray to silvery green

- Matilija poppy (*Romneya coulteri*), with bluish gray leaves

- St. Catherine's lace and other buckwheats (*Eriogonum giganteum*), with felted gray to whitish wool on leaves

The aesthetic effects of leaf texture are much more subtle than color but every bit as important. Texture, defined as the overall impression of leafy branches as they appear from a distance, may range from delicate and light to heavy and dark; from lacy and fragile to chunky and bold. Myriad adjectives describe these details, but full consensus is lacking in what they mean. The best advice for interpreting them is to look at a wide variety of different species during different seasons, so as to know what appearances exist to be described.

Although textures of similar values help harmonize and unify an area (for example, a simple hedge, foundation planting, backdrop, or barrier where there is simplicity in the plantings it accompanies), opposing textures lend a dynamic quality to plantings when properly balanced. Just as with leaf color contrasts, keep the textures repeatable and simple: bold playing against lacy, for example. Such design practices enliven any landscape.

Finally, don't forget that winter bare branches and twigs also have texture. The finely branched slender twigs of snowberries (*Symphoricarpos* spp.) play in high contrast against the bold branches of California buckeye (*Aesculus californica*). Imagine the repeatedly forked branching of maples (*Acer* spp.) against the umbrellalike tiers of twigs found on western azalea (*Rhododendron occidentale*) branches, or the horizontally tiered, pagodalike branches of California hazelnut (*Corylus cornuta californica*) opposite the vertically directed branches of cascara sagrada (*Rhamnus purshianus*).

BARK

For deciduous shrubs, bark becomes the focal point during the winter, but evergreen shrubs may also offer beautiful bark. With evergreens judicious pruning or thinning of lower branches reveals the lower bark, as can planting position—high placement of shrubs lets you look up into them.

Bark can be characterized by its color, texture, and pattern. Shrubs with striking bark colors include the red, smooth bark of manzanitas, the reddish purple bark of hopbush and desert willow, the silver bark of bitter cherry, and the ghostly white-gray bark of buckeye. On some shrubs it's the newer bark that is dramatic, while the older bark is a rather nondescript shade of brown or gray; examples include the bright red new twigs of creek dogwood, coffee berry, and red buckthorn.

Bark patterns and designs can be subtle or bold, insignificant or arresting. Strong patterns may be created, for example, by the pattern in which older bark peels away to reveal new bark, or by the shapes and clustering of the lenticels (breathing pores). The madroña, *Arbutus menziesii*, is an example of a tree with beautiful patterns of new and old bark: the oldest bark forms thin, narrow reddish brown strips periodically criss-crossed by horizontal breaks; newer bark is a smooth, polished orange-red; the youngest bark is sometimes smooth and green. Another striking pattern is found on the native sycamore, *Platanus racemosa*, where a jigsaw-puzzle-like pattern of different layers of bark takes on shades of gray, brownish, cream, and near white. Unfortunately, few true shrubs exhibit such striking patterns, though designs of lenticels highlight some. Hopbush, *Ptelea crenulata*, has smooth bark sprinkled with tiny circular white lenticels, as does also the bronzish bark of water birch, *Betula occidentalis*. Many of the native cherries, including bitter cherry, *Prunus emarginata*, have circular clusters of lenticels that form rings or bands scribed on the silvery bark.

The majority of shrubs have relatively nondescript bark; in these cases, lower branches may be left alone as long as they remain healthy. Nothing is gained by pruning to expose the bark to view.

FLOWERS

Perhaps no one feature is deemed as important as flowers, although shrubs are often chosen mainly for their habit, leaves, and bark, the features visible year-round. Even though all the bedding plants, bulbs, annuals, and perennials planted in front of shrubs are selected for their flowers, considering the flowering of shrubs can enhance plantings as well.

To be sure, there are several shrubs whose flowers are disappointing or inconspicuous—use these for foliage and bark alone. Here is a list of shrubs whose flowers add little or nothing (in fact, you might even wish to trim them off):

- Coyote bush (*Baccharis pilularis pilularis*) has tiny heads of creamy flowers in fall.

- Sagebrushes (*Artemisia* spp.) carry minute heads of greenish yellow flowers in spikes in late summer and fall.

- Brickel bush (*Brickellia californica*) bears spikes of small heads of greenish white flowers in fall (but they are deliciously fragrant!).

- Mountain mahoganies (*Cercocarpus* spp.) bear small, pendant, axillary creamy saucers in late spring or early summer (but these are followed by wonderfully ornamental fruits).

- Buckthorns, including coffee berry (*Rhamnus* spp.), have small clusters of tiny greenish yellow stars.

On the other hand, many shrubs feature floral displays that are truly inspiring and that deserve a show-off position in the garden. Just about every color of the rainbow is represented by some shrub, although the preponderance of colors are in the whites, blues, purples, and yellows. Thus, when you consider what shrubs to plant side by side, it's important to consider flower colors that complement each other (at least if they flower during the same season). Pleasing combinations include:

- blues and purples
- blues and yellows
- blues and whites
- yellows and whites
- blues, yellows, and whites
- blues, purples, and pinks
- pinks and blues
- reds and yellows
- oranges, reds, and yellows

Besides flowers' colors, their shapes, sizes, and arrangements give floral "texture" to shrubs, especially from a distance. Shrubs such as ceanothuses, spiraeas, chamise, and creambushes have dozens of tiny flowers massed into complex panicles, giving a frothy look. Encelias, dogwoods, azaleas, rhododendrons, carpenteria, and mock orange bear bold, large flowers. Others fall between these extremes. Flower shape may also enhance the display, especially seen up close. Here are some examples of distinctive shapes:

- Manzanitas, white heather, summer holly, and mission manzanita have nodding urn- to bell-shaped flowers.

- Rhododendron and azalea have large, flared trumpet-shaped flowers.

- Fremontias, carpenteria, bush and Matilija poppies, and philadelphus have saucer-shaped flowers.

- Western spicebush has multiple-petaled, water-lily-like flowers.

- Currants and gooseberries have horizontal to hanging tubular flowers ending in flared "skirts."

- Hummingbird fuchsia has tubular flowers flared at their ends into trumpets.

- Service berry, oso berry, ninebark, hawthorn, and several others have single roselike flowers.

- Penstemons, salvias, wooly blue curls, and bush monkeyflowers have snapdragonlike or two-lipped flowers.

- Encelias, haplopappuses, vigueras, desert asters, and other composites have daisylike flowers.

Flower color, size, and shape are the major attributes of any flowering shrub, but a few have the bonus of pleasant fragrances. These odors may occur at specific times of the day (often in late afternoon or evening, for example). Some carry well to several feet away, while others are for close sniffing. Here are the best:

- Brickel bush releases a sweet, long-distance fragrance late in the day.

- Western azalea wafts a sweet, powerful long-distance fragrance throughout the day.

- Mock orange has attributes similar to western azalea.

- Carpenteria flowers provide a somewhat less sweet perfume than mock orange at close range.

- Western spicebush flowers have the odor of old wine at close range.

- Ceanothus blossoms smell like corn tortillas at medium range.

- Wild roses have the fine rose fragrance of old-fashioned garden roses close up.

- Blue elderberry releases a potent, sweet perfume at day's end, which carries long distances.

- Desert lavender has a delicate lavender fragrance close up.

Seasonality is another factor to consider about flowering. Included here are shrubs that flower practically every month, so it's possible to plan a garden that always has seasonal color from flowers, or from fruits, or a combination. The majority of shrubs bloom in spring (March through May), but here are others:

- October to March for various flowering currants

- November to March for bay trees (*Umbellularia californica*)

- December to February for many manzanitas

- December to February for silk-tassel bush

- February onward for prickly phlox and bush poppy

- May to June for California buckeye

- May to June for blue elderberry

- June for chamise

- June through August for many mountain shrubs

- summer for most penstemons

- summer (sometimes into fall) for bush monkeyflowers

- summer to fall for most buckwheats

- midsummer to fall for gumweeds

- late summer to fall for California fuchsias

- late summer to fall for fernbush

- fall for rabbitbrush

In addition, several shrubs that bloom in spring will have a second (but minor) flowering in fall, if autumn days are sunny and warm. This happens because day length and temperature are usually what trigger flowering, and fall weather may be a repeat of spring. Expect ceanothuses, in particular, to follow this pattern.

FRUITS

Often forgotten are the various seed pods, berries, and other seed-bearing structures, all of which we call fruits. Fruits follow after successful flowering, pollination, and fertilization. Many shrubs are as enhanced by their fruits as they are by flowers, and many become advantageously (or not) the focus of attention by birds and other animals seeking a meal. Choose your shrubs accordingly.

Fruits fall into two categories: those that shed their seeds from pods (or other containers that split open), and those that retain their seeds inside a fleshy berry or dry, nutlike fruit. Those with fleshy fruits are most often commented on for their display, since most "berries" turn distinctive colors before they're plucked and eaten. Here are some of the best:

- Toyon has bright red-orange berries in late fall.

- Holly grapes bear bluish purple (occasionally red) berries in summer.

- Elderberries have flat-topped clusters of blue or bright red berries from midsummer to early fall.

- Redberry buckthorn has translucent red berries in fall.

- Manzanitas display small, apple-shaped berries of rose, bronze, pink, or green splotched red from late spring to summer.

- Huckleberries make dark purple or bright red berries by fall.

- Summer holly has red berries in late summer to fall.

- Sugarbush and lemonade berry show deep red, "frosted" berries in late summer or fall.

- Salmonberry is loaded with salmon-red "raspberries" in early to midsummer.

- Wild roses bear fiery, orange-red hips in fall.

- Snowberries have close clusters of large white berries in fall.

Certainly another plus for many of these berries is their edibility; among the possibilities are:

- blue elderberries cooked or fermented

- manzanita berries cooked into jelly or as "cider"

- huckleberries eaten fresh or cooked

- salmonberries eaten any way (fully ripe)

- blackberries eaten any way (fully ripe)

- thimbleberries eaten any way (dead ripe)

- holly grapes cooked with sugar
- June berries cooked with sugar or dried
- oso berries cooked with sugar or dried

- rose hips cooked as jam or made into tea (remove fuzzy "seeds" inside)
- wild grapes cooked as jam or jelly
- salal berries eaten fresh or cooked with huckleberries

Other kinds of fruits vary in their attractiveness; those that remain on the shrub indefinitely, turning brown as they ripen, are often considered unsightly. Four shrubs worth remembering for this tendency are:

- Santa Cruz Island ironwood (*Lyonothamnus floribundus*)
- creambushes (*Holodiscus* spp.)
- chamise (*Adenostoma fasciculatum*)
- red shanks (*Adenostoma sparsifolium*)

Yet other fruits have such interesting design or pick up the light in such a fashion that they are definite pluses for attractiveness alone. A few worth noting are:

- cercocarpuses, with long, white-plumed tails attached to one-seeded fruits
- Apache plume and cliff rose, with similar long-plumed tails that often turn pink
- spicebush, with cup-shaped pods decorated in fluted designs
- ninebark, with pink to rosy, pointed seed pods
- vine maple, with rosy-winged samaras
- redbud, with deep wine-mauve pea pods

FRAGRANCE

Besides fragrant flowers, discussed under "flowers" above, some shrubs are notable for fragrant leaves, and occasionally bark. Fragrances of leaves differ from those of flowers in purpose. Flowers' odors attract pollinators such as bees, butterflies, and moths. Fragrant leaves usually contain volatile oils, with chemicals that deter would-be leaf munchers and are also implicated in preventing germination of competing seeds in the soil around the base of the shrub. These oils evaporate rapidly on hot days. Even on cool days they are released by crushing the leaves or, if you're an insect intent on making a meal from such leaves, by chewing on them.

All of this means that, compared to floral fragrances, leaf fragrances are quite different in nature and quality—often they are strong, penetrating odors referred to as resinous, turpentinelike, camphorous, minty, sagey, piny, or citruslike, qualities with which everyone is acquainted. Humans often find these fragrances appealing in small quantity, but on hot days some shrubs can be overwhelming (for example, white sage, pitcher sage, mountain misery, and bay laurel). No two people agree on which scents are pleasant and which are downright malodorous; whether fragrant leaves are a plus or minus is an individual preference. Use fragrant-leafed shrubs only when you're familiar with their fragrance, or you may regret planting them in your landscape. Note that it is mostly the drought-tolerant species that are fragrant. Here is a list of some of the more popular shrubs with fragrant leaves:

- western spicebush (allspice-scented bark and leaves)
- California bayberry (a subtle odor often first experienced in bayberry candles)
- flowering currants (sagey odor)
- evergreen currant (lemony odor)
- rabbitbrush (strong, bitter, resinous odor of the high desert)
- salvias (strong sage odors)
- sagebrushes (strong, bitter sage odor)
- wooly blue curls (turpentine-sage odor)
- monardellas (sage odor)

- coyote bush (resinous, sweet odor on hot days)
- incienso (resinous odor)
- hopbush and bush rue (rue or bitter citrus odor)
- elderberries (strong odor somewhat suggestive of bitter peanut butter!)
- tobacco brush ceanothus (strong, sweet-tobacco odor)
- creambushes (sweet, fruity odor)
- thimbleberry (sweet sage odor on hot days)
- laurel sumac (lemony odor)
- yerba santas (minty-sagey odor on hot days)
- mat juniper (strong piny odor)

SPEED OF GROWTH

This characteristic is too seldom given its due in planning a landscape. Shrub species vary greatly in the speed with which they grow, although speed is also influenced by climate and soils. Two points need be emphasized concerning speed of growth.

1. First, don't space young shrubs as though this will be their permanent girth. Crowded planting encourages spindly growth and ugly individual shrubs because of undue stress and competition between them. Please allow ample room for future growth, even though the initial planting looks sparse.

2. Second, don't assume that the shrubs you plant will always remain their present height. Instead, check the heights given in the Encyclopedia section, and integrate this information with the speed of growth to arrive at a realistic height within the foreseeable future of your garden. The most common mistake is to assume that shrubs will not become very tall; many do have that capability even within the span of a few years.

Also take into account the following factors in speed of growth:

- Light-loving shrubs often grow tall faster when shaded, in an attempt to reach for light. This encourages spindly, unhealthy, unattractive growth.

- Heavy nitrogen fertilizers may speed growth but often do so at the expense of growth that is weaker and more susceptible to fungal diseases and the attacks of insects.

- "Rich" soils, with many kinds of nutrients available to plant roots, generally encourage faster growth than "poor" soils, with fewer nutrients. Since these terms are relative it is difficult to define a particular soil's degree of richness, but generally rich soils have a deep color, and poor soils a light, bleached look.

- Summer water sometimes speeds growth, but often at the expense of weakening the shrub by preventing it from taking a rest. Many shrubs react by becoming vulnerable to soil fungal diseases and dying.

- Pruning or cutting back encourages vigorous juvenile growth when done at the right time—usually at the beginning of the growing period, in spring. Remember, however, that pruning causes a bushier shape. When certain shrubs are cut back to the ground the new growth may be vigorous and rapid, but there are obvious limits on the size possible using this method.

Factors that may slow the rate of growth include:

- shade, with no apparent light source to direct the shrub's growth;

- poor, nutrient-starved soils;

- lack of fertilizer;

- no extra watering, especially during summer;

- excessively cold winters for tender species. If the shrub is not killed outright in this way it may be killed back to the roots, which will take time to grow a new top;

- cold spells during the height of the spring growth cycle. Such cold may kill back the tender new growth and greatly reduce the amount of growth produced during that year. Shrubs may be protected from winter cold by a light cover or, if growing close to the ground, by a thick mulch;

- Repeated cutting back or pruning. While a single pruning may stimulate growth, multiple prunings within a single season can weaken a plant and slow its progress;

- shallow soil or use of small containers where roots are restricted and become root bound. This is sometimes an effective way of creating a low-maintenance bonsai.

LANDSCAPES USING NATIVE SHRUBS

THE WOODLAND GARDEN

If you are lucky enough to have trees already in place, you already have the primary requisite for establishing a woodland garden. One can be built beneath a wide variety of native and nonnative trees; only a few trees, such as many eucalyptuses and acacias, are inimical to growth underneath. Trees for woodland gardens include conifers (pines, redwoods, firs, spruces, Douglas fir, incense cedar, red cedar, and cedars), and various broadleaf trees (oaks, maples, ashes, birches, alders, sycamores, bays, and madrones; of these, oaks are among the most outstanding).

Conifers—because they're evergreen—create a denser all-year shade than deciduous, broadleaf trees, and their needles often create an acid soil. Underplanting them requires acid-tolerant plants that also tolerate moderate to deep shade. Since many (though not all) coniferous trees have shallow roots and so need summer water, the companion plants in their root zone must need or tolerate summer water as well.

Many broadleaf trees are deciduous (for example, several kinds of oak, alders, and sycamores, and all ashes, maples, and birches). Such trees provide ample light during late fall, winter, and early spring months for understory plantings and provide shade of varying densities from mid-spring through fall. Many of these trees require summer water, but one outstanding exception is the oaks, be they evergreen (live) or deciduous. Oaks slowly die from surface watering in summer, which promotes oak root fungus. Plantings under oaks need, therefore, to be summer drought tolerant.

One other note about choice of trees is to avoid those that sucker rampantly from the root crown; to this category belong most willows, cottonwoods, and poplars.

Suckers create an unkempt appearance and create greater demands on soils for water and nutrients.

Design in a woodland garden should be natural and free, not formal or contrived. Shrubs can be highlighted in several ways:

- as a border following a path or other prominent feature. Such a border may have more than one "layer" of shrubbery, starting with low shrubs near the path and ending with tall ones in the background;

- as naturally occurring clumps or islands in various positions under trees. Here, the important consideration is light needs. Remember that most shrubs understood to be shade-loving really don't tolerate deep or dense shade, such as is found next to the trunks of densely branched conifers;

- as a backdrop or background to a woodland setting where they define the far boundary of the garden. Here shrubs requiring light shade may be used, and should be planted to create a dense screen. Shrubs best fitted to this role are the tallest ones.

Naturally, other kinds of plants are part of a woodland setting, for woody plants seldom dominate as the main understory or ground cover. Instead, herbaceous perennials, various seasonal bulbs, and ferns occupy the bulk of the space. For more complete coverage of these necessary plants, turn to pages 30–32 in the companion book *Complete Garden Guide to the Native Perennials of California*.

The following lists provide many kinds of shrubs to try for the woodland garden. With regard to plants requiring summer water, most do well in even shade, while for drought-tolerant plants, light or partial shade may be required. For the latter group I have included cultural information to indicate this need.

Low Shrubs that Need Summer Water

Arctostaphylos nummularia (Fort Bragg manzanita)
Cornus canadensis (bunchberry, technically a creeping woody plant, behaving like an herbaceous perennial)
Mahonia aquifolium (Oregon grape)
Mahonia nervosa (northern holly grape)
Paxistima myrsinites (Oregon boxwood)
Ribes binominata (dwarf gooseberry)
Rosa spithamea (ground rose)

Medium Shrubs that Need Summer Water

Calycanthus occidentalis (western spicebush)
Gaultheria shallon (salal)
Osmaronia cerasiformis (oso berry)
Physocarpus capitatus (ninebark)
Ribes bracteosum (stink currant)
Ribes menziesii and *californicum* (canyon and California gooseberries)

Rosa gymnocarpa (wood rose)
Rosa woodsii (wood's rose)
Rubus parviflorus (thimbleberry)
Spiraea douglasii (steeple bush)
Vaccinium ovatum (evergreen huckleberry)
Vaccinium parvifolium (red huckleberry)

Tall Shrubs that Need Summer Water

Acer glabrum and *circinatum* (mountain and vine maples)
Arctostaphylos columbiana (Columbia manzanita)
Cornus nuttallii (flowering dogwood)
Cornus stolonifera (and other creek dogwoods)
Corylus cornuta californica (California hazelnut)
Crataegus douglasii (native hawthorn)
Menziesia ferruginea (mock azalea)

Myrica californica (California bayberry)
Philadelphus lewisii (mock orange)
Prunus subcordata (Sierra plum)
Rhamnus purshiana (cascara sagrada)
Rhododendron macrophyllum (rosebay rhododendron)
Rhododendron occidentale (western azalea)
Rubus spectabilis (salmonberry)
Sambucus callicarpa (red elderberry)

Low Shrubs that Need Little Summer Water

Arctostaphylos uva-ursi (kinnikinnick; light shade)
Ceanothus prostratus (mahala mats; light shade)
Chamaebatia foliolosa (mountain misery)
Chrysolepis sempervirens (mountain chinquapin)
Mahonia repens (creeping barberry; very light shade)

Pachystima myrsinites (Oregon boxwood; in coastal areas)
Rhus trilobata (squaw bush; light shade)
Ribes viburnifolium (evergreen currant)
Rosa spithamea (ground rose; in coastal areas)
Symphoricarpos rivularis (snowberry)
Vancouveria spp. (inside-out flowers; often considered perennials)
Whipplea modesta (modesty)

MEDIUM SHRUBS THAT NEED LITTLE SUMMER WATER

Carpenteria californica (bush anemone; light shade in coastal areas)

Holodiscus discolor (creambush)

Mahonia pinnata (California holly grape; light shade)

Prunus emarginata (bitter cherry; light shade)

Rhamnus californica (coffee berry; light shade in inland areas)

Ribes speciosum (fuchsia-flowered gooseberry)

Rosa pisocarpa and *pinetorum* (pine roses; in cool climates)

TALL SHRUBS THAT NEED LITTLE SUMMER WATER

Ceanothus integerrimus (deerbrush; light shade)

Cercis occidentalis (western redbud; light shade)

Comarostaphylis diversifolia (summer holly; light shade)

Heteromeles arbutifolia (toyon; light shade in inland gardens)

Lithocarpus densiflorus echinoides (shrub tan oak; light shade)

Ptelea crenulata (hop bush; light shade)

Ribes aureum (golden currant; light shade)

Ribes sanguineum (flowering currant)

Sambucus mexicana/caerulea (blue elderberries; light shade)

Styrax officinalis (snowbell bush)

THE WATER GARDEN

Even in times of drought, when it may seem contradictory to talk of water gardens, in fact such gardens fool the senses by presenting water in an unwasteful fashion. The centerpiece for the water garden can be a fountain or a pond. In both cases, water is simply recirculated via a low-cost pump. Water cools the surroundings and soothes the soul, and although there is inevitable evaporation, the small amount lost is negligible compared to the mood created (unless the pond is very large).

THE FOUNTAIN

This is a wonderful feature for a recessed corner, patio, or courtyard and is particularly effective with a building of Spanish or Mediterranean style, with red tile roof and adobe walls. The focal point is, of course, the fountain itself, but the pool and catchments should be of material matching or complementing the roof: red tile or some neutral earth color such as terra cotta or sandstone. Refer to books specializing in this subject, or to a local specialty nursery, for further ideas.

Plants displayed in a courtyard are often in a variety of attractive containers, themselves of earth tones, sometimes ornate, sometimes simple. Too many different designs detract from unifying the whole; the use of one dominant theme holds everything together. Containers can range from small pots to large urns several feet tall. In addition, there may be several small open beds arranged in geometric design around the fountain itself.

Plantings chosen for containers and beds usually heighten the drama between the play of water and the feel of architectural materials: plentiful water is juxtaposed with drought-tolerant, xeric plants. Plants of bold design belong in containers, where they are displayed by themselves, while plants of complementary design grace beds surrounding the fountain. In addition to native shrubs, consider succulents, small trees, and splashes of color provided by flowering annuals and perennials. The following lists suggest some native shrubs and some other nonshrubby bold native plants for containers.

Native Shrubs for Containers

Adenostoma sparsifolium (red shanks)

Agave desertii (native agave)

Arctostaphylos glauca or *viscida* (bigberry or white-leaf manzanita)

Artemisia californica ('Canyon Gray' weeping form, California sagebrush)

Artemisia pycnocephala (dune sagebrush)

Artemisia tridentata (common sagebrush)

Dendromecon rigida (bush poppy)

Encelia farinosa (incienso)

Galvezia speciosa (island snapdragon)

Isomeris arborea (bladder pod)

Lavatera assurgentiflora (malva rosa)

Leptodactylon californica (prickly phlox)

Lyonothamnus floribundus asplenifolius (Santa Cruz Island ironwood)

Mahonia haematocarpa or *nevinii* (prickly holly grapes)

Monardella spp. (coyote mints)

Penstemon centranthifolius (scarlet bugler)

Penstemon palmeri (Palmer's penstemon)

Rhus laurina (laurel sumac)

Salvia apiana (white sage)

Simmondsia chinensis (jojoba)

Trichostema lanatum (wooly blue curls)

Yucca schidigera (Mojave yucca)

Yucca whipplei (our lord's candle)

BOLD NATIVE PLANTS FOR CONTAINERS

Agave spp. (magueys or century plants)
Cereus spp. (cereus cacti)
Cupressus forbesii (Tecate cypress)
Dalea spinosa (smoke tree)
Ferocactus and *Echinocactus* spp. (barrel cacti)
Juniperus californica (California juniper)

Opuntia spp. (prickly pears)
Pinus monophylla (single-needle pinyon pine)
Pinus sabiniana (gray pine)
Washingtonia filifera (California fan palm)
Yucca brevifolia (Joshua tree)

OTHER BOLD PLANTS, NOT NATIVE TO CALIFORNIA

Aloe spp. (aloes)
Citrus spp. (citruses: oranges, lemons, and others)
Cupressus arizonica (Arizona cypress)
Cynara cardunculus (artichoke)
Echium spp. (pride-of-Madeira, tower-of-jewels)
Ficus carica (fig)

Lagerstroemia indica (crepe myrtle)
Laurus nobilis (Greek laurel)
Myrtus communis (myrtle)
Nerium oleander (oleander)
Olea europea (olive)
Pinus edulis (pinyon pine)
Pinus pinea (Italian stone pine)

The last list above includes trees that for all intents and purposes are grown as miniatures or large bonsais, by confining the roots and periodically removing the plant from its container to prune back roots. Shaping the top also keeps these plants compact and in scale with their setting. Slow-release fertilizer, such as the pellets sold under the name Osmacote, may be used to dress the surface of the soil to compensate for the confinement of roots.

Open beds should contain lower-growing plants that don't visually block the fountain. Beds may be devoted exclusively to flowering perennials or annuals or, in more formal designs, permanent, low-growing shrubs. Shrubs used should repeat certain design elements by careful choice of leaf color and texture. Again, native shrubs may be used exclusively or in a mixture of native, Mediterranean, and South African shrubs. For more ideas on possibilities, turn to the lists under The Herb Garden, page 55.

THE POND

The pond is one of the less formal possible design elements that works well against a backdrop of dense shrubberies or trees. It can unify an open meadow or lawn area with the contrasting shade of woody plants, and is ideal where a natural stream or drainage already exists. Refer to specialty books for advice on actual design and construction of the pond, but bear these recommendations in mind:

- An asymmetrical shape is best.
- The pond should have a gradual slope along at least part of its periphery to allow planting of plants that grow only in shallow water.
- Use material of dark color so as not to make it obvious that the pond has been constructed.
- Use rocks at many places along the rim of the pond, and partly submerge them to give a natural effect.
- Create an island off-center in the pond for a more graceful feel.
- Be sure to include mosquito fish, which take care of mosquito larvae.
- Take care that the pond does not leak before permanently filling and planting it.

Choose plants to encircle your pond that are tolerant of wet conditions and poorly aerated soil. Use clumps of grasslike plants especially toward the back of the pond, to enhance its naturalness. Also lend it bold design, with tall-growing perennials such as lilies (*Lilium* spp.) and large ferns, including chain fern (*Woodwardia fimbriata*), lady fern (*Athyrium filix-femina*), and spiny wood fern (*Dryopteris dilatata*). Finally, fill in with shrubs behind the immediate periphery, with a few gracefully draped branches just above the pond's back edge. Use different tiers or layers to wed the pond to the woods behind it, where trees create a backdrop. Here are lists of shrubs by height for this purpose:

SHORT SHRUBS FOR THE POND PERIPHERY

Arctostaphylos nummularia (Fort Bragg manzanita)
Arctostaphylos uva-ursi (kinnikinnick)
Ledum glandulosum (Labrador tea)
Leucothoe davisae (Sierra laurel)
Mahonia nervosa (northern holly grape)
Osmaronia cerasiformis (oso berry)
Paxistima myrsinites (Oregon boxwood)

MEDIUM SHRUBS FOR THE POND PERIPHERY AND BACKGROUND

Gaultheria shallon (salal)
Mahonia aquifolium (Oregon grape)
Ribes aureum (golden currant)
Ribes bracteosum (stink currant)

Ribes sanguineum (flowering currant)
Ribes speciosa (fuchsia-flowered gooseberry)
Rubus parviflorus (thimbleberry)

TALL SHRUBS FOR THE BACK OF THE POND

Calycanthus occidentalis (western spice bush)
Carpenteria californica (bush anemone)
Cornus nuttallii (flowering dogwood)
Cornus stolonifera (creek dogwood)
Corylus cornuta (California hazelnut)
Euonymus occidentalis (western burning bush)

Lonicera involucrata (twinberry honeysuckle)
Physocarpus capitatus (ninebark)
Rhamnus purshianus (cascara sagrada)
Rhododendron macrophyllum (California rosebay)
Rhododendron occidentale (western azalea)
Sambucus callicarpa (red elderberry)

SHRUBS FOR HEDGES AND BARRIERS

Little explicit detail need be given for use of shrubs as hedges and barriers; the terms are self-explanatory. The distinction between the two is merely one of practicality: hedges only screen one area from another, while barriers impede movement as well.

More concerns than mere practicality weigh in choice of material, however: leaf color, texture, whether leaves are deciduous or evergreen, and the bonus of showy flowers or fruits are important considerations. Also worth considering is whether the site is sunny or shaded, and summer cool and watered or summer hot and dry.

Finally, the initial spacing of shrubs should be close for shrubs that grow slowly, and farther apart for speedy growers. In any case, for hedges and barriers allow smaller spaces between shrubs than you would in other garden situations, so that the desired effect is achieved with dispatch.

HEDGE PLANTS FOR FULL SUN

(All are evergreen except as noted.)
Aesculus californica (buckeye; deciduous)

Ceanothus griseus (coastal ceanothus)
Dendromecon rigida (bush poppy)
Garrya buxifolia (boxleaf garrya)

Heteromeles arbutifolia (toyon)
Prunus ilicifolia/lyonii (holly-leaf and island cherries)
Quercus vaccinifolia (huckleberry oak)
Rhamnus californica (coffee berry)
Rhus integrifolia (lemonade berry)

Rhus laurina (laurel sumac)
Rhus ovata (sugar bush)
Salvia leucophylla (purple sage)
Simmondsia chinensis (jojoba)
Xylococcus bicolor (mission manzanita)

HEDGE PLANTS FOR SHADE

(For locations with summer water every few weeks.)
Carpenteria californica (bush anemone)
Chrysolepis chrysophylla minor (bush chinquapin; summer water, but minimal)
Comarostaphylis diversifolia (summer holly; summer water, but minimal)
Gaultheria shallon (salal; low barrier only)

Heteromeles arbutifolia (toyon)
Lithocarpus densiflorus echinoides (shrub tan oak)
Mahonia pinnata (California holly grape)
Myrica californica (California bayberry)
Umbellularia californica (shrub form of California bay laurel)
Vaccinium ovatum (evergreen huckleberry; a slow grower)

BARRIER PLANTS

(All are evergreen except as noted.)
Agave deserti (desert agave, low barrier only)
Ceanothus incanus and *leucodermis* (white-thorn and coastal white-thorn ceanothus)
Ceanothus spinosus (red-heart ceanothus)
Forestiera neomexicana (desert olive; deciduous)
Leptodactylon californica (prickly phlox; low barrier only)

Mahonia dictyota (veined holly grape)
Mahonia haematocarpa (desert holly grape)
Mahonia nevinii
Pickeringia montana (chaparral pea)
Prosopis juliflora (mesquite; deciduous)
Ribes menziesii and *californica* (canyon and California gooseberries; deciduous with shade)
Yucca schidigera (Mojave yucca)
Yucca whipplei (low barrier only)

THE CHAPARRAL GARDEN

Recreating one of California's most typical landscapes—the chaparral—is an idea whose time has come. Chaparral is that tough, dense cover of evergreen shrubs thickly clothing (as it seems from a distance) rocky hillsides with full summer sun and heat. It has been referred to as elfin forest, since a small animal could walk underneath its canopy much in the way we would walk through the corridors of a full-sized forest. Chaparral is the best indicator of the Mediterranean climate most of us garden in: mild, wet winters and warm to hot, dry summers. Its colors blend and harmonize with the subtle browns and ochres of rocky mountainsides, sometimes a monotone with few species, other times a rich tapestry of complementary, widely varied colors.

Chaparral consists primarily of woody plants—one might say it is *the* domain of drought-tolerant shrubs. It is here that manzanitas, ceanothuses, bush poppies, rhamnuses, garryas, salvias, and many others reach their peak of diversity. Flowers punctuate the mix of green and gray tones, with splashes of bright color: blues, purples, whites, and yellows. Shrubs flower almost any month, but the best displays occur from February through June.

Other kinds of plants are rare here; the bulbs, bunchgrasses, perennials, and annuals so typical of woodlands, forests, and grasslands are nearly absent. Yet two specialized niches provide home for some of these: the chaparral edge—along road cuts, road banks, rock outcroppings, and stream sides—and the entire community after a fire. Where burns have blackened shrubs, great swaths of annual and bulbous wildflowers cover slopes for one or more years before shrubs are restored to their original condition. Certain kinds of wildflower seeds remain hidden in the soil until a fire releases them from their imprisoning seed coats, even after ten to twenty years.

Why might it be desirable to recreate this phenomenon termed chaparral in a garden? Here are a few reasons:

- Chaparral blends beautifully with such natural settings as rocky hillsides and already-existing scrub, or provides contrast against a backdrop of mature oak woodland and open grassland.

- The shrubs require no water when fully established.

- The shrubs require little special care, except for periodic replacement as they decline in vigor or health.

- There is subtle beauty here, which reveals itself a little differently at each time of the year.

One caveat must be mentioned, however: chaparral shrubs are noted for their adaptations to fire—to remain healthy, shrubs need to be burned periodically, on the order of every twenty to thirty years. What this means to the homeowner is that these shrubs become a fire hazard with time. Although old, dead branches may be removed periodically through pruning, the volatile oils produced by leaves on hot days render many chaparral species susceptible to sustaining and transmitting fire. If yours is a small garden, and you wish to incorporate some chaparral shrubs, plant them far from flammable structures including fences, trees, and sheds, and water them occasionally in summer. For larger properties, a chaparral garden may be safely planned by providing a broad perimeter around the house. Within this perimeter use plants with low combustibility (particularly those with fleshy leaves or thirsty roots).

Given these guidelines, how should you approach the design of a chaparral garden? Start with the landform first. A south-facing slope provides the perfect setting. It may be graded into a number of irregular shelves to display shrubs at different levels. Once a pleasing landform is achieved, the next step is careful placement of rocks of different sizes for contrast with shrub foliage. Bear these rules in mind:

- One unifying rock texture and color should be used. Particularly pleasing would be granite rocks for a mountain garden and rounded, cinnamon-colored sandstone rocks for a foothill garden. The bluish or green colors of serpentine rock are also highly decorative.

- Rocks of varying sizes should appear to be placed more or less randomly. Avoid using a single rock size at each level.

- Rocks should be buried so that only one-third to one-quarter actually shows above ground. This gives a natural appearance.

- Rocks should be clustered in several places rather than sitting singly by themselves.

After the rocks have been installed, it's time to think about what shrubs to use and their proper location. Although the tallest shrubs should go toward the crown of the hill and the shortest near the bottom, a pleasing mix of different sizes should be used on each level so that the planting does not look contrived. As with rocks, shrubs should be planted sometimes singly and other times in small informal groupings, again for the most natural effect. Shrubs should also be chosen for their complementary leaf textures and colors and for pleasing harmonies in flower color. Grays and deep greens provide beautiful contrasts; so do fine and bold textures. Blue or purple flowers enliven yellow or orange kinds; white flowers help unify other colors. Cool flower colors recede, while warm colors come forward. Finally, a limited number of species should be chosen, to create harmony and avoid a cluttered effect. For a large garden, between ten and twenty species could be incorporated into a pleasing design.

In this garden shrubs provide the main context, but don't forget the chaparral edge where other plants wander in. Such edges are provided along pathways, by rocks, or toward the bottom of the hill, where smaller plants are readily visible and provide needed contrast with those massive shrubs. Border plants can be interwoven with some of the lower shrubs so that a nearly seamless transition is created; in fact, many of the border plants can simply be very low shrubs, such as the prostrate manzanitas and ceanothuses, or half-shrubby plants such as buckwheats and penstemons. In addition, bold succulents, rock ferns, and seasonal perennials and annuals serve to enliven the scene.

LARGE CHAPARRAL SHRUBS

Adenostoma sparsifolium (red shanks)
Arctostaphylos andersonii (heartleaf manzanita)
Arctostaphylos glauca (big-berry manzanita)
Arctostaphylos insularis (island manzanita)
Arctostaphylos manzanita (Parry manzanita)
Arctostaphylos mariposa (Mariposa manzanita)
Arctostaphylos pallida (pale-leaf manzanita)
Arctostaphylos viscida (white-leaf manzanita)
Ceanothus arboreus (tree ceanothus)
Ceanothus integerrimus (deerbrush)
Ceanothus sorediatus (Jimbrush)

Ceanothus spinosus (redheart)
Ceanothus thyrsiflorus (blueblossom)
Cercis occidentalis (western redbud)
Cercocarpus spp. (mountain mahoganies)
Fremontodendron hybrids (flannel bush)
Garrya spp. (silk-tassel bushes)
Heteromeles arbutifolia (toyon)
Lithocarpus densiflorus echinoides (shrub tan oak)
Prunus ilicifolia and *lyonii* (holly-leaf and Lyon's cherries)
Quercus dumosa and others (scrub and other oaks)
Styrax officinalis (snowbell bush)
Umbellularia californica (shrub form of California bay laurel)

MEDIUM CHAPARRAL SHRUBS

Adenostoma fasciculatum (chamise)
Arctostaphylos densiflora (some forms of Vinehill manzanita)
Arctostaphylos glandulosus (Eastwood manzanita)

Arctostaphylos patula (green-leaf manzanita)
Arctostaphylos silvicola (silver-leaf manzanita)
Arctostaphylos stanfordiana (Stanford manzanita)

Arctostaphylos tomentosus (shaggybark manzanita)

Baccharis pilularis consaguinea (coyote bush)

Calystegia cyclostegius and *occidentalis* (wild morning glories, woody climbers)

Carpinteria californica (bush anemone)

Ceanothus cuneatus (buckbrush)

Ceanothus griseus (coastal ceanothus)

Ceanothus leucodermis (spiny ceanothus or white-thorn)

Ceanothus papillosus (wartleaf ceanothus)

Ceanothus parryi (Parry's ceanothus)

Ceanothus purpureus (Napa ceanothus)

Ceanothus ramulosus (coastal buckbrush)

Ceanothus velutinus (tobacco brush)

Clematis lasiantha (virgin's bower, a woody climber)

Dendromecon rigida (bush poppy)

Keckiella cordifolius (heartleaf or climbing penstemon, a woody climber)

Lepechinia fragrans (island pitcher sage)

Malacothamnus spp. (bush mallows)

Pickeringia montana (chaparral pea)

Prunus emarginata (bitter cherry)

Rhamnus californica (coffee berry)

Rhamnus crocea (redberry buckthorn)

Rhus spp. (sugar bush, lemonade berry, laurel sumac)

Ribes indecorum and *malvaceum* (white and chaparral currants)

Romneya coulteri (Matilija poppy)

Salvia mellifera and *leucophylla* (black and purple sages)

Low Chaparral Shrubs

Arctostaphylos hookeri (Monterey manzanita)

Arctostaphylos myrtifolia (myrtle-leaf manzanita or Ione manzanita)

Arctostaphylos nummularia (Fort Bragg manzanita)

Arctostaphylos pungens (Mexican manzanita)

Artemisia tridentata and *californica* (common and California sagebrushes)

Baccharis pilularis pilularis (creeping coyote bush)

Ceanothus cordulatus (snowbrush)

Ceanothus foliosus (littleleaf ceanothus)

Ceanothus griseus horizontalis (Carmel creeper)

Ceanothus jepsonii (Jepson's ceanothus)

Ceanothus lemmonii (Lemmon's ceanothus)

Ceanothus rigidus (snowball ceanothus)

Chrysolepis sempervirens (mountain chinquapin)

Chrysothamnus nauseosus (rabbitbrush)

Cneoridium dumosum (bush rue)

Encelia californica (incienso)

Eriogonum arborescens (Santa Cruz Island buckwheat)

Eriogonum fasciculatum (flat-top buckwheat)

Eriogonum giganteum (St. Catherine's lace)

Galvezia speciosa (island snapdragon)

Haplopappus spp. (bush sunflowers)

Leptodactylon californicum (prickly phlox)
Lotus scoparius (deerbroom lotus)
Penstemon antirrhoindes (bush snapdragon)
Penstemon corymbosus (red-flowering rock penstemon)
Quercus vaccinifolia and others (huckleberry and other oaks)

Rhamnus crocea (redberry buckthorn, in some forms)
Salvia apiana, dorrii, and others (white and other sages)
Solanum umbelliferum and *xantii* (blue nightshades)
Trichostema lanatum (wooly blue curls)

PROSTRATE CHAPARRAL SHRUBS

Adenostoma fasciculatum (chamise's prostrate form)
Arctostaphylos edmundsii (Pt. Sur manzanita)
Arctostaphylos imbricata (shingle-leaf manzanita)
Arctostaphylos nevadensis (pinemat manzanita)
Arctostaphylos uva-ursi (kinnikinnick)

Artemisia californica ('Canyon Gray')
Ceanothus gloriosus (glory mat)
Ceanothus hearstiorum (Hearst ceanothus)
Ceanothus prostratus (mahala mats)
Juniperus communis saxatilis (mat juniper)
Ribes viburnifolium (Island currant)
Salvia sonomensis (Sonoma sage)

ACCENT PLANTS FOR CHAPARRAL

Chrysopsis villosa (golden aster)
Coreopsis maritima (sea dahlia)
Dicentra chrysantha (golden eardrops)
Dudleya brittoni
Dudleya pulverulenta (chalk lettuce)
Erigeron glaucus (seaside daisy)
Eriogonum spp. (buckwheats)
Helianthemum scoparium (sunrose)

Monardella spp. (coyote mints)
Penstemon spp. (penstemons or beard-tongues)
Solanum wallacei (island nightshade)
Solidago californica (California goldenrod)
Yucca whipplei (chaparral yucca)
Zauschneria spp. (California fuchsias)

ROCK FERNS FOR CHAPARRAL

Aspidotis californica (California lace fern)
Aspidotis densa (Oregon cliffbrake)
Cheilanthes gracillima (lace fern)

Pellaea andromaedifolia (coffee fern)
Pellaea mucronata (birdsfoot fern)
Pityrogramme triangularis (goldback fern)

ANNUALS FOR CHAPARRAL

Emmenanthe penduliflora (whispering bells)

Lupinus benthamii (Bentham's lupine)

Lupinus hirsutissimus (nettle lupine)

Lupinus stiversii (harlequin lupine)

Mentzelia lindleyi (Lindley's blazing star)

Papaver californicum (fire poppy)

Phacelia campanularia (wild Canterbury bells)

Phacelia grandiflora (large-flowered phacelia)

Phacelia minor (bell phacelia)

Phacelia viscida (sticky phacelia)

Salvia carduacea (thistle sage)

Salvia columbariae (chia)

Stylomecon heterophylla (wind poppy)

THE HERB GARDEN

Herb gardens embody many principles of xeriscaping—the growing of drought-tolerant plants—since our familiar herbs come from the Mediterranean basin, where summer-dry climates dominate. Historically, herbs have come down to us through our Greek-Roman heritage, beginning as valuable medicines, evolving through the need to preserve foods from spoiling, and later developing as culinary adjuncts for flavoring foods. This rich heritage is reflected in the modern herb garden, which brings together herbs for medicine, culinary use, potpourri, perfume, or pleasure—in a combination that is aesthetically pleasing.

Today's herb gardens usually are in one of two designs. Formal designs have intricately woven patterns of carefully clipped and pruned herbs of contrasting leaf colors and textures. The culmination of this type is the knot garden. In natural designs herbs are incorporated into pleasing mounds, drifts, and shrubberies, often in a tiered setting in which rocks complement herbs.

Although both designs are appropriate for California climates, the natural design lends itself to the use of native shrubs, many of which have highly scented leaves, as do traditional herbs. Native shrubs' leaves have scents describable, for example, as minty, resinous, sagey, parsleylike, baylike, or licoricelike. Further, because traditional herbs and scented native shrubs are both adapted to Mediterranean climates, their leaf textures and colors often match or offset one another. Finally, California shares several genera with Old World herbs, including *Artemisia* (sagebrushes), *Satureja* (savories), *Salvia* (sages), *Tanacetum* (tansies), *Mentha* (mints), *Heracleum* (cow parsnip), *Angelica* (angelica), and *Sanicula* (sanicles). Other genera differ but may have close counterparts: *Monardella* with *Origanum* (oregano, marjoram),

Ligusticum (lovage) with *Apium* (celery), *Umbellularia* (California bay laurel) with *Laurus nobilis* (European bay).

For these reasons, a traditional herb garden—replete with contrasting leaf textures and colors and of pleasing informal composition of mounds, creeping carpets, drifts, and shrubberies—can mix traditional herbs with California counterparts for an exciting new design. The following lists give California native shrubs and herbs together with their European foils and counterparts.

In the following lists cultural information has been included in parentheses for small plants that need extra summer water or shade.

TREES FOR THE BACKDROP OF THE HERB GARDEN

Calocedrus decurrens Incense cedar: tall tree to over a hundred feet; fragrant piny, scalelike, vivid green foliage and cinnamon bark. Small, birdlike seed cones. California native. Compare to next for usage and fragrance.

Cedrus spp. Cedars: tall trees with broad spread; fragrant piny needles in bunches, dark green or blue-green, with dark brown bark. Dramatic, candlelike seed cones borne on uppermost branches. Old World only: Atlas cedar (*C. atlantica*), deodar cedar (*C. deodara*), and cedar of Lebanon (*C. lebanii*).

Cupressus spp. Cypresses: bushy to medium-sized trees of several shapes; fragrant piny, gray-green to deep green scalelike foliage and cherry red to pale brown bark. Tightly closed, globe-shaped seed cones. Old World and California species: Monterey cypress (*C. macrocarpa*), pygmy cypress (*C. pygmaea*), Sargent's cypress (*C. sargentii*), and Italian cypress (*C. sempervirens*).

Laurus nobilis European or Grecian laurel: bay odor. Old World tree and the original source of bay leaves for cooking. Compare to *Umbellularia*.

Pseudotsuga menziesii Douglas fir: very tall tree with comely shape when young; strong pine- to lemon-scented dark green needles and deeply sculpted dark brown bark. Curious pendant seed cones with three-pronged bracts between rounded scales. California native.

Torreya californica California nutmeg: modest tree with pendant side branches; astringent strongly scented, glossy, sharp needles and dark brown bark. Prunelike, fleshy seed cones. California native.

Umbellularia californica California bay laurel: penetrating bay odor. California native.

TALL SHRUBS FOR THE BACK EDGE OF THE HERB GARDEN

Aloysia citriodora Lemon verbena: green folded leaves, strong lemon odor. Tender shrub from the Old World. Compare to *Rhus laurina* for usage and fragrance.

Artemisia tridentata Desert sagebrush: grayish leaves, attractive bark, strong
   sage scent. California native. See other artemisias in the Medium-sized
   Shrubs and Herbaceous or Nonwoody Plants lists below for other species
   with similar odors.

Calycanthus occidentalis. Western spicebush: deciduous dark green leaves, allspice
   odor. California native (summer water and light shade).

Citrus spp. Citruses: lemons, oranges, and others; broad, tough evergreen leaves
   with the strong scent of the fruits. Old World natives.

Eriodictyon spp. Yerba santa: green to wooly gray leaves, deep sagey or minty odor.
   California natives.

Leptospermum spp. Australian tea trees: green to gray-green needlelike leaves,
   strong resinous odor. From Australia and New Zealand.

Myrica californica California bayberry: evergreen wavy green leaves, subtle bay
   odor. California native (summer water and light shade). Compare to
   Umbellularia (California bay laurel) and *Laurus* (Roman laurel) under Trees,
   above, for odor and usage.

Ptelea crenulata Hopbush: deciduous trifoliate green leaves with purplish bark,
   strong bitter citrus odor. California native (some summer water). Compare to
   Citrus for odor.

Rhus laurina Laurel sumac: bright green leaves, its new growth red in spring;
   lemony odor. California native. Compare to *Aloysia* (lemon verbena) and *Citrus*
   (lemon tree) for fragrance.

Medium-Sized Shrubs for the Back Area of the Herb Garden

Artemisia abrotanum Southernwood: deeply divided, greenish leaves, bitter-lemon
   odor, and insignificant flowers. Old World. Compare to other artemisia entries
   here and under Tall Shrubs, above, or Herbaceous or Nonwoody Plants, below.

Artemisia absynthium Wormwood: lacy gray leaves, strong and deep sage scent.
   Old World.

Artemisia californica California sagebrush: finely textured, gray-green leaves, strong
   sage scent. California native.

Cistus ladanifer Rockrose: narrow, quilted, deep green leaves, sweet, pungent
   smell, and large, saucer-shaped flowers of pink or purple. Old World.

Encelia farinosa Brittlebush: broad silvery leaves (summer-dormant), resinous odor,
   and large yellow daisy flowers. California native.

Haplopappus ericoides Mock heather: narrow, green, heathlike leaves, piny odor,
   and dense clusters of small yellow daisies. California native.

Hyptis emoryi Desert lavender: wandlike stems with summer-dormant, minty leaves and tall whorls of pale purple flowers. California native. Compare to *Lavandula* (lavenders) for odor.

Isomeris arborea Bladderpod: trifoliate, dull green leaves, strong, ruelike odor, and short racemes of yellow flowers followed by balloonlike pods. California native.

Lavandula spp. Lavenders: narrow green to gray-green leaves, minty or sagey aroma, wandlike spires of deep to pale blue-purple flowers. Old World. Compare to *Hyptis emoryi* (desert lavender) for odor.

Lepechinia spp. Pitcher sage: quilted, dull green leaves, penetrating, stale sage odor, and racemes of inflated white to purple flowers. California native. Compare to salvias (sages) under Medium-sized Shrubs, above, and Herbaceous or Nonwoody Plants, below, for odor and usage.

Pelargonium spp. Scented geraniums: scalloped to deeply divided, pale green to deep green leaves; fruity, minty, spicy or roselike odors; and small pale purple to whitish flowers. Old World.

Rosmarinus officinalis Rosemary: bright green needlelike leaves, rosemary odor, and showy, sea- to sky-blue flowers. Old World.

Ruta graveolens Rue: low mounds of blue- or gray-green, scalloped leaves, strong rue scent, and yellowish green flowers. Old World.

Salvia apiana White or bee sage: broad, whitish green leaves, penetrating sage aroma, and tall spikes of white to pale purple flowers. California native. Compare to other salvias here and under Herbaceous or Nonwoody Plants, below.

Salvia clevelandii Cleveland sage: quilted, dull green leaves, sage aroma, and tiered whorls of blue-purple flowers. California native.

Salvia leucophylla Purple sage: quilted, grayish leaves, strong sage aroma, and tiered whorls of pale purple flowers. California native.

Salvia officinalis Culinary or cooking sage: dull green to variegated quilted leaves and tiered whorls of pale purple flowers. Old World.

Santolina spp. Cotton lavenders: bright green to gray narrow, fluted leaves, strong sage odor, and pale yellow, pincushionlike flowers. Old World.

Trichostema lanatum Wooly blue curls: narrow green leaves, strong turpentine-sage odor, and racemes of wooly red-purple and blue-purple flowers. California native.

HERBACEOUS OR NONWOODY PLANTS FOR THE FOREGROUND TO MIDDLE OF THE HERB GARDEN

Achillea spp. Yarrows: widely spreading plants with fine, ferny foliage, strong sage odor, and flat-topped clusters of yellow, pink, rose, or white flowers. Old and New worlds.

Allium spp. Wild onions: low to medium-sized bulbs that are mostly summer dormant; long, narrow, flattened grasslike leaves, strong onion or garlic odor, and umbels of white, pink, or purple flowers. California natives.

Allium sativum, tuberosum, and *schoenoprasum* Garlic, garlic chives, and chives: may or may not be summer dormant. Long, cylindrical to flattened grasslike leaves, strong garlic or onion odor, and umbels of white to purplish flowers. Old World.

Andropogon schoenanthus Lemon grass: medium-sized grass, strong lemon odor and insignificant flowers. Asiatic (frost tender). Compare to *Hierchloe* (vanilla grass).

Anethum graveolens Dill: annual with finely divided, ferny green leaves, dill odor, and flowering stalks with umbels of yellow-green flowers. Old World.

Angelica archangelica, breweri, and *hendersonii* Angelica: large, coarsely divided, dark green leaves, strong angelica odor, and tall flowering stalks with broad umbels of whitish flowers. First, Old World; latter two, California natives.

Artemisia douglasiana and *vulgaris* Mugworts: widely spreading plants with deeply slashed, green and gray leaves (winter-dormant), strong sage scent, and insignificant flowers. Former, California native; latter, Old World.

Artemisia dracunculus Tarragon: widely spreading plants with narrow, lance-shaped leaves, strong sage-tarragon odor, and insignificant flowers. Old and New worlds.

Artemisia pycnocephala Dune sagebrush: ferny leaves covered with white to gray wool; little odor; insignificant flowers. California native.

Carum carvi Caraway: biennial with ferny, green leaves, caraway odor, and umbels of white flowers followed by scented seeds. Old World.

Coriandrum sativum Coriander: annual with ferny, coarsely divided green leaves, strong cilantro odor, and umbels of white flowers followed by scented seeds. Old World. Compare to *Saniculum* (poison sanicle) for fragrance.

Foeniculum vulgaris Fennel: invasive annual with finely divided, ferny, bright green leaves, strong anise odor, and tall stalks with umbels of yellow flowers. Old World. Compare to *Osmorhiza* (sweet cicely) for fragrance.

Hierchloe occidentalis Vanilla grass: medium-sized clump-forming grass with pale green grasslike leaves, sweet vanilla odor, and spikes of whitish insignificant flowers. California native (summer water, shade). Compare to *Andropogon* (lemon grass) for form.

Horkelia spp. Horkelia: low, matted plants with pale green, ferny leaves, strong sage odor, and tiny white flowers. California native.

Lomatium spp. Indian biscuit roots: finely divided, ferny, green to whitish green leaves, strong parsley odor, and umbels of yellow, whitish, or purplish flowers. California natives. Compare to *Petroselinum* (parsley) for odor.

Melissa officinalis Lemon balm: tall clumps of wrinkled, bright green leaves, lemon odor, and tiers of whitish flowers. Old World. Compare to *Aloysia* (lemon verbena) and *Citrus* (lemon tree) for odor.

Mentha spp. Mints: widely spreading and invasive plants with quilted or wrinkled broad leaves, strong mint aromas, and tiers of purple to whitish flowers. (Includes spearmint, peppermint, apple mint, and pennyroyal.) Old World.

Mentha arvensis Field mint: widely spreading plants with quilted, broad, dull green leaves, strong mint odor, and tiers of pale purple flowers. Strong mint aroma. California native.

Monarda spp. Bee balms: clumps of dull green leaves, sage odor, and handsome heads of purple, pink, or red flowers. Eastern United States. Compare to *Monardella* (coyote mint) for odor and arrangement of flowers.

Monardella spp. Coyote mints: matted to mounded plants, dull to bright green leaves, and heads of purple, whitish, or red flowers. California natives.

Origanum spp. Oregano and marjoram: dull green leaves, sage or oregano scent, and spikes of pale purple flowers. Old World.

Osmorhiza chilensis Sweet cicely: small clumps of ferny, dark green leaves, anise odor, and insignificant flowers. California native (shade, summer water).

Petroselinum spp. Parsleys: crisped, curly, or coarsely divided, ferny green leaves, strong parsley odor, and small umbels of yellow-green flowers. Old World. Compare to *Lomatium* (Indian biscuit root) for odor.

Salvia leucantha Mexican purple sage: widely spreading plants with narrow, lance-shaped dull green leaves, strong sage odor, and tiered spikes of deep blue-purple, wooly flowers. Mexico. Compare various salvias here and under the preceding lists Medium-sized Shrubs and Tall Shrubs for similar yet different fragrances.

Salvia sclerea Sclary sage: bold, light green leaves, sage odor, and tiered whorls of pale purple flowers. Mediterranean.

Salvia spathacea Hummingbird sage: widely wandering plants with quilted, pale green leaves, sweet sage odor, and tiered spikes of rose-pink flowers. California native.

Sanicula bipinnata Poison sanicle: ferny, green leaves, strong cilantro odor, and umbels of yellow, buttonlike flowers. California native. Compare to *Coriandrum* (coriander) for fragrance.

Satureja montana Savory: narrow, dark green leaves, savory scent, and whitish to pale purple flowers. Old World. Compare to *Satureja douglasii* (yerba buena) under Ground Covers, below.

Stachys albens White or wooly woodmint: widely spreading plants with wooly, gray to silvery leaves, penetrating sage aroma, and tiers of whitish flowers. California native. Compare to lamb's ears, immediately below, for fragrance and leaf texture.

Stachys olympica Lamb's ears: low, cushion-forming plants with broad, wooly, gray-white leaves, penetrating sage aroma, and low flowering stalks with tiers of white or purplish flowers. Old World.

Tanacetum camphoratum and *douglasii* Dune tansies: low clumps of handsome, ferny leaves on wandering roots, grayish or green leaves, strong, bitter sage odor, and small clusters of modest yellow daisies. California natives. Compare to tansy, immediately below, for fragrance and leaf texture.

Tanacetum vulgaris Tansy: narrow clumps with green, ferny foliage, strong, bitter sage odor, and flat-topped clusters of small yellow daisies. Old World.

Thymus spp. Thymes: matted plants, tiny dull green to grayish leaves, strong thyme or sage odor, and small clusters of pale to purple flowers. Old World.

Zingiber zerumbet Ginger root: subtropical, tender herb from rhizomes, with broad, dark green leaves, ginger scent, and short spikes of pale yellow flowers. Asiatic (frost tender). Compare to ground cover *Asarum* (wild ginger) for fragrance.

Ground Covers for the Herb Garden

Asarum spp. Wild ginger: coarse ground cover of large, round, dark green leaves, ginger scent, and hidden spidery, maroon flowers. California natives (summer water and shade). Compare to *Zingiber* (ginger root), immediately above this list, for fragrance.

Chamaemeleum spp. Chamomile: low, ferny mat with bright green leaves, chamomile odor, and yellow buttons or white and yellow daisy flowers. Old World.

Juniperus 'Tam.' Tam juniper: coarse, woody ground cover with needlelike, grayish leaves, strong, piny odor, and insignificant cones. Old World. Compare to mat juniper, immediately below, for fragrance and similar usage.

Juniperus communis saxatilis Mat juniper: cascading woody ground cover with needlelike, silvery green leaves, strong, piny odor, and purplish berries (female plants). California native.

Mentha requenii Corsican mint: very low, tight ground cover with minute leaves, strong mint odor, and tiny purplish flowers. Old World. Compare to other mints (*Mentha* spp.) for odor.

Origanum dictamnus Dittany of Crete: coarse mats of rounded, silver-gray leaves, strong sage or oregano odor, and short spikes of tiered, purple bracted flowers. Old World. Compare to oregano (*Origanum* spp.) for fragrance.

Ribes viburnifolium Evergreen currant: coarse, woody ground cover with broad, shiny, light green leaves, lemon odor, and tiny maroon-purple flowers. California native (light shade).

Salvia sonomensis Sonoma sage: cascading, subwoody ground cover with dull green, quilted leaves, strong sage odor, and tiered spikes of blue-purple flowers. California native.

Satureja douglasii Yerba buena: very low, cascading ground cover with elliptical, light green leaves, mint odor, and tiny whitish flowers. California native (occasional summer water, light shade). Compare to *Satureja montana* (savory) for nonnative species used as a culinary herb.

Thymus spp. Thymes: very low mats of subwoody ground cover with tiny, elliptical, dull green to gray leaves, strong sage or thyme odor, and tiny spikes of purplish flowers. Old World.

Fragrant Flowers for the Herb Garden

Situate these fragrant flowers according to height and the carrying power of their odor.

Boronia megastigma Brown boronia: low to medium evergreen shrub with bitter-citrus-scented leaves and nodding, saucer-shaped, brown and yellowish flowers. Delightful chocolate odor. Australia (some summer water).

Brickelia californica California brickel bush: small, winter-deciduous shrub with resinous scented, dull green leaves, and greenish white spikes of inconspicuous flowers. Strong, carrying, sweet perfume in late afternoon to evening. California native. Compare to *Cestrum* (night-flowering jasmine) for fragrance.

Brugmansia spp. Angel's trumpets: tall, evergreen shrubs with leaves foul-scented, flowers very large, hanging, and trumpet-shaped in white, orange, pink, or red. Penetrating, sweet odor at night. South America. Compare to Datura in this list for fragrance and form of flower.

Calycanthus occidentalis Western spice bush: medium-sized, deciduous shrub with spice-scented leaves and water-lily-like red-maroon flowers. Odor of old wine close up. California native (summer water, light shade).

Carpenteria californica Bush anemone: medium-sized, evergreen shrub, with unscented leaves and large, single, roselike white flowers. Mild, sweet scent at close range. California native (some summer water, light shade).

Ceanothus spp. Wild lilacs: medium to large shrubs, with usually unscented leaves and dense spires of white, pink, blue, or purple flowers. Corn tortilla odor at moderate to close range. California natives (most need full sun and are drought tolerant). Compare to *Syringa* (lilac) in this list for usage and arrangement of flowers.

Cestrum jasminoides Night-flowering jasmine: lank, medium-sized, deciduous shrub with fuchsialike, unpleasantly scented leaves and unshowy long, tubular, greenish flowers. Penetrating sweet jasmine odor at night. South America. Compare to *Trachelospermum* (star jasmine) for fragrance.

Citrus spp. Citruses: medium-sized, shrubby trees with tough, evergreen, citrus-scented leaves and small clusters of white blossoms. Strong, sweet, lilac odor at medium to long range. Old World. Compare to *Philadelphus* (mock orange) for fragrance.

Convallaria majalus Lily-of-the-valley: low, bulbous plant spreading by rootstocks, with unscented leaves and nodding, white bell flowers. Sweet, delicious fragrance at close range. Old World (summer water and light shade). Compare to *Smilacina (fat false Solomon's seal) in this list for fragrance.*

Daphne odora and spp. Daphnes: medium-sized to low, evergreen shrubs with unscented leaves and tight clusters of starry, white to purple flowers. Heavy sweet perfume, which carries. Old World (some summer water, light shade).

Datura meteloides Datura: coarse, perennial herb with large, dark green, unpleasantly scented leaves and very large, flared, trumpet-shaped white flowers that fade purple. Strong, penetrating, sweet scent from late afternoon through evening. California native. Compare to *Brugmansia* (angel's trumpet) for fragrance and flower shape.

Dianthus spp. Pinks: low, matted plants with narrow, silvery to gray, unscented leaves. Flowers are in small clusters or single; fringed, carnationlike, and white, pink, or rose. Strong clove scent at medium range. Old World. Compare to *Lilium washingtonianum* (Washington lily) for fragrance.

Erysimum spp. Native wallflowers: low- to medium-sized biennials with unscented, narrow leaves and racemes of mustardlike, creamy white, yellow, or orange flowers. Sweet fragrance at close range. California natives.

Gardenia spp. Gardenia: small, evergreen shrubs with unscented, shiny leaves and large, mostly double white flowers. Strong, sweet odor. Old World and American tropics (summer water, light shade).

Hedychium gardnerianum Yellow ginger lily: tall perennial herb from rhizomes (winter dormant), with unscented, bananalike leaves, and spikes of spidery, pale yellow flowers. Strong, sweet odor with overtones of ginger. Asiatic (summer water, light shade).

Lilium regale Easter lily: bulb, extending upward to two and a half feet, with whorled, unscented leaves and large, regal white trumpets. Strong, penetrating, sweet scent. Asiatic. Compare all liliums (lilies) for flower fragrance.

Lilium rubescens Chaparral lily: bulb, extending upward to six feet, with whorled, unscented leaves and medium-sized lily flowers opening pale pink and fading deep rose. Less prominent scent than Washington lily. California native.

Lilium washingtonianum Washington lily: bulb, extending upward to six-plus feet, with whorled, unscented leaves and large, white trumpet flowers fading pink-purple. Strong, penetrating, sweet clove odor. California native.

Lupinus albifrons White-leaf bush lupine: low, evergreen shrub with unscented grayish leaves and spikes of blue-purple flowers. Sweet, carrying odor in afternoon and evening. California native.

Mirabilis froebellii and others. Wild four o'clocks: smaller than four o'clock below (compare them also in flower shape and fragrance). Perennial herbs with tuberous roots (noninvasive) and handsome, flared, trumpetlike, purple, pink, or white flowers. Sweet scent late afternoon through evening. California natives.

Mirabilis jalapa Four o'clock: coarse perennial herb with large, tuberous, invasive roots, unpleasantly scented leaves, and small, trumpet-shaped pink, white, red, or yellow flowers. Strong, penetrating, sweet scent late afternoon through evening. South America.

Narcissus poeticus Paper-white narcissus: medium-sized bulbs, narrow, grasslike, unscented leaves, and umbels of white flowers with shallow, yellow cups. Intense, sweet, long-range fragrance. Old World.

Philadelphus lewisii Mock orange: large, deciduous shrub with unscented leaves and large, pure white roselike flowers in short clusters. Strong, sweet odor. California native (summer water, light shade). Compare to *Syringa* (lilac) for fragrance.

Rhododendron fragrantissima Fragrant azalea: medium-sized, evergreen shrub with unscented leaves and clusters of pure white, rhododendron flowers. Long-range, sweet, powerful odor. Asiatic (summer water and light shade). Compare to western azalea, immediately below, for usage, shape, and fragrance.

Rhododendron occidentale Western azalea: tall, deciduous shrub with unscented leaves and clusters of large, showy, rhododendron flowers in white and yellow or pink and yellow. Long range, sweet, powerful odors. California native (summer water and light shade).

Rosa spp. Roses: medium-sized deciduous shrubs with unscented leaves and thorny branches, and with large, single to very double, pink or white flowers (other colors also). Some with deep, sweet perfume at close range. Old World (summer water). Compare to next for usage, shape, and fragrance.

Rosa spp. Wild roses: low- to medium-sized deciduous shrubs, with unscented leaves and thorny branches, and with small- to medium-sized, single rose flowers. Deep, sweet perfume close up. California natives (some summer water, light shade).

Smilacina racemosa Fat false Solomon's seal: tuberous plant spreading slowly by rhizomes, in time forming large clumps with unscented leaves and sprays of tiny, cream-colored flowers. Lily-of-the-valley scent at medium range. California native (summer water and light shade). Compare to *Convallaria* (lily-of-the-valley) in this list for usage and fragrance.

Syringa vulgaris Lilac: large, deciduous shrub, with unscented leaves and dense spires of white, purple, or pinkish flowers. Strong, sweet odor (with winter chill). Old World.

Trachelospermum jasminoides Star jasmine: low, semisprawling, evergreen shrub with unscented, shiny leaves and clusters of small, white, pinwheel-shaped flowers. Strong, penetrating, sweet odor. Old World (summer water, light shade). Compare to *Cestrum* (night-flowering jasmine) in this list for odor.

Viola odorata English violet: invasive ground cover with unscented, heart-shaped leaves and dark blue, pink, or white violet-shaped flowers. Sweet, medium-range fragrance. Old World (some summer water, light shade).

PART TWO

ENCYCLOPEDIA

of NATIVE SHRUBS

In the following entries native shrub species are listed by genus, and the genus names are listed alphabetically. Heading each entry are one or more species names, the common name(s), the family, and encapsulated information. The abbreviations used stand for:

HT: overall height of shrub

LVS: whether the leaves are evergreen or deciduous

FLWS: attributes of flowers, including color, showiness, and flowering time

SMR WTR: whether shrubs require summer water

PROP: methods of propagation

EXP: required exposure to the sun

Following this encapsulated information, entries detail shrubs' assets and liabilities, special cultural requirements, garden uses, habitat and place of origin, and other pertinent aspects.

The following is a cross-reference of common names to genus and species names, with the page number for each.

IMPORTANT NOTE ON NAMING

The scientific names in this book do *not* reflect the many name changes in the recently published *Jepson Manual*. Rather, the names that are already likely to be familiar to the gardening public and in the nursery trade have been used here.

CROSS-REFERENCES OF
COMMON TO SCIENTIFIC NAMES

COMMON NAME	GENUS AND SPECIES NAME	PAGE
Agave, desert	*Agave deserti*	82
Alder, mountain	*Alnus tenuifolia*	83
Alyssum, desert	*Lepidium fremontii*	186
Anemone, bush	*Carpenteria californica*	106
Antelope brush	*Purshia* spp.	222
Apache plume	*Fallugia paradoxa*	157
Ash, flowering	*Fraxinus dipetala*	161
mountain	*Sorbus* spp.	251
Aspen, quaking	*Populus tremuloides*	217
Aster, desert	*Machaeranthera tortifolia*	195
Azalea, mock	*Menziesia ferruginea*	202
western	*Rhododendron occidentale*	228
Azalea-flowered monkeyflower	*Diplacus bifidus*	143
Barberry	*Mahonia* spp.	198
Barrel cactus	*Ferocactus acanthodes*	157
Bayberry, California	*Myrica californica*	204
Bay laurel, shrub	*Umbellularia californica*	262
Beargrass	*Nolina parryi*	208
Beavertail cactus	*Opuntia basilaris*	209
Berry rue	*Cneoridium dumosum*	131
Birch, resin	*Betula glandulosa*	103
water	*B. occidentalis*	102
Bladdernut	*Staphylea bolanderi*	253
Bladderpod	*Isomeris arborea*	179
Blueblossom	*Ceanothus thyrsiflorus*	120
southern	*C. cyaneus*	111
Blue curls, wooly	*Trichostema lanatum*	261
Blue witch	*Solanum umbelliferum & xantii*	251

70

NATIVE SHRUBS, BY GENUS

Acalypha californica. California Copperleaf. Spurge family (Euphorbiaceae)

HT: 10 to 40 inches. LVS: evergreen. FLWS: inconspicuous, greenish to reddish, in short spikes; April to May. SMR WTR: little. PROP: cuttings. EXP: full sun

California copperleaf is a short shrub with broadly ovate leaves, attractively copper-red when young. It forms a rather compact shrub for the foreground in drought-tolerant plantings. It can take full sun and plenty of heat. The flowers are in short spikes, the male reddish, the female greenish to reddish and sticky. Although easily propagated from half-ripened wood, copperleaf is rather tender and does poorly where winters are wet and cold.

Use California copperleaf in a desert-style garden as an edging for taller or bolder plants, or in a droughty mixed border where the leaves can add bold and definitive detail in the front or middle section.

Acamptopappus shockleyi. Goldenhead. Sunflower family (Asteraceae)

HT: to 20 inches. LVS: evergreen. FLWS: golden daisies on single stalks; April to June. SMR WTR: none. PROP: cuttings (use bottom heat); seeds (stratify). EXP: full sun

Goldenhead is a trim shrub of mid to high deserts, where it grows fully exposed to the heat of the summer sun. Its white bark with evergreen, spoon-shaped to elliptical leaves, and late-spring display of yellow daisies are appealing. Once established it should be reliable without summer water and should blend well into a desert planting. Two attributes that place it in the foreground, besides size, are the attractive bark and dark green leaves; many other desert shrubs defoliate in summer and fall. Goldenhead can be used in lieu of or with the more widely distributed bush sunflower *Haplopappus linearifolius* and any of the companion shrubs recommended for it.

Acer circinatum. Vine Maple. Maple family (Aceraceae)

HT: 3 to 20 feet. LVS: winter deciduous. FLWS: delicate chains of small reddish flowers; early spring. SMR WTR: moist soil. PROP: cuttings; layering; seeds (stratify). EXP: shade

Vine maple is the essence of grace as a large shrub or small tree. Although the common name suggests a viny growth form, this is seldom the case. Vine maple is outstanding for seasonal changes: pretty bare reddish twigs in winter, graceful, half-drooping clusters of dull red and white flowers in early spring (accompanying the unfolding of new leaves), delicate, many-lobed leaves through spring and summer, pink winged samaras in late summer or early fall, and scarlet autumn leaves (less intensely colored in mild-winter climates). Vine maple is not for areas with dry summers; its forte is in the moist forest garden. Areas of plentiful winter rains and generous summer fogs befit it best. Although tolerant of deep shade, dappled shade provides healthier, more rapid growth.

Vine maple's biggest liability is its slow growth; it can take many years to attain mature size, especially from seed. Establishing a mature specimen is faster from cuttings or layering, but even then patience is needed. Vine maple is tolerant of cold winters and withstands freezing temperatures quite well. It also withstands very hot summers, when given adequate shade and water.

In the landscape, use vine maple as a backdrop for a forest or woodland garden, against the shaded side of a house, behind a pond, or as a specimen. Its leaves complement many other forest plants, such as rhododendrons, azaleas, ferns, fuchsias, and camellias. It should be planted to show off the leaves as well as possible. Consider it also as a striking specimen plant in lieu of Japanese maple (*Acer palmatum*).

Acer glabrum. Sierra or Rocky Mountain Maple. Maple family (Aceraceae)

HT: 6 to 20 feet. LVS: winter deciduous. FLWS: inconspicuous, pale yellow; early spring. SMR WTR: some deep watering. PROP: cuttings; layering; seeds (stratify). EXP: light shade

Sierra maple makes a small tree or can be trained easily as a bushy shrub. It is a subdued version of a maple, with neither the delicacy of the vine maple nor the grand manner of big-leaf maple, but it is an excellent choice for the mountain garden, where winters are severely cold and summers warm. Like most maples it lives naturally near streams or along lake margins and so must have summer water to succeed.

Sierra maple has small, few-lobed leaves, but they have a glowing sheen when reflecting late afternoon sun. Flowers and fall leaf color are unlikely to elicit strong comment, yet this maple is an altogether pleasant companion for a naturally wooded garden, as an underplanting for pines or firs. It should stand alone or be planted in company with others of its kind to make the best garden statement. If you grow it with other shrubs, be sure those shrubs have a bold and different leaf pattern.

Adenostoma fasciculatum. Chamise. Rose family (Rosaceae)

HT: 3 to 10 feet. LVS: evergreen. FLWS: showy plumes of tiny white flowers; late spring. SMR WTR: none. PROP: cuttings (use bottom heat); seeds (stratify). EXP: full sun

Chamise is a densely branched, rounded or angular shrub of hot, dry, rocky slopes. It inhabits some of the poorest soils in exposed situations in the chaparral. The first years of growth are rapid, tapering off later. The mature height depends upon the richness of soils; on sands and serpentine, shrubs remain stunted.

Chamise has thick clusters of short, polished green, needlelike leaves that clothe the shrub all year. In hot weather leaves carry a volatile oil that makes plants combustible, so be sure to plant shrubs well away from flammable structures. Flowers are borne in small dense sprays reminiscent of spiraea, covering plants with a creamy froth in late spring. Blossoms dry to a rusty brown and remain on shrubs throughout the summer.

Chamise is a wonderful shrub for naturalizing on steep and rocky slopes. (Remember its liability near houses owing to its susceptiblity to burning.) There is also a variety with creeping to decumbent habit from Santa Cruz Island, excellent as a tough ground cover for places with little foot traffic and with the bonus of seasonal flower color.

Adenostoma sparsifolium. Red Shanks. Rose family (Rosaceae)

HT: 6 to 20 feet. LVS: evergreen. FLWS: similar to those of chamise, above; late spring. SMR WTR: none. PROP: cuttings; seeds (stratify). EXP: full sun

In the same degree that its relative chamise is mundane in chaparral settings, red shanks is bold and dramatic there. Its tall stems develop into trunks with handsome red strips of peeling bark, and it can be easily trained into tree form. The branches create an open cloud of pale green foliage with narrow, almost needlelike leaves. The flowers, a pretty addition in late spring, sometimes highlight the plant as chamise's flowers do, and they contrast well with the rest of the plant.

Red shanks is adapted to hot summer climates and rocky soils, and it will tolerate some winter chill. Long lived, it may take several years to reach maturity but is well worth the wait. This shrub is ideal as a bold specimen, backdrop, or foundation plant in a xeriscape or desert garden. Its handsome bark and leaf combination is hard to beat.

Aesculus californica. California Buckeye. Horse-chestnut family (Hippocastanaceae)

HT: to about 25 feet. LVS: deciduous fall and winter. FLWS: candles of white flowers; late spring. SMR WTR: occasional deep watering. PROP: cuttings; seeds (plant immediately). EXP: full sun or very light shade

California buckeye grows naturally as a small tree, with a broad, beautifully rounded canopy. Pinching back the new shoots encourages it instead to bush out and create a large shrub. Here is a fine plant for seasonal interest: silvery gray bark that's shown to advantage from fall through winter; fanlike, palmately compound apple green leaves in spring and early summer; tight candles of nearly pure white, sweetly fragrant flowers in May or June; and curious, leathery pear-like seed pods with glossy brown seeds like chestnuts in fall. Note that buckeye seeds are not, however, edible, though they resemble the edible seeds of chestnuts. The large seeds contain an abundant food reserve but fare poorly, shriveling if not planted immediately; prompt planting assures easy germination and vigorous seedlings. Growth is rapid for the first few years. Decent size for the shrub requires only a few years with abundant water and sun.

California buckeye is adapted to especially hot, dry summers once its roots are well established, but it will retain leaves longer and grow more steadily when given occasional deep summer waterings. It can be grown as a focal point in a small garden, yet it is capable of growing tall enough to provide shade for a one-story building. It also can be pruned as a hedge or foundation planting. Two liabilities: lots of leaf litter in fall, and poisonous leaves and seeds. This is not an appropriate plant where young children wander. In a large-scale garden, buckeye can be grown to tree size with live oaks and digger pines for a natural effect.

Agave deserti. Desert Century Plant or Agave. Agave or maguey family (Agavaceae)

HT: out of flower, to about 2 feet. LVS: tough and evergreen. FLWS: enormous panicles of yellow flowers in 10 to 15 years. SMR WTR: none. PROP: pups from parent plant; seeds. EXP: full sun

The agaves are a tough, drought-resistant lot with bold design, perfect for desert gardens. They make dramatic rosettes of tough, gray, large fleshy leaves, each tipped by a wicked spine and edged with murderous sawlike teeth. These leaves were universally used by early peoples for their tough fibers. New leaves overlap one another and make impressions where their teeth lie, lending a sculpted beauty to mature leaves.

Agaves are monocarpic: they grow for several years to accumulate enough reserve food for one "big-bang" flowering. At first the flowering stalk resembles a giant asparagus. It may soar to ten or more feet, finally opening in a broad panicle of tubular yellow flowers dripping with nectar and sought out by hummingbirds and bees alike. The seed pods ripen slowly over the next few months, finally turning brown and opening. At the same time the leaves gradually turn brown; the whole plant dies from its mammoth reproductive effort. Generally, however, the parent makes a circle of pups before passing on. These are easily severed and start the cycle all over with minimum fuss; seeds germinate freely but take much longer to reach maturity.

Place this agave where it can be the center of attention: an island in a desert garden or the bold element among various smaller cacti or succulents. Use it also in a large container. It is difficult to integrate into conventional garden designs, because of its unique structure and shape.

Two other agaves for consideration are A. *shawii*, from the southernmost coast of San Diego County, with green leaves and immense panicles of bright yellow flowers, and the rare *A. utahensis*, a miniature with short, very spiny leaves and short flowering stalks.

Alnus tenuifolia. Mountain Alder. Birch family (Betulaceae)

HT: 3 to 10 feet. LVS: winter deciduous. FLWS: male catkins, late winter; female catkins inconspicuous. SMR WTR: moist soil at all times. PROP: layering; seeds. EXP: light shade

Mountain alder is familiar to mountain climbers: it forms dense, impenetrable thickets along rushing brooks, often just below timberline. It is irrevocably associated with bright mountain days and wildflower meadows. A plant that elicits this order of nostalgia deserves a trial in a natural garden. Bear two things in mind: alders grow prolifically and rapidly and so must have ample space (they spread by running roots); and they die if they dry out.

Mountain alder is seldom more than a densely branched bush with arching trunks and resilient, springy branches. It is easy to propagate by layering or from cuttings. It lends a natural feel to streamsides planted by itself, although it can wage turf battles with other vigorous riparian shrubs, such as willows. It is of seasonal interest for its long dangling male catkins in late winter to early spring before leaves reappear; the shorter upright female catkins are seldom noticed, until they develop into conelike fruits, which decorate branches into winter. Because it is bare twigged half the year, mountain alder can be underplanted with pretty, moisture-loving wildflowers such as enchanter's nightshade (*Circaea alpina*), glacier lilies (*Erythronium* spp.), western bleeding heart (*Dicentra formosa*), *Corydalis caseana*, and smooth yellow violet (*Viola glabella*). Or it can serve as protection for taller-growing stream followers such as tower larkspur (*Delphinium glaucum*), lilies (*Lilium* spp.), ranger's buttons (*Sphenosciadium capitellatum*), monkshood (*Aconitum columbianum*), and cow parsnip (*Heracleum lanatum*).

Ambrosia dumosa. Burro Bush. Sunflower family (Asteraceae)

HT: to 2 feet. LVS: summer deciduous. FLWS: tiny yellow-green heads in short spikes; through spring months. SMR WTR: none. PROP: seeds (stratify or scarify). EXP: full sun

Burro bush is a small shrub dominant in California's warm deserts, frequently interspersed with the taller creosote bush (*Larrea divaricata*). In that setting it lends a pleasing contrast, for creosote bush wears shiny, dark green leaves; burro bush is decked out in soft gray foliage. The leaves are deeply pinnately slashed and lobed, giving a pretty pattern to the branches. The flowers, on the other hand, are negligible, borne in short spikes of tiny yellow-green heads, male above female, the female covered with spiny bristles.

Burro bush will never find a place in the ordinary garden, but because of its tough nature—adaptation to high summer heat, low winter rainfall, and sandy soils—it is perfect for a low-maintenance desert garden. There it contrasts nicely with green-leafed shrubs such as creosote bush, yellowheads, and desert trixis.

Amelanchier pallida. Service Berry or June Berry. Rose family (Rosaceae)

HT: 3 to 20 feet. LVS: winter deciduous. FLWS: abundant, white applelike blossoms; midspring. SMR WTR: periodic deep watering. PROP: cuttings (use bottom heat); suckers; seeds (stratify). EXP: full sun to light shade

Service berry is an overlooked, deserving ornamental shrub with several fine qualities: seasonal masses of attractive applelike white flowers; a picturesque branching pattern; and malleable habit. In lowland forests it can attain near-tree stature; on wind-blown coastal knolls or mountain heights it becomes a prostrate, woody ground cover flowing prettily over boulders. Consequently, the gardener can select the form he or she wishes: prune it severely to create a bold ground cover in a rock garden; train it against a wall as an espalier; or allow it to grow naturally into a large shrub in an open woodland garden or behind a pond.

Service berry is a modest shrub out of flower, with soft, pale green to gray-green leaves, distinctively toothed on the upper half and smooth on the lower. Its berrylike rosy pomes, which ripen in early summer, are tasty dried or used for jams or jellies. Neither cuttings nor seeds are easy to handle, requiring considerable patience, and growth is relatively slow. Layering of lower branches might also prove effective in propagation.

Amorpha spp. False Indigo. Pea family (Fabaceae)

HT: 3 to 10 feet. LVS: winter deciduous. FLWS: dark purple in dense spikes; early summer. SMR WTR: occasional deep watering. PROP: root divisions; layering. EXP: light shade

California's two species of false indigo are closely similar: A. *californica* has prickles on stems and leaves; A. *fruticosa* does not. Both grow as low to medium shrubs with creeping roots so that eventually loose colonies are formed; both have odd-pinnately compound, deciduous leaves of typical pea form; both have a pleasing resinous odor obvious on hot days; and both produce slender spikes of unusual, dark indigo-purple flowers complemented by orange stamens. The flowers, unlike typical peas, have only one petal, the banner, but the combination of indigo purple and orange is very attractive close at hand, and butterflies seek out the blossoms for nectar.

False indigo is a good shrub for the edge or backdrop of an open woodland garden, or along a seasonally dry stream. Its open growth and wandering habit mean it needs "elbow" room, and its distinctive form places it away from other shrubs. A striking natural combination in southern Arizona is false indigo on banks above a streambed lined with golden columbine (*Aquilegia chrysantha*) or bordered by clumps of coral

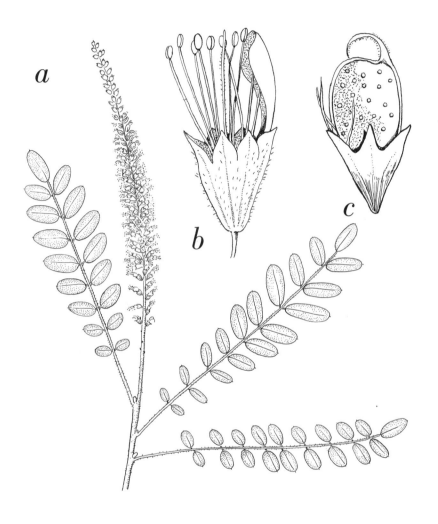

a

b

c

False Indigo (*Amorpha californica*)
a. flowering branch   *b*. flower detail   *c*. fruit detail

bells (*Heuchera sanguinea*). California natives of similar form are red columbine (*Aquilegia formosa*) and common alumroot (*Heuchera micrantha*).

Arctostaphylos spp. Manzanitas. Heather family (Ericaceae)

HT: 2 inches to 20 feet. LVS: evergreen. FLWS: racemes of white to pink urn-shaped flowers; winter to spring. SMR WTR: none for most. PROP: cuttings (use bottom heat); seeds (scarify and stratify). EXP: full sun for most

Manzanitas are one of the best known Californian shrubs and well established in the nursery trade. Even with a broad description of so many kinds, I have excluded some species and varieties.

Manzanitas are handsome, durable shrubs for the garden, and they deserve even wider recognition. They all share lovely polished, red-purple bark, and stiff evergreen, ovate to elliptical leaves, which are vertically oriented in species receiving full sun. Some manzanitas produce basal burls at the root crown; those with burls are capable of stump sprouting after fire, allowing regeneration of plants without seeds. All bear copious racemes of nodding white to rose-pink, urn-shaped flowers, which appear early in the season for their particular habitat. All also produce quantities of small applelike berries, which slowly turn from green to pink, rose, or mahogany brown. Berries are edible but have uncommonly large bonelike seeds in the center. Their best uses are for jelly or for a sort of hot cider.

Since manzanitas vary from low, sprawling ground covers to small trees, their use is dictated by kind. They are all highly drought tolerant and favor slightly acid but well-drained soils, and the majority perform best in full sun. Most live happily in rocky or sandy soils low in nutrients. A few need light shade or cool summer conditions; this is indicated for each species. Manzanitas do not transplant easily and so are best grown to vigorous condition in gallon cans, then moved into permanent positions in the garden, preferably in late fall or early winter. They are most often propagated by cuttings; creeping kinds may already have roots attached along their stems. Propagation by seed is recommended only for those willing to subject seeds to filing, soaking in acid, stratifying for long periods, or a combination of these. Be sure the potting mix drains well and is free of fungal pathogens.

The larger manzanitas make wonderful specimen shrubs or trees, standing by themselves as focal points. They may also be combined with other chaparral shrubs to create a planting with floral color over a long period (for example, with ceanothuses, bush poppies, fremontias, and garryas). Many lend themselves to creating informal barriers or hedges, but use care in pruning them, since fungal pathogens have the potential to enter the stems where the stems have been opened by cutting. The low-growing kinds are excellent in front of taller shrubs or as an integral part of a dry mixed border. The prostrate kinds create low-maintenance, woody ground covers, as long as any foot traffic is minor. Manzanitas are a real asset for their masses of flowers in the winter, their handsome bark and foliage all year, and their colorful berries. The following are short descriptions of species with garden potential:

A. andersonii. Heartleaf manzanita. Large shrub to twelve feet tall, with clasping pale to dark green, heart-shaped stalkless leaves, white to pink flowers in mid to late winter, and red-brown berries. No burl. Full sun near coast, light shade inland.

A. auriculata. Mt. Diablo manzanita. Similar to heartleaf manzanita but more compact, with felted, grayish foliage. Very attractive, distinctive, and drought tolerant. Full sun.

A. bakeri. Serpentine or Baker's manzanita. Medium shrub to six or eight feet, similar in many respects to Stanford manzanita. No burl. Twigs and branchlets dark with fine, sticky hairs and longer shaggy hairs; flowers slightly larger, pale pink. Can take full sun on nutrient-poor serpentine soils. Handsome shrub for northern California.

A. canescens. Downy-leaf or hoary manzanita. Small upright or sprawling shrub, up to six feet tall. No burl. Select either form according to garden need. Leaves pale green, stalked, covered with white, hoary hairs when young; flowers white to pinkish, in winter and spring according to elevation; berries covered with white fuzz. Full sun to light shade; tolerates summer heat.

A. cinerea. Del Norte manzanita. Semidecumbent, spreading shrub to about five feet. With burl. Leaves ashy green; twigs with very short hairs; flowers white to pink in spring. Fruits dark red-brown. Good for summer-hot areas; tolerates poor soils.

A. columbiana. Columbia or hairy manzanita. Large shrub sometimes with single trunk (or can be pruned that way) to ten feet tall. No burl. Leaves and new stems have shaggy white hairs. Leaves are gray-green, flowers white to pale pink in spring. Good for cool climates; accepts light shade; needs acid soil. Good with other heather relatives such as huckleberries and salal.

A. crustacea. Brittle-leaf manzanita. Medium-sized shrub to six feet with basal burl and deep red-purple, smooth bark. Leaves bright green, stalked; twigs covered with close felty hairs in addition to long bristly hairs. Flowers in open panicles, white to pink, late winter to spring. Berries red. Handsome in coastal gardens, requiring little water. The variety *rosei*, localized around Lake Merced in San Francisco, is lower growing and is especially fine for its display of pink flowers followed by deep red berries.

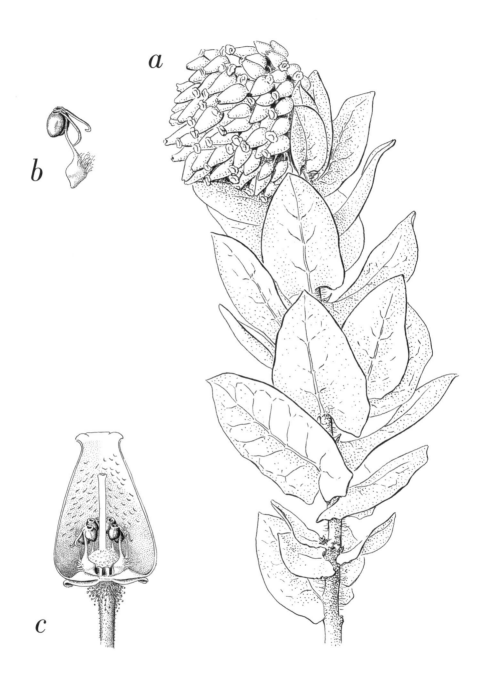

Heartleaf Manzanita (*Arctostaphylos andersonii*)
a. flowering branch *b.* flower detail *c.* stamen detail

A. densiflora. Vinehill manzanita. Low semiprostrate or mound-forming shrub to one or two feet, but variable in stature, especially when hybridized with other species. No burl. Stems root freely as they contact soil. Leaves shiny green, sharply pointed. Flowers in short, dense clusters, white to pink, in spring. One of the most widely used parents for selected cultivars and hybrids for garden purposes.

A. edmundsii. Little Sur manzanita. Widely spreading, half-prostrate shrub without burl. Broad green, stalked leaves; hairy stems; pink flowers, in early to mid winter; berries brown. Excellent ground cover for coastal areas or in rock gardens. Roots as it grows.

A. glandulosa. Eastwood manzanita. Shrub to eight feet tall with dense, often twisted or crooked branches. Large basal burl. Leaves pale green, stalked, with glandular hairs at base; short panicles of white flowers midwinter to mid spring; brownish-red berries. Very variable species; good all-around shrub for hot, dry areas.

A. glauca. Big-berry manzanita. Large shrub, trainable as small tree to twenty feet. No burl. Handsome smooth whitish leaves; dense panicles of white to pinkish flowers from midwinter to early spring; uncommonly large brown to red, sticky berries. Accepts rocky soils in hot sun. Handsome specimen.

A. hearstiorum. Hearst manzanita. Prostrate version of Monterey manzanita, forming broad mats. No burl. Small clusters of flowers. Good ground cover for warm, coastal situations.

A. hookeri. Monterey manzanita. Low mound-forming shrub to three feet. No burl. Bright shiny green, stalked leaves; small white to pinkish flower clusters winter to mid spring; bright red berries. Excellent shrub for rock gardens in coastal areas, or as coarse ground cover. Tolerates sandy soils.

A. hooveri. Hoover's manzanita. Tall shrub, to eighteen feet. No burl. Handsome heart-shaped, grayish leaves with shaggy hairs, on stalks. White flowers. Excellent large shrub for summer-hot situations, where large size and gray color are wanted.

A. imbricata. Shingleleaf manzanita. Unusual sprawling shrub, which covers large areas over time and roots as it grows. No burl. Bright green, smooth leaves overlap one another like shingles on a roof; white flowers in winter to early spring. Difficult to grow, and rare, but a superlative and unusual ground cover. Tolerates rocky soils with good drainage.

A. *insularis*. Island manzanita. Large shrub (probably trainable as small tree) to sixteen feet tall. No burl. Bright green, shiny, stalked leaves; open, drooping panicles of white flowers from late winter to early spring; brown berries. Handsome specimen for coastal gardens. Tolerates light shade inland.

A. *intricata*. Black-bark manzanita. Handsome, upright shrub to six feet, with unusual near-black bark. Basal burl. Stalked, dull green leaves with short, wooly hairs; flowers white to rose-pink, in spring. Good shrub for its interesting bark color; well adapted to summer heat and poor soils.

A. *manzanita*. Common or Parry manzanita. Striking large shrub or small tree to twenty feet or more. No burl. Pale green, stalked leaves and open, drooping panicles of white to pink flowers from midwinter to spring, according to elevation. Berries deep red. Handsome specimen plant; full sun. One of the best all-around.

A. *mariposa*. Mariposa manzanita. Similar to A. *viscida*, with white leaves and no burl, but leaves and twigs and sepals bear sticky, glandular hairs. Handsome for hot-summer areas. From the central and southern Sierra foothills.

A. *mewukka*. Indian or Miwok manzanita. Shrub to about eight feet high, with deep red-purple bark. Basal burl. Pale, gray-green leaves are hairless and on stout stalks; flowers white to pink, in early spring. Fruits deep red or red-brown. Midelevation Sierra shrub; should adapt well to relatively cold winters and warm or hot summers. Excellent for mountain gardens.

A. *montana*. Mt. Tamalpais manzanita. Low, sprawling, mat-forming shrub, with leaves and flowers somewhat resembling Mexican manzanita. Flowers white, appearing in late winter to early spring. Excellent for poor, exposed, summer-hot soils; from serpentine outcroppings.

A. *myrtifolia*. Ione manzanita. Miniature spreading shrub to about two and a half feet high, with lower branches rooting on contact with soil and shreddy bark on branchlets. No burl. Shiny, pale green, myrtlelike leaves and small clusters of white to pinkish flowers, late winter. A charming shrub but difficult to grow; give hot summer sun. Tolerates poor soils.

A. *nevadensis*. Pinemat manzanita. Widely spreading, prostrate shrub with dense, often tangled branchlets. No burl. Roots as it grows. Smooth bright green leaves; small dense, upright clusters of white flowers in late spring to early summer. Seeks open forests in the mountains; not easily adaptable to low elevations, but excellent for ground cover in mountain gardens.

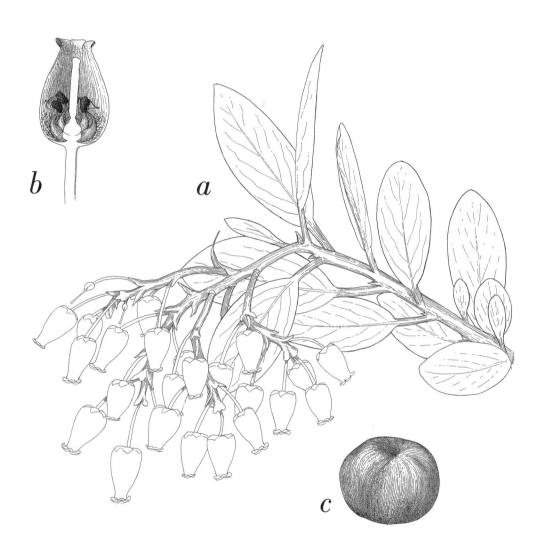

b *a* *c*

Common Manzanita (*Arctostaphylos manzanita*)
a. flowering branch   *b.* flower cut-away detail   *c.* fruit detail

A. *nummularia*. Fort Bragg manzanita. Small, dense shrub to four feet, often lower and sprawling. No burl. Miniature ovate to elliptic, dark green, shiny leaves, sometimes curled under along their edges; small clusters of white, miniature flowers in spring; green berries. Lovely miniature shrub for coastal gardens. Likes cool foggy conditions, acid soils, and some summer water. Ideal for the edge of a wooded garden.

A. *obispoensis*. San Luis Obispo manzanita. Shrub to ten feet high, with dark red-purple bark. No burl. Twigs and leaves covered with close, grayish, wooly hairs; leaves often heart shaped at base, with or without stalk. Flowers white to pink, late winter to early spring. Fruit orange- or red-brown. Excellent choice for poor, rocky soils with summer heat. Tolerates serpentine.

A. *pallida*. Pale-leaf manzanita. Similar to heartleaf manzanita, but becoming a small tree to fifteen or more feet with smooth, pale green leaves and handsome, white flowers in mid to late winter; red berries. No burl. Rare. Use as a specimen in full sun to light shade.

A. *patula*. Green-leaf manzanita. Dense, much-branched shrub to about six feet tall. With burl. Some forms are semiprostrate. Nearly round bright green, smooth, stalked leaves; attractive clusters of pink flowers mid to late spring. Tolerates hot summers and cold winters, light shade. Excellent for mountain gardens. The vivid green leaves set off gray-leafed plants.

A. *pringlei*. Pink-bracted manzanita. Tall shrubs to about fifteen feet, sweet scented. No burl. Leaves gray-green, nearly hairless, stalked; flowers with conspicuous pink bracts and stalks, petals rose colored, in late winter to spring. Fruit red and sticky. Superb shrub for its floral display, and is adapted to cold winters. Fine choice for the mountain garden, but worthy of trial in any summer-hot situation.

A. *pumila*. Dwarf or dune manzanita. Sprawling to rounded low, dense shrub to about two and a half feet, with branches that root freely. No burl. Shreddy bark; pale green leaves, narrow and spoon shaped; small, tight clusters of white to pink flowers from late winter to mid-spring; brown berries. Excellent for coastal areas, especially to bind sandy soils or in the rock garden. Light shade inland.

A. *pungens*. Mexican manzanita. Much-branched, dense shrub to about nine feet tall. No burl. Leaves green and smooth, sharply pointed, stalked; small white to deep pink flowers in tight clusters in late winter; red-brown berries. Excellent shrub for hedge or barrier and easy to cultivate. Full sun.

A. *sensitiva*. Sensitive manzanita. A charming, dense shrub to six feet tall with nearly round leaves and erect branches. No burl. Closely related to Fort Bragg manzanita, but in gardens it tolerates more summer heat and needs little extra water.

A. *silvicola*. Silver-leaf manzanita. Upright, branched shrub to eight feet tall. No burl. Handsome, silver-gray leaves closely felted with hairs; short, drooping flower clusters with wooly hairs and white, nodding flowers from late winter to early spring; red-brown berries. Specimen shrub or for contrast of its foliage with green-leafed shrubs. Tolerates nutrient-poor sandy soils. Coastal areas are best. Can take light shade. Should be used more, for its beautiful foliage.

A. *stanfordiana*. Stanford manzanita. Small, upright shrub with slender branches to seven feet. No burl. Bright green shiny, smooth, stalked leaves; open, drooping clusters of pink flowers from late winter to mid-spring; bright red berries. Handsome specimen; one of the best for gardens. Give full sun. Variety *repens* is a rare kind from Sonoma County that trails along the ground. It should make an excellent ground cover for summer-hot areas.

A. *subcordata*. Santa Cruz Island manzanita. A handsome shrub to seven feet, with enlarged basal burl. Leaves dark green, stalked, on twigs with fine and glandular hairs. Flowers in dense panicles, white, late winter to early spring. Fine shrub for rocky places, but possibly frost tender.

A. *tomentosa*. Shaggybark manzanita. Upright shrub with dense, spreading branches to eight feet tall, beautiful shreddy bark. Basal burl. Leaves are pale green above and white felted below, stalked; white flowers in dense wooly panicles winter to early spring; brown berries. Handsome specimen for its bark and interesting leaves. Light shade. Cool coastal conditions are best.

A. *uva-ursi*. Kinnikinnick or bearberry. Low, prostrate, trailing plant. No burl. Stems root as they grow. Leaves leathery, oval, shiny, bright to pale green; small, tight clusters of white to pinkish flowers in spring; bright red berries. This is one of the most popular woody ground covers, with several named cultivars. It is outstanding for sandy soils, preferring coastal situations, and tolerates light shade. Forms from mountainous areas of the West will be better adapted to mountain gardens.

A. *viscida*. White-leaf manzanita. Large, open-branched shrub to fourteen feet (trainable as a tree). No burl. Handsome whitish, stalked, smooth leaves; sticky branchlets; open panicles of white to pink flowers from late winter to mid-spring; red to brownish berries. Handsome specimen plant, or use leaf color as a foil for green-leafed plants. Takes full, hot sun or tolerates light shade.

Artemisia californica. California Sagebrush. Sunflower family (Asteraceae)

HT: 2 to 4½ feet. LVS: evergreen or partially summer deciduous. FLWS: inconspicuous spikes of greenish heads. SMR WTR: occasional. PROP: cuttings; layering. EXP: full sun

California sagebrush is a small, compact, densely branched shrub with finely divided gray-green, sage-scented leaves. It looks attractive all year with light pruning and occasional pinching to keep it from growing straggly. It does best where summers are warm to cool; coastal fogs are particularly to its liking. It also thrives where soils drain rapidly (or are sandy) and winter cold does not linger. Given these conditions, California sagebrush needs only periodic deep waterings to look good; without water, shrubs persist but look sickly and become almost leafless at the height of summer drought. Flowers and fruits are insignificant, and for all intents and purposes can be ignored, since they add little visually.

California sagebrush has several horticultural merits: foliage that adds both fine texture and gray color, pleasant scent (some may find it overpowering on hot days), and bushy habit when properly pruned. It is excellent in a mixed dry border or as the foreground for taller, darker-leafed shrubs. The cultivar 'Canyon Gray' is a fine, low, creeping form from the Channel Islands, which cascades over rocks or serves as a graceful, woody ground cover of great beauty.

California sagebrush tends toward short life, and can unpredictably rot and die. It is especially vulnerable to root fungi and long periods of wet and cold conditions. Since it grows rapidly to full size, so that new plants reach maturity quickly, this vulnerability is seldom a problem.

Artemisia pycnocephala. Dune (Sandhill) Sagebrush. Sunflower family (Asteraceae)

HT: 1 to 2 feet. LVS: evergreen. FLWS: insignificant greenish heads in spikes; late summer. SMR WTR: occasional deep watering. PROP: cuttings. EXP: full sun

Dune sagebrush is a borderline shrub, only half-heartedly woody. It is included here because it is closely related to other decidedly woody artemisias. This low subshrub makes few-branched, tight mounds of lovely soft, wooly, white to silvery foliage, but without the typical sage aroma. It tends toward straggliness in late summer when the short, terminal flowering spikes—of no redeeming value—appear; it's best to remove these. Allowing for this shortcoming, dune sagebrush is a superb plant for texture and leaf color in a rock garden or mixed border or in front of larger shrubberies. Plants should be selected for leaf color, as individuals vary considerably in their wooliness and shade of gray.

Give dune sagebrush cool summers for the longest life and least need for supplemental watering. It adapts well to sandy soils (and should have good drainage in any case) and is wind- and salt-spray tolerant, but may not thrive in hot climates. It combines naturally with other sand dune plants, such as dune bursage (*Ambrosia chamissonis*), sand verbena (*Abronia* spp.), beach sweet-pea (*Lathyrus littoralis*), and bluff gumweed (*Grindelia stricta venulosa*).

Artemisia tridentata. Desert Sagebrush. Sunflower family (Asteraceae)

HT: 2 to 10 feet. LVS: evergreen. FLWS: inconspicuous yellow-green heads in spikes; late summer. SMR WTR: none. PROP: cuttings; seeds (stratify). EXP: full sun

Desert sagebrush is the little-appreciated shrub that dominates vast expanses of high desert through the Great Basin: Nevada, eastern California, Utah, Arizona, and New Mexico. There it may be the only conspicuous all-year element in the landscape. When brought into the garden it makes a first-rate ornamental shrub that is tough, needs little or no water, and is amenable to bitterly cold winters. Desert sagebrush grows surprisingly fast under good conditions, and it is tolerant of moderately wet winters and a variety of soils. Shrubs mature within ten years.

Desert sagebrush often grows from a single stem, which may become a beautifully twisted and contorted trunk carrying tight mounds of gray, three-toothed, sage-scented leaves. The odor can be overwhelming on hot days. Although the flowers are insignificant, they seldom detract from the overall beauty; tiny, greenish-yellow heads are carried in slender candles above the foliage. In the garden desert sagebrush can be used as a bold specimen (especially old ones pruned to reveal the trunks or even as bonsai subjects) or in desert gardens can create striking contrasts with cacti and antelope brush (*Purshia*). In a mixed dry border it contributes interesting foliage texture and color, and it forms a pleasing backdrop in an herb garden or in the forefront of taller, drought-tolerant shrubs. Note also that there are smaller-scale desert sagebrushes, attractive for gardens in their compact form and durable foliage: these include A. *cana* and A. *arbuscula*, from high-desert mountains. Their adaptation to lowland gardens has scarcely been tested.

Asclepias albicans and subulata. Desert Milkweeds. Milkweed family (Asclepiadaceae)

HT: 3 to 6 feet. LVS: short-lived, summer and drought deciduous. FLWS: umbrellas of curiously shaped, greenish to yellow-brown flowers; late spring. SMR WTR: none. PROP: cuttings; root divisions; seeds. EXP: full sun

These two milkweeds constitute an unusual pair of subshrubs—bushy plants woody at their bases. Both consist of multiple canelike stalks that tend to be leafless most of the year (except after rains). *Asclepias albicans* is so named because of its striking waxy, whitish stems, while A. *subulata* has pale white-green stalks. Both bear umbrellalike clusters of curious flowers near the tops of these stems: the former with

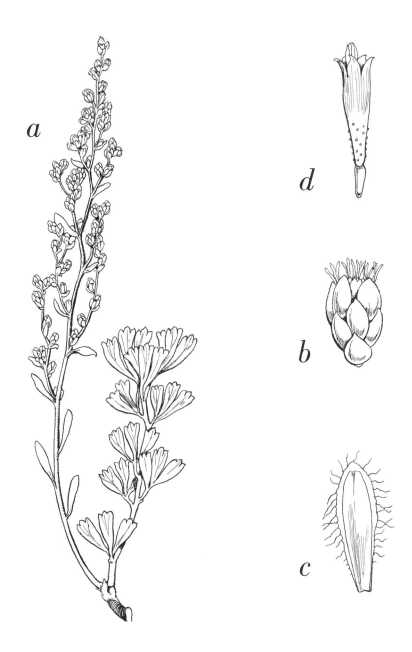

Desert Sagebrush (*Artemisia tridentata*)
a. flowering branch   *b*. flower head detail   *c*. fruit detail
d. single floret, enlarged

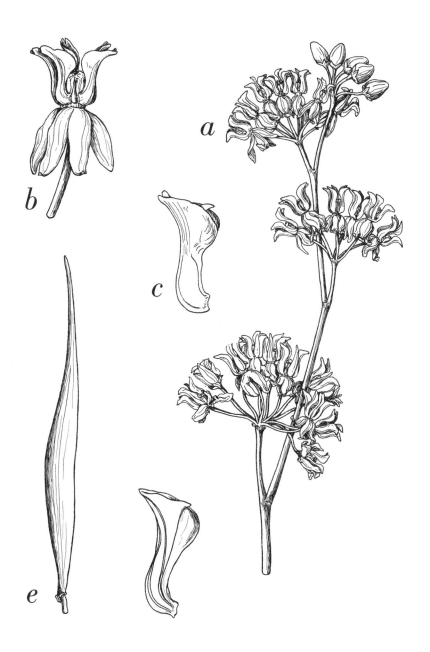

Desert Milkweed (*Asclepias subulata*)
a. flower clusters   *b.* flower detail   *c.* nectar hood of flower
d. inside nectar hood   *e.* seed pod detail

greenish-white flowers topped by rather ornate nectar "hoods," the latter with greenish flowers flushed pink or brown and with shorter, pale yellow hoods. Both bear close inspection as curious manifestations of special pollination by butterflies and possibly bumblebees. The hoods, stamen details, and stigmatic slots add intrigue to pollination mechanisms.

These two milkweeds differ from other native milkweeds in their negligible small leaves and in their adaptation to hot, rocky places in the low deserts. You can use them to striking effect for their unusual and dramatic form, pointing up the shapes that fill the desert with real character. Plant several in bunches to contrast with fat globular cacti, or for shorter scale, next to the tall, wandlike branches of ocotillo. The flowers are a bonus strictly for those who love the bizarre.

Atriplex hymenelytra. Desert Holly. Goosefoot family (Chenopodiaceae)

HT: 1 to 4 feet. LVS: evergreen. FLWS: in small terminal clusters, reddish, dioecious; midwinter. SMR WTR: none. PROP: cuttings. EXP: full sun

Desert holly is at once a distinctive and beautiful shrub, surely the best of the atriplexes California has to offer. Its unusual white-silver leaves are stiff, tough, evergreen, and hollylike, and in midwinter it bears pretty clusters of dark red flowers, male and female on separate plants. It has had limited garden use thus far, and its adaptability to the garden is still uncertain. Because it comes from some of the most inhospitable desert environments—scorching hot, dry summers in alkaline to saline soils—it should handle these conditions like few other shrubs. However, it would be less than happy with cool, moist coastal garden sites.

Desert holly is a small shrub and hence suitable to containers, the backs of rock gardens, or ideally as a focal point in a desert garden. Its distinctive and compact shape and color give it a unique character; plant it separately in several mounds spaced apart, with gravel or scree between.

Atriplex lentiformis. Quail Bush. Goosefoot family (Chenopodiaceae)

HT: 3 to 10 feet. LVS: evergreen. FLWS: tiny greenish flowers in dense terminal panicles, dioecious; summer to fall. SMR WTR: none. PROP: cuttings. EXP: full sun

Quail bush is a fairly dense, much branched, grayish silver bush retaining leaves all year. Although flowers are borne in dense panicles, they're inconspicuous, with the male and female on separate bushes. The best feature of quail bush is the attractive, broadly triangular to oval leaves. It grows in full sun with no extra water and tolerates alkaline or saline soils. In such situations there are few better choices, and quail bush grows quite rapidly as well.

Quail bush can be clipped to shape its new growth and kept dense enough to form

Desert Holly (*Atriplex hymenelytra*)
flowering branches

a screen or informal hedge. It is also an excellent filler in the background of desert gardens, hiding the leafless branches of many summer-deciduous shrubs.

Baccharis pilularis ssp. pilularis. Dwarf Coyote Bush. Daisy family (Asteraceae)

HT: 1 to 4 feet. LVS: evergreen. FLWS: insignificant heads, cream-color (male) or whitish & bristly (female), dioecious; fall. SMR WTR: little or none. PROP: cuttings. EXP: full sun

Dwarf coyote bush is a subspecies of the common, invasive pioneer shrub, but unlike the latter it has good garden behavior. It occurs naturally on coastal promontories and dunes, where wind helps trim it to low, tight mounds of dense, green foliage year-round. In the garden (unless in exposed sites) it remains low and mounded in comparison to its common brother (*Baccharis pilularis* ssp. *consanguinea*), but it still grows considerably taller than where winds keep it low. Periodic mowing or shearing of top growth maintain both vigor and low stature.

Dwarf coyote bush is propagated exclusively from cuttings of the male plant, since the female form, when it goes to seed, creates masses of wind-sown, white-tufted, messy fruits. The male plant bears inconspicuous but innocuous heads of creamy disc flowers. Since seed-grown plants are unpredictable as to gender, cuttings are the only way to go. The dense, shiny green, small rounded leaves remain attractive through the year, a real plus in summer drought or winter wet. On warm days, leaves may become resinous and aromatic with a pleasing and subtle fragrance.

Dwarf coyote bush has wide appeal for holding steep banks, and it is a low-maintenance, woody ground cover or creates attractive mounds in front of taller shrubbery. It is also good as a low, dense hedge for lining paths and walks. It is tough, is drought and heat resistant, and grows most rapidly in mild coastal areas.

Baccharis viminea/glutinosa. Mulefat or Seep Willow. Sunflower family (Asteraceae)

HT: 6 to 14 feet. LVS: evergreen. FLWS: densely arranged heads of white male or female flowers; spring and summer. SMR WTR: none when established. PROP: suckers; seeds. EXP: full sun

Mulefat is a characteristic feature of the stony, dry arroyos throughout the drier foothills of California. Its second name—seep willow—alludes to its similarity to true willows (*Salix* spp.) in appearance and also in habitat, although few true willows will tolerate a significantly lowered water table in summer, as do these shrubs. This tolerance indicates deeply probing roots, useful in situations where water may be hidden below the surface but not readily apparent.

Both species have shiny, willow-shaped evergreen leaves—B. *glutinosa* with serrated edges and B. *viminea* with smooth margins—and both produce a profusion of small white flower heads late in the season. The flowers are of no particular horticul-

Mulefat (*Baccharis viminea*)
a. flowering branch   *b.* flower head detail   *c.* floral bract detail
d. floret detail   *e.* fruit detail

tural value, although they provide nectar sources for bees and other insects. The best use, since these shrubs multiply by slowly wandering roots, is in large-scale landscapes, in places where you wish to suggest a dry streambed without the need for summer water. They would serve well as a backdrop to showier plantings in such places.

Beloperone californica. Chuparosa. Acanthus family (Acanthaceae)

HT: 1 to 3 feet. LVS: summer-winter deciduous. FLWS: tubular, two-lipped scarlet flowers in short racemes; spring. SMR WTR: occasional deep watering is beneficial. PROP: cuttings. EXP: full sun

Chuparosa, the hummingbird flower par excellence, is a seasonally colorful subshrub from California's warm deserts. Like so many other small desert shrubs it is dormant much of the year, with closely felted, greenish twigs and no leaves. But after rains and through spring the small, ovate leaves appear, followed by short clusters of bright scarlet flowers, their long tubes and abundant nectar a mainstay of nectar-feeding hummingbirds. In fact, chuparosa lives mostly along the edges of oases and desert washes where cottonwoods and fan palms provide shelter for birds and the water table is high—often beside pools. Chuparosa is a rather straggly shrub with horizontally arched branches, comely in flower, unexceptional out of flower.

For best effect in the garden, use chuparosa as a bold contrast planting near a water feature in a dry or desert garden. It could line a dry, stony watercourse or be massed next to a small pond, where roots could seek a bit of summer water. The striking flower color also provides a startling effect with the golden daisies of brittle bush (*Encelia farinosa*) or the purple and yellow daisies of desert aster (*Machaeranthera* spp.). Its flowers can be followed by other hummingbird favorites in hot reds, such as hummingbird fuchsia (*Zauschneria californica*) or cardinal lobelia (*Lobelia cardinalis*).

Betula occidentalis/glandulosa. Water Birch. Birch family (Betulaceae)

HT: up to 25 feet. LVS: winter deciduous. FLWS: male in catkins in early spring; female inconspicuous. SMR WTR: needs constant moisture. PROP: cuttings; layering; seeds. EXP: full sun or very light shade

Water birch is truly one of the undiscovered gems of the shrub world. It can also be trained as a small tree with rounded crown. It lines the sides of rocky streambeds on the east side of the Sierra and high desert mountains, where its seasonal changes create outstanding beauty. In spring its new triangular leaves flutter in breezes after the dangling male catkins have finished shedding their pollen to the winds. By summer's end, female catkins have developed into short, fat, conelike structures, which shatter as days shorten. In October, leaves turn a buttery gold before dropping. Winter shows off the handsome, burnished bronze bark, sprinkled with elliptical white lenticels.

Water birch has proven amenable to garden conditions even in mild coastal climates, although leaves do not wear their autumn colors there. A moderately fast grower, water birch succeeds well with moist soil and tolerates light shade; it will go through mild to hot summers and cool to very cold winters equally well.

Water birch has much to recommend it as a container plant, and it is also ideal behind a pond or, several together, lining a stream. A copse would be delightful as a special, shaded place to commune with nature. Underplant it with natural companions such as Jeffrey's shooting stars (*Dodecatheon jeffreyi*), swamp onion (*Allium validum*), *Potentilla gracilis*, snowy rein orchid (*Habenaria dilatata*), or polemoniums.

A second little-known species, resin birch (*Betula glandulosa*), is a largely untried bushy shrub to about seven feet tall. Its rounded leaves are prettily scalloped, rather than sharply toothed as in water birch. Resin birch would be especially worth trying in a mountain setting, with open sun and moist soil.

Brickellia californica. California Brickel Bush. Sunflower family (Asteraceae)

HT: 1 to 3 feet. LVS: winter deciduous. FLWS: small greenish white rayless heads in panicles; late summer and fall. SMR WTR: none. PROP: cuttings (include some wood); seeds. EXP: full sun

The brickel bushes are a poorly known group of small shrubs from dry, rocky, summer-hot habitats: in deserts, with coastal sage and at chaparral edges, and often by dry arroyos. Although there are other species for garden consideration, the most widespread kind aptly illustrates merits and limitations; California brickel bush is a multiple-branched, half-woody shrub covered with pale green, triangular leaves coarsely serrated and pleasantly scented, deciduous in winter (the whole plant may die back in cold climates). The clusters of whitish green flower heads are drab and of little redeeming horticultural value even though they appear at the end of the dry season, August to October. Yet these flowers provide one of the best-carrying garden fragrances; from late afternoon through evening they send forth a powerfully scented, sweet perfume. They are certain to be a source of confusion for those who look for the typical large white blossoms of many evening bloomers. Instead, brickel bush keeps company with the likes of *Sarcococca* and night-flowering jasmine (*Cestrum jasminoides*), both also with totally insignificant flowers but heady evening perfume.

Brickel bush grows easily and rapidly even after it has been frozen to the ground, but very cold winters (where the soil is frozen) will kill the roots. It needs a place in the sun and heat of the garden, and it could be planted with such floriferous neighbors as penstemons, monardellas, and bush monkeyflowers (*Diplacus* spp.). The foliage is a pleasant feature through the growing season. Also brickel bush could form the backdrop to low-growing herbs, such as thymes (*Thymus* spp.) and savory (*Satureja* spp.).

Bursera microphylla. Elephant Tree or Torote. Bursera family (Burseraceae)

HT: 3 to 10 feet. LVS: summer and drought deciduous. FLWS: tiny, greenish white, in small clusters; early summer. SMR WTR: none. PROP: perhaps cuttings; seeds (stratify). EXP: full sun

The elephant tree is well named, for its often-twisted, multiple limbs suggest elephantine form in shape and bark, the large platelets of pale whitish brown bark like layers of skin peeling from a thick hide. Leafless much of the year, the shiny, resinous, pleasantly scented, pealike leaves appear shortly after rains, then fall when soils dry again. The tiny greenish white flowers are of little consequence but are followed by pleasantly scented, dark red-purple berries.

Elephant tree is rare in California, favoring localized arroyos and canyons in the Anza Borrego country of the Colorado Desert, where it grows in small "groves" or colonies on gravelly soils. Its use in the garden is as a focal point for its curious shape and bark, providing drama among cacti, agaves, yuccas, and other specialized desert forms. It can also be grown as a large container plant, suggesting a jovial bonsai from another planet.

Calliandra eriophylla. Fairy Duster Bush. Pea family (Fabaceae)

HT: to 18 inches. LVS: summer deciduous. FLWS: showy, pink powder puffs; late winter to early spring. SMR WTR: none. PROP: perhaps cuttings; seeds (scarify). EXP: full sun

This small shrub is a delightful surprise in the desert, when after substantial rains the branches grow light green, pealike leaves and burst into colorful bloom. Each flower cluster—really a tight head of tiny flowers with long, showy, pinkish stamens—bursts out at the ends of a branch like a fluffy powder puff. Like so many other desert shrubs, fairy duster rests most of the year, quickly losing leaves when the climate dries and, when seeds ripen, dropping long green pea pods.

Because of its seasonal drama fairy duster is a lovely shrub to plant among shrubs with more permanent, evergreen leaves, such as some bush daisies, pygmy cedar, or green-stemmed ephedras. It would also be appropriate for large terra-cotta containers, where its bare summer form could suggest a harsh environment, or it could be moved to a place of less prominence when flowers have passed.

Calycanthus occidentalis. Western Spicebush or Sweetshrub. Sweetshrub family (Calycanthaceae)

HT: 3 to 10 feet. LVS: winter deciduous. FLWS: showy, curious maroon-red "water lilies"; late spring and summer. SMR WTR: some summer water. PROP: layering; cuttings. EXP: full sun to dappled shade

Western spicebush lines permanent streams or clusters around seeps in cool coastal or midmountain forests. It is a bold shrub with numerous branches from the base, the

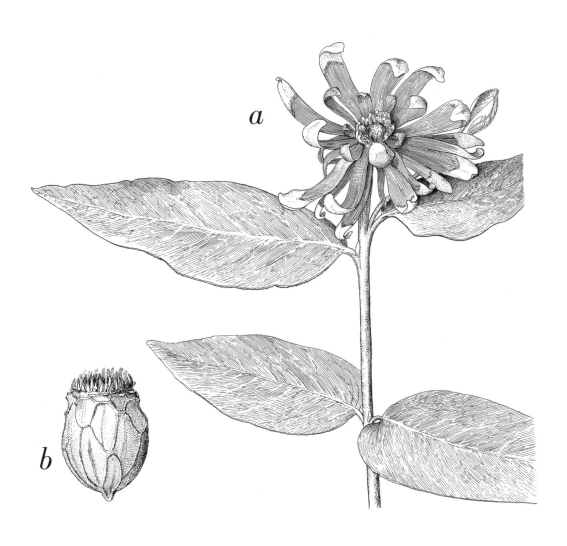

Western Spicebush (*Calycanthus occidentalis*)
a. flowering branch   *b*. fruit detail

ultimate form a comely, rounded shape, with large, soft, fragrant ovate leaves. Seasonal interest includes a generous sprinkling of large maroon-red flowers that look like closed-up water lilies and smell of old wine. These are replaced by large, cup-shaped seed pods decorated with scalelike bracts, which persist into winter long after leaves have been shed. Spicebush also has shreddy brown bark, which is heavily scented with the essence of allspice.

Western spicebush is a lovely shrub that is happy as a trimmed hedge or foundation planting, a natural adjunct to a stream side in a woodland garden or by itself, as long as it receives adequate summer water. Near the coast it will take full sun; inland it does better in light shade. It is a rapid grower, often reaching full size within a season or two. Good companions include western azalea (*Rhododendron occidentale*), service berry (*Amelanchier pallida*), chain fern (*Woodwardia fimbriata*), flowering currant (*Ribes sanguineum glutinosum*), and ninebark (*Physocarpus capitatus*).

Carpenteria californica. Bush Anemone. Mock orange family (Philadelphaceae)

HT: 3 to 10 feet. LVS: evergreen. FLWS: large, showy white platters; late spring. SMR WTR: some deep watering. PROP: cuttings; seeds (scarify). EXP: light shade

Bush anemone is a rare shrub in the wild, but with assured survival because of its exceptional ornamental qualities. It is a dense, unevenly shaped shrub with handsome, polished, deep green, narrowly ovate leaves all year. This alone recommends it as an informal hedge or foundation shrub. The best feature, however, is the striking large white flowers, filled with yellow stamens and looking for all the world like single camellias. Flowers continue for some time in late spring; close up they exude an odd, sweet scent.

Bush anemone grows moderately fast, is strong, and usually is trouble free, and although recommended for dry shade, it will thrive with occasional deep summer watering. It can be sheared to maintain better shape, and is excellent as a background in the natural woodland garden. Good companions include western spicebush (*Calycanthus occidentalis*), fuchsia-flowered gooseberry (*Ribes speciosum*), and western azalea (*Rhododendron occidentale*).

Cassia armata. Desert Senna. Pea family (Fabaceae)

HT: 2 to 4½ feet. LVS: seasonal, appearing after rains. FLWS: showy butter yellow; mid spring. SMR WTR: none. PROP: seeds (scarify). EXP: full sun

Desert senna is a low, rounded shrub with intricate pale green branches. Out of flower, it is an unimposing—even drab—shrub, which leafs out only after rains. Even then, leaves are small and olive-green with barely discernible leaflets. However, when flowers appear the shrub is transformed into a mass of gold, with countless open flowers like those of the tropical cassias.

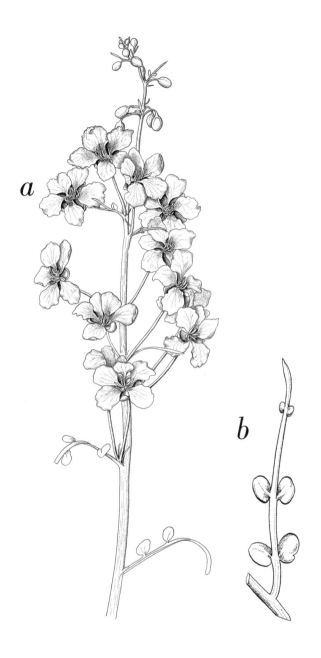

Desert Senna (*Cassia armata*)
a. flowering raceme   *b*. leaf detail

Desert senna grows where soils are sandy, temperatures soar in summer, and rains are sparse in winter. It's a great shrub for a desert garden, perhaps as part of an open border with various seasonally beautiful shrubs including paperbag bush (*Salazaria mexicana*), desert aster (*Machaeranthera cognatus*), apricot mallow (*Sphaeralcea ambigua*), and incienso (*Encelia farinosa*). It should not be used where its unassuming habit interferes with the harmony of a planting.

Cassiope mertensiana. White Heather. Heather family (Ericaceae)

HT: 4 to 12 inches. LVS: evergreen. FLWS: white and pink bells in short clusters; summer. SMR WTR: moist soil. PROP: cuttings (use bottom heat); seeds (stratify). EXP: full sun to light shade

White heather joins such other stalwart mountain companions as red heather (*Phyllodoce* spp.) and mountain laurel (*Kalmia polifolia*) to create pictures of great beauty in the rarefied air of the alpine. Together they compose perfect pictures around granite boulders and sedge meadows, as the snows slowly melt. White heather is half-spreading, half-upright, but never awkward, with branches that drape themselves over nearby boulders or intertwine to form compact clumps. Leaves are reduced to bright green scales that clothe the branches, while dainty tresses of white bells—trimmed with rose-pink sepals—hang from branch tips. Plants are adapted to boggy, acid soils, where the growing season is short—only two to three months per year—and the soils frozen the rest of the time.

Given these conditions, few gardeners can create even a rough approximation of this habitat in the garden. Attempts to grow it in the lowlands result in plants that languish in vigor and slowly die. The best way to try white heather is from seeds, with the hope that a few might adapt early in life to different conditions, but in the long run the only reasonable thing to do is reserve it for mountain gardens, where a boggy spot in summer (but with drainage) should suit it well.

Ceanothus. Wild Lilacs. Buckthorn family (Rhamnaceae)

HT: 2 inches to 20 feet. LVS: evergreen; occasionally deciduous. FLWS: many tiny saucers borne in rounded umbels, cymes, or complex panicles; blue, purple, pink, or white; spring to summer. SMR WTR: little or none for most. PROP: cuttings (use bottom heat); seeds (stratify). EXP: full sun to light shade

Perhaps no other group of shrubs surpasses the ceanothuses for practical use in the garden; many species and cultivars are available at a large number of nurseries. In many ways, the ceanothuses parallel the manzanitas (*Arctostaphylos* spp.) for variety of form and habitat. The prostrate ones are excellent low maintenance ground covers; there are miniatures for the forefront of the garden, medium-sized shrubs for foun-

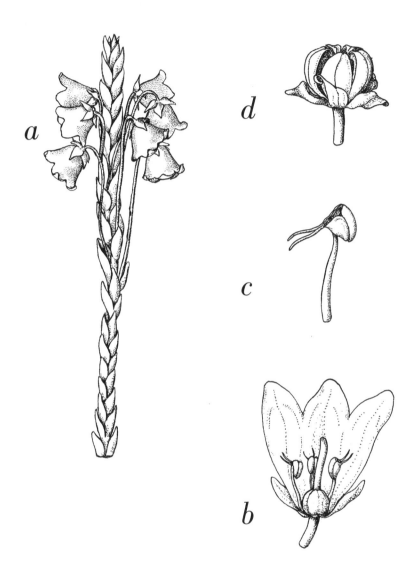

White Heather (*Cassiope mertensiana*)
a. flowering branch   *b*. flower detail   *c*. stamen detail
d. seed pod detail

dation plantings, and tall treelike ones for specimens. Most prefer open, well-lighted situations, but they vary in their adaptability to intense summer sun.

Few ceanothuses do well with copious summer water; in fact, many are prone to oak root fungus and other water molds, which are promoted by summer-wet soils. Most are short lived in the garden for this and other reasons, often reaching large size in few years, then succumbing to overly active growth or root infections brought on by wet, soggy winter conditions. It is not uncommon to see part of a large specimen dead from such causes; judicious pruning to remove the infected growth may bring about a cure, but often pruning only puts off the day when the whole plant dies. For this reason, it is wise to regard each plant as temporary (averaging four to six years), with provision made for replacement, although some plants may persist for more than ten years, eventually reaching great size.

Despite the problem of life span, ceanothuses are noteworthy for their brilliant flushes of lilaclike clusters of flowers, mostly in the spring. They are great panicles or cymes of blue, purple, pinkish, or white flowers, perfumed on warm days (a close approximation is that blossoms smell like corn tortillas). The flowers may be rubbed in water as a soap substitute. The bees are fond of ceanothuses, and great numbers hover around the blossoms on sunny days. The fruits are three-sided capsules, at first appearing fleshy—almost berrylike—but later drying and splitting open. A few species have ornamental capsules flushed red, and with decorative "horns" on the tops.

The leaves are also attractive, usually tough and evergreen, sometimes shiny above and paler beneath, occasionally thin and deciduous. Some are elliptical, others spoon-shaped, long and narrow (by curling under), or oval; many have smooth margins, but quite a number have hollylike teeth. The undersides of several species show three major veins running the length of the leaf; others have a finely wrought, pinnate vein pattern. A few have fragrant leaves. Branching varies from dense and intricate to open, sometimes with branchlets arching, other times with branchlets held stiff and rigid.

Most ceanothuses benefit from tip pruning to keep the shape compact. Most of the bigger kinds should have the lower interior branches pruned away to open up the plant, so as to avoid what otherwise would become an ugly tangle of half-dead branches.

The uses of ceanothuses in the landscape run the gamut from low-maintenance ground covers (but without supporting foot traffic) to informal hedges (there are even species with spine-tipped branches) to foundation shrubs or handsome single specimens. They require little attention except for shaping, and most get by with no summer water or fertilizer. (In fact many have special nitrogen-fixing nodules on their roots.) Here are some of the numerous recommendable ceanothus species:

C. arboreus. Tree ceanothus. Dense shrub or small tree (one main trunk can be developed by pruning) with gray bark, up to twenty feet in height. Leaves broadly oval, up to three inches long, and evergreen, green above and whitish beneath with a fine felt, finely serrated along the margins. Dense plumes of pale blue flowers appear from late winter through mid spring. Excellent as a bold feature in the landscape or as a specimen—lovely behind a wildflower meadow. For mild climates; good in coastal gardens.

C. cordulatus. Snowbrush. Low mounded and densely branched with arching branchlets, gray to whitish bark, and spine-tipped twigs. Ovate, evergreen leaves are blue-green on top and grayish below, with smooth margins. Dense, broad flower clusters are snowy white to cream colored from late spring to early summer. Good informal low barrier plant, or, for its mounded effect, good in front of taller shrubs. Best adapted to mountain conditions; tolerates light shade, and probably requires winter dormancy to do its best.

C. crassifolius. Thickleaf ceanothus. Tall shrub, to twelve feet, with stiff branches, grayish to white bark, and thick, leathery, elliptical leaves. Leaves are often curled under, have coarse teeth, and are glossy above but covered with dense, white hairs below. Flowers are borne in dense globe-shaped clusters from early to mid-spring. Excellent for the dry garden in full sun, with summer heat. White flowers contrast well with those of blue-flowered species.

C. cuneatus. Buckbrush. Rigidly branched large shrub, to twelve feet, with grayish bark. Leaves are borne on spur shoots—small, leathery, wedge- to spoon-shaped and dull green. Flowers are borne in dense umbels, white to off-white. One of the toughest ceanothuses for hot, dry summers, but not the most decorative. Best used where the garden gradually blends into a natural landscape.

C. cyaneus. Southern blueblossom. Large treelike shrub (prunable to one or a few trunks) to sixteen feet, with gray-green branches. Leaves tough and evergreen, oval to elliptical, and up to two inches long, green above with smooth to slightly saw-toothed margins and pale beneath. Flowers are in compound clusters, intense blue. One of the best for flower color. Especially fine in southern California; needs minimal water.

C. divergens var. *confusus.* Rincon ceanothus. Creeping, woody ground cover, the ends of branchlets sometimes turned up but the entire plant only two to four inches high. Small, elliptical leaves are glossy above, lined with more or less prominent teeth, but grayish underneath. Tight clusters of blue flowers appear in

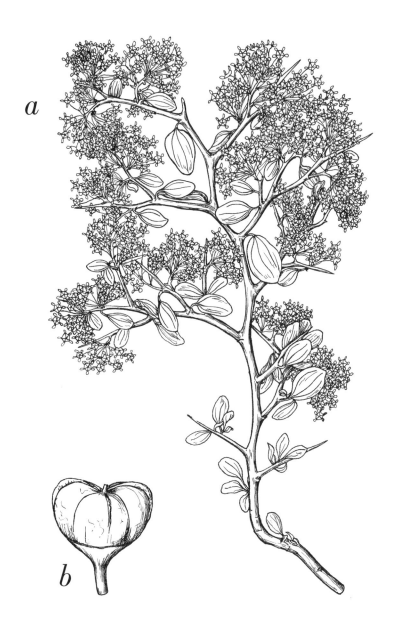

a

b

Snowbrush (*Ceanothus cordulatus*)
a. flowering branches   *b.* seed pod detail

early spring. A fine candidate as ground cover for steep, dry, open banks, with summer heat. Intolerant of summer water.

C. diversifolius. Pinemat ceanothus. Creeping woody ground cover seldom exceeding four inches tall, rooting as it grows. Evergreen, round-elliptical, thin pale green leaves are silky-haired above with closer hairs beneath. Half-inch clusters of white to pale bluish flowers bloom profusely in late spring. Excellent ground cover for shaded banks, especially with conifers, but should be more adaptable to gardens than the ground cover *C. prostratus*, and it tolerates hot summers.

C. ferrisae. Mt. Hamilton ceanothus. Erect shrub to around six feet, with stiff branches; side branches are short. Leaves are evergreen, nearly round, smooth and dark green above and pale whitish below, with few or no teeth along the edge. Dense umbels of white flowers in early spring give a frothy effect to the shrub. Good companion to blue-flowered species; drought and summer-heat tolerant.

C. foliosus. Littleleaf ceanothus. Small, rounded shrub to a maximum of three feet (often much less). Oblong to elliptical leaves seldom exceed half an inch in length, are glossy green above and pale beneath, and have minute, sticky teeth along the edges, which sometimes turn under. Flowers are borne in close globe-like clusters in spring and are clear blue. Excellent for the front of a mixed border or in a rock garden. Full sun and summer heat. A charming miniature.

C. gloriosus. Glorymat ceanothus. Mostly a prostrate shrub with stout branches, rooting as it goes. Handsome evergreen, elliptical to nearly round, glossy, dark green leaves (pale beneath) with sharp teeth along the margins. Dense, showy umbels of blue to purplish flowers in spring. Excellent coarse ground cover; especially appropriate for steep coastal banks or sand dunes. A notable variety, *exaltatus*, is an erect shrub up to six feet tall from similar situations (requiring cool, foggy summers in light shade). The variety *porrectus*, a sprawling shrub from the Point Reyes peninsula, is also sometimes available.

C. griseus. Blueblossom. Large shrub, to twelve or more feet with dense branching, the ultimate branchlets arching. Handsome evergreen, rounded to elliptical leaves to two inches long, shiny and smooth above with silky grayish hairs underneath. The margins have tiny teeth and are sometimes curled under. Dense panicles of bluish purple flowers through spring. Similar to *C. thyrsiflorus*, and horticulturally treated the same way. Use as large specimen shrub or for background. Great in combination with fremontias and bush poppies (*Dendromecon*). The variety *horizontalis* is widely used in the nursery trade for its lower-growing, half-sprawling shape. The best-known cultivar of this variety, 'Carmel Creeper,' differs in being a widely spreading, partly prostrate shrub well adapted to ocean bluffs. In the garden, though, it grows up to four or five feet tall and needs pruning to retain its low profile. Excellent for a coarse, low-maintenance woody ground cover.

C. hearstiorum. Hearst ceanothus. Very low, prostrate plants with creeping stems, developing into large mats over time. Small, oblong, vivid green leaves with a wrinkled upper surface, covered with white, wooly hairs underneath. Vivid blue flowers in late spring. Fine, drought-tolerant ground cover for coastal areas.

C. impressus. Lompoc ceanothus; see *C. papillosus.*

C. incanus. Coastal white-thorn; see *C. leucodermis.*

C. insularis. Island bigpod ceanothus; see *C. megacarpus.*

C. integerrimus. Deerbrush. A large, openly branched shrub to twelve feet, with newer branchlets greenish. Ovate to elliptical leaves to three inches long are winter deciduous, green above and pale below, and with smooth margins. Large compound, frothy plumes of flowers appear in late spring; many are pure white, but there are also pale bluish and pinkish forms. Use different color forms side by side for a stunning backdrop. Tolerates light shade and winter freezes.

C. jepsonii. Jepson's ceanothus. Dense, low-spreading shrub to two feet with rigid, arching branchlets. Leaves hollylike with four or five teeth on each side, green above but whitish beneath, the edges of the leaves often partly folded together. Flowers pale purple in small umbels in spring. Excellent shrub for the toughest rocky embankments with no summer water, but difficult to establish and not particularly showy. Favors serpentine soils in nature. The variety *albiflorus* is an altogether better choice, being a more upright shrub to three feet with pure white flowers. The latter tolerates very hot, dry summers.

C. lemmonii. Lemmon's ceanothus. Low, broadly spreading shrubs to two-and-a-half feet with grayish white bark. Evergreen, elliptical to oblong leaves, green above and paler beneath with silky hairs, margins nearly smooth to slightly toothed. Dense, simple clusters of bright blue blossoms in mid-spring. An excellent subject to place in front of shrubberies or to combine with a mixed border. Fine flower color with careful selection. Amenable to hot, dry summers.

C. leucodermis. White-thorn ceanothus. Broadly spreading shrub to twelve feet with arching, rigid branches, pale green to whitish bark, and twigs stoutly spine tipped. Evergreen, ovate to elliptical leaves to about an inch long, bluish gray on both sides and with nearly smooth margins. Flowers in simple plumes in mid- to

Deerbrush (*Ceanothus integerrimus*)
a. flowering branch   *b.* seed pod detail

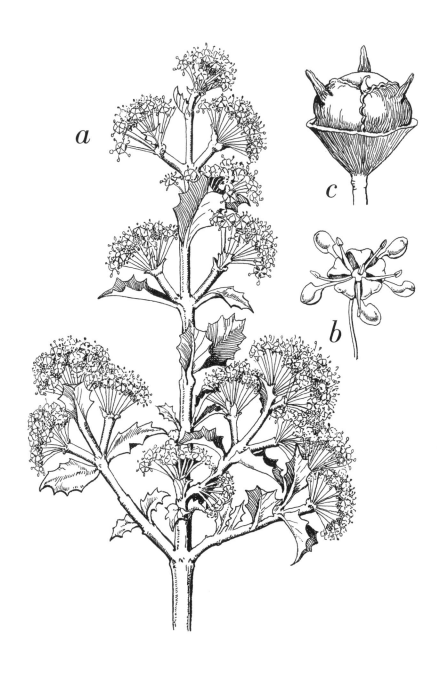

Jepson's Ceanothus (*Ceanothus jepsonii*)
a. flowering branches   *b.* flower detail   *c.* seed pod detail

late-spring, white to bluish. Excellent informal barrier shrub; drought tolerant; full sun. A similar species, *C. incanus* (coastal white-thorn) has leaves to three inches long and compound plumes of white flowers, and prefers coastal conditions, tolerating light shade.

C. megacarpus. Bigpod ceanothus. A dense shrub to sixteen or more feet, with brownish gray bark and rigid branchlets. The half-inch leaves are tough, dull green, and wedge to spoon shaped, often with the edges curled under. The small flower umbels are white. This species looks much like *C. cuneatus*, but it prefers milder winters and dry, moderately hot summers. Its variety *insularis*, from the Channel Islands, has somewhat larger leaves and seed pods and is appropriate for coastal gardens of southern California with mild winters.

C. papillosus. Wartleaf ceanothus. Large, open-branched shrub to fifteen feet tall with sticky new twigs. The evergreen leaves are mostly oblong with strongly curled-under margins giving the impression of being narrow; upper surfaces are densely covered with sticky "warts" or bumps. Flowers in simple, narrow plumes, deep blue, in mid to late spring. An unusual specimen or foundation shrub tolerant of a wide range of summer temperatures. Excellent for its fine flower color. A related species, *C. impressus* (Lompoc ceanothus), is noted for its contribution to popular cultivars; it is a low, mounded shrub that has short, nearly round leaves with a deeply textured upper surface, and has especially deep blue flowers in mid-spring. Perhaps its finest cultivar is 'Julia Phelps,' a small- to medium-sized shrub with intense, deep indigo-blue flowers.

C. parryi. Parry blueblossom. Medium to large shrub, to sixteen feet, with angular branchlets. Evergreen, elliptical leaves are shiny green above, closely white-felted below, with nearly straight but sometimes recurved edges. Flowers in complex panicles, bright blue. A handsome species for northern California gardens, especially in summer-hot areas.

C. prostratus. Mahala mats, prostrate ceanothus. Totally prostrate shrub forming widely spreading mats that may cascade over embankments, rooting as they grow. Handsome inch-long, wedge-shaped, evergreen leaves with three or more sharp, hollylike teeth, dark green above and pale beneath. Small globe-shaped clusters of pale to dark blue flowers smother plants from mid to late spring, followed by decorative reddish, horned seed pods. Superb ground cover, but difficult in lowland gardens. Adapted to the pine belt in the mountains. Perhaps the subspecies *occidentalis* would give better results, for it lives at two thousand to three thousand feet in the northern Coast Ranges.

C. purpureus. Napa ceanothus. Three- to six-foot erect shrub with widely spreading, rigid branches and reddish bark. Attractive evergreen, hollylike leaves are

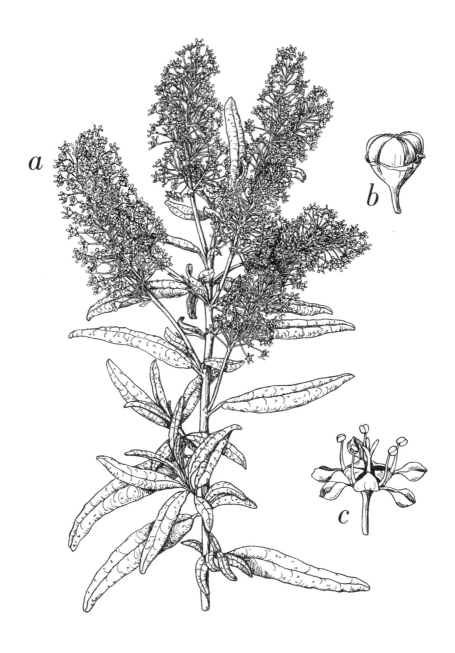

Wartleaf Ceanothus (*Ceanothus papillosus*)
a. flowering branches   *b.* flower detail   *c.* seed pod detail

shiny dark green above, pale beneath, with wavy, spiny margins. Tight umbels of deep blue or blue-purple flowers from early to mid-spring. Decorative, horned seed pods. Tolerates summer heat and drought well. Use as a specimen or part of shrubbery. Choice, but rare and hard to find.

C. ramulosus. Coast buckbrush. Widely branching shrub to ten feet tall with arching branches. Wedge-shaped to elliptical evergreen leaves one inch long, dark green and smooth above, paler beneath with fine whitish hairs. Flowers in dense umbels, pale purplish to whitish from midwinter to midspring. A tough shrub, for poor soils and dry summers; plant with kinds that have contrasting deeper flower color to prolong the spring floral pageant.

C. rigidus. Monterey ceanothus. Densely branched shrub, forming large mounds to six feet tall, with arching branches. Small, wedge-shaped to rounded evergreen leaves, glossy and dark green above and pale beneath, sometimes with tiny teeth toward tips. Small umbels of blue flowers from late winter to mid-spring. A common cultivar is 'Snowball,' with lower habit and pure white flowers. Distinctive and handsome.

C. sanguineus. Oregon tea-tree. Erect shrub to ten feet with flexible, red-purplish twigs. Prunable as a tree. Leaves rounded or elliptical to four inches long, thin and deciduous, with fine teeth along margins. Flowers in dense panicles, white. An attractive large specimen for northern and mountain gardens— accepts much winter rain (with drainage) and hot summers.

C. sorediatus. Jimbrush. Large, densely branched shrub to fifteen feet with stiff, rigid branches and gray-green bark. Evergreen, elliptical leaves to one and a half inches long, glossy smooth above and pale beneath, with tiny sticky teeth. Dense panicles of pale to dark blue flowers from late winter through spring. Good background or foundation shrub, or for informal hedges. Drought tolerant, likes plenty of summer sun.

C. spinosus. Redheart ceanothus. Large shrub to small tree (forms a single trunk with pruning) to twenty feet, with drab green bark and short, stiff, spine-tipped branchlets. Evergreen, elliptical to oblong leaves to one inch long, glossy bright green above and pale beneath, without teeth. Large intricate plumes of pale blue to whitish flowers from late winter through spring. Excellent background shrub or for informal hedges. Tolerates plenty of heat and needs no water. Especially appropriate for coastal southern California gardens.

C. tomentosus. Wooly-leaf ceanothus. Densely branched, upright shrub to ten feet with brownish to rusty bark. Evergreen, elliptical to ovate leaves to one inch long, glossy green above but covered beneath with fine whitish wool, the margins with tiny teeth. Flower plumes complex but short, often brilliant blue, in mid to late spring. Excellent shrub for fine seasonal color; excellent contrast with bush poppy (*Dendromecon*) and chaparral pea (*Pickeringia montana*). Tolerates hot, dry summers.

C. thyrsiflorus. Blueblossom ceanothus. Similar to C. *griseus* (described above) but may grow up to twenty feet tall (prunable to a single trunk). Leaves tend to be a bit narrower and are flat, without the edges turned under. Flowers are sky blue, blooming in spring months. This shrub has many cultivars and has been hybridized with a number of other species. Forms are available with snowy white flowers (such as 'Snow Flurry'). It is one of the easiest and fastest to grow, and is handsome as a specimen tree, background shrub, or even pruned as a hedge. Tolerant of coastal conditions.

C. thyrsiflorus var. *repens*. A naturally occurring variety, with low, sprawling stems, wind-pruned on coastal bluffs to inches high but with the same leaves and flowers as the regular upright shrub. Excellent woody ground cover for coastal gardens.

C. velutinus. Tobacco brush. Densely branched, rounded shrubs to six feet or more. Unusual, handsome, oval to elliptical, evergreen leaves to three inches long. They are glossy dark green and varnished above (sticky on hot days), pale and whitish-felted beneath, with the margins curling under strongly on hot days. Leaves have strong, sweetish aroma in summer. Flowers in large complex plumes, snowy white, from midspring to midsummer, according to elevation. Unusual specimen shrub; use flowers as contrast to blue species. Also good hedge. Excellent for mountain gardens; tolerates heat, drought, and winter cold.

Celtis douglasii. Desert Hackberry. Elm family (Ulmaceae)

HT: 6 to 20 feet. LVS: winter deciduous. FLWS: insignificant, green; males in small flat-topped clusters, females single; mid-spring. SMR WTR: occasional deep watering. PROP: cuttings (use bottom heat); seeds (scarify or stratify). EXP: full sun

Desert hackberry is our only native member of the elm family. Uncommon in nature, it is found along permanent seeps or streams in the middle deserts, where it is often accompanied by such other thirsty plants as willows, cottonwoods, native reed (*Phragmites communis*), and oasis goldenrod (*Solidago spectabilis*). Although the flowers are totally insignificant, the colorful orangy-brown, one-seeded fruits are pretty in early fall or late summer. Except during the coldest months the shrubs wear a mantle of bright green, elmlike leaves, narrowly ovate with uneven (oblique) base and finely serrated teeth along the edge. The near-white bark is handsome played against the leaves, or by itself in winter.

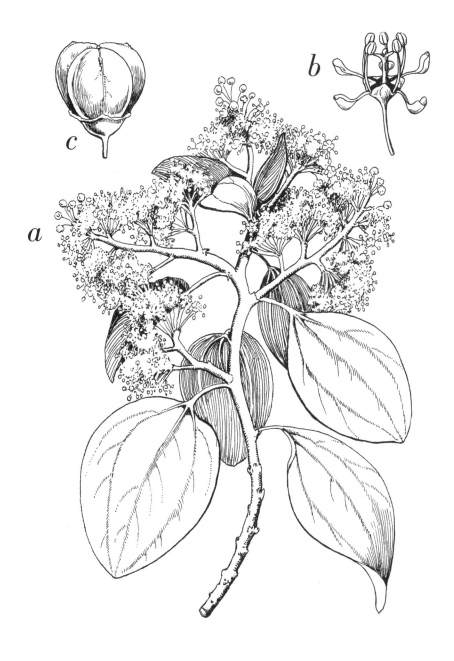

Tobacco Brush (*Ceanothus velutinus*)
a. flowering branch   *b*. flower detail   *c*. seed pod detail

Desert hackberry is for a garden where summers are hot, but unless the water table is already high it does well only with some deep summer irrigation. Its bold design could be used around a desert oasis theme, accompanying desert olive, desert willow, and mesquite, or by itself underplanted with yerba de mansa (*Anemopsis californica*), oasis goldenrod, and brook orchid (*Epipactis gigantea*), or with wild roses.

Cephalanthus occidentalis. Button Bush or Button Willow. Coffee family (Rubiaceae)

HT: 6 to 30 feet. LVS: winter deciduous. FLWS: ball-shaped heads of white flowers; summer. SMR WTR: deep watering. PROP: cuttings; suckers. EXP: full sun to light shade

Button bush is an unassuming, large shrub, at times becoming treelike. It lines watercourses throughout the hot foothill country surrounding the Central Valley and has deep but thirsty roots, so requires some summer water for good performance. Pale green, narrowly ovate leaves are borne in pairs; flowers are individually small but massed in globelike heads.

All in all, button bush is a modest plant with no truly outstanding traits. It fills a niche where a fast-growing border is needed along watercourses in summer heat.

Cercidium floridum. Palo Verde. Pea family (Fabaceae)

HT: up to 30 feet. LVS: seasonal; after rains. FLWS: showy bright yellow racemes; midspring. SMR WTR: little or none. PROP: seeds (scarify). EXP: full sun

Palo verde is usually a tree, but it is included here because it can assume the form of a large shrub. It is an altogether distinctive and beautiful addition to any desert setting. In nature it seeks out gravelly washes in the hot southern Colorado desert, where the water table stands high. With time it develops deeply penetrating roots. Among palo verde's attributes are handsome smooth, green, skinlike bark, a plumelike crown, and a veritable profusion of golden, cassialike flowers in midspring. Leaves are ephemeral, pinnately compound in the typical fashion of other pea leaves. Branches are spine-tipped.

Palo verde deserves a special spot as a specimen in the desert garden and can stand alone. One brilliant and daring color combination would be to grow it next to the scarlet-red wands of ocotillo (*Fouquieria splendens*), a slender cactuslike shrub with multiple branches and flamboyant, tubular flowers. It revels in hot temperatures, full sun, and mild winters. Severely cold or wet winters are not appropriate. Palo verde could also be closely pruned into a dense barrier or hedge.

Cercis occidentalis. Western Redbud. Pea family (Fabaceae)

HT: 6 to 18 feet. LVS: winter deciduous. FLWS: smothering the shrub in rose-purple; early to mid-spring. SMR WTR: occasional deep water. PROP: seeds (scarify, stratify, or use burn treatment). EXP: full sun or very light shade

Western redbud is one of California's outstanding shrubs. Like so many other fine shrubs, it has great seasonal interest: intricate, contorted twigs in winter; clouds of rose-purple, pealike flowers in early to midspring; curious leathery, kidney-shaped leaves from spring through fall; and showy, pendant, rose-purple seed pods in late spring. Because of its showy fruits, western redbud is like a plant that flowers twice.

Western redbud is typical of the interior hot foothill area of California, a familiar sight in company with California buckeye (*Aesculus californica*), digger pine (*Pinus sabiniana*), and blue oak (*Quercus douglasii*). Its stature varies from dense shrub to small tree, and it can be shaped accordingly in the garden. It makes a superb specimen or can be combined with other showy shrubs, sometimes to startling effect: with fremontia (*Fremontodendron* species and hybrids), bush anemone (*Carpenteria californica*), or various ceanothuses. A nice background complement would be a festoon of virgin's bower (*Clematis lasiantha*) smothered with creamy, starlike flowers.

Patience is required in the germination of western redbud's oversized, pealike seeds. One method is to bring water to a boil, remove it from heat, and immerse seeds for several minutes; others are to scarify or to stratify them. Once established, redbud grows slowly. It is sensitive to excessive winter moisture but is tough, and resistant to freezing temperatures.

Cercocarpus betuloides. Chaparral Mahogany. Rose family (Rosaceae)

HT: 6 to 25 feet. LVS: usually evergreen. FLWS: small greenish yellow saucers; mid-spring. SMR WTR: none. PROP: seeds (stratify); cuttings (use bottom heat). EXP: full sun

Chaparral mahogany is a large shrub, and can be pruned (by removing suckers) to form a tree. It is typical of foothill chaparral where summers are hot and dry, and there are several varieties sometimes treated as separate species—among them variety *blanchae* and variety *traskiae* from the Channel Islands—that differ in minor ways. It grows moderately fast with many upright, whiplike branches clothed with small, thick, fuzzy, birchlike leaves bearing an imprinted pinnate vein pattern on the upper surface. Bark is smooth and silvery gray; flowers are tiny, scarcely noticed, yellow-green saucers; the real show comes in summer, when fruits grow long, white-plumed tails. When backlit, a well-fruited shrub seems to glow with a special light. It is this feature and the handsome bark that make chaparral mahogany— named for its hard wood—highly garden worthy.

Chaparral mahogany is a malleable bush; for special effect, it can be espaliered

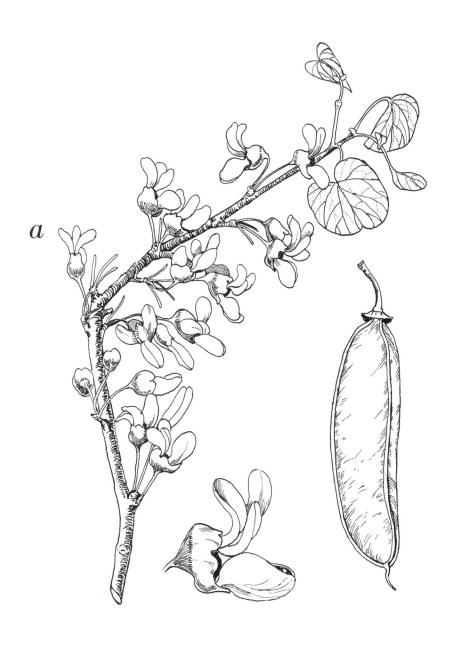

Western Redbud (*Cercis occidentalis*)
a. flowering branch   *lower center.* flower detail
lower right. seed pod detail

against a warm southern wall. It can also be used as an informal hedge or as a complementary shrub to flashier, spring-flowering shrubs. It deserves space in the larger drought-tolerant garden for its showy fruits.

Cercocarpus ledifolius. Mountain (Curl-Leaf) Mahogany. Rose family (Rosaceae)

HT: 6 to 30 feet. LVS: evergreen. FLWS: small, greenish yellow saucers; mid to late spring. SMR WTR: none. PROP: cuttings (use bottom heat), seeds (stratify). EXP: full sun

Mountain mahogany is a large shrub or, frequently, a multitrunked tree whose shape reflects the harsh environment it survives in: rocky slopes on the rain-shadow side of high mountains, where very cold winters, scant moisture, and hot summers are the rule. Plant height, branching pattern, and vigor all relate to local conditions, with many specimens beautifully "tortured" into picturesque and elegant patterns by winds, snows, and droughts.

Mountain mahogany has leathery leaves, dark green above and whitish beneath, with strongly curled margins that protect much of the upper surface from excessive exposure to drying. Strong trunks and beautiful red-brown bark, silvery on newer twigs, add to the "character" of this plant. Flowers are closely similar to those of chaparral mahogany, and the white-plumed fruits are just as spectacular.

In the garden, expect mountain mahogany to grow slowly but be a tough customer, with few worries about summer water or winter cold—wet winters and poor drainage are its enemies. Mountain mahogany is a superb specimen plant, blends well with a high desert setting in the company of sagebrush (*Artemisia tridentata*), antelope brush (*Purshia*), rabbitbrush (*Chrysothamnus*), desert peach (*Prunus andersonii*), and fern bush (*Chamaebatiaria millefolium*). It lends quiet elegance to a spartan planting, or could be trained as an unusual bonsai subject.

Chamaebatia foliolosa. Mountain Misery or Kitkadizzie. Rose family (Rosaceae)

HT: 8 inches to 2 feet. LVS: evergreen. FLWS: single white roses in flat-topped clusters; late spring to summer. SMR WTR: little or none. PROP: stem divisions; cuttings. EXP: light shade

Mountain misery is a low subshrub forming extensive mats—often excluding other vegetation—as a woody carpet under ponderosa pines and other conifers. Anyone who has driven across the Sierra in summer has experienced this plant, if not by sight then by smell, for on hot days the glandular leaves give off an unmistakable odor (justifying the common name). Here is a quick-growing ground cover for dry shade, which will tolerate snow and winter chill yet withstands the blistering summer heat of the foothills. Up close its broad, fernlike leaves are quite handsome (although not agreeable to the touch on hot days because of sticky resins). Modest clusters of single, white, roselike flowers complement leaves in early summer.

For most gardeners, mountain misery's liabilities offset its assets: sticky and stinky leaves are a fire hazard because of their high resin content, and the foliage carries on chemical warfare with neighboring plants. Nonetheless, it creates a special niche for a garden under pines, where summer drought must be borne, and it stabilizes soils of steep embankments.

Chamaebatiaria millefolium. Fern Bush. Rose family (Rosaceae)

HT: 2 to 6 feet. LVS: evergreen or winter deciduous. FLWS: showy spikes of white single roses; late summer to fall. SMR WTR: none. PROP: cuttings; seeds. EXP: full sun

Fernbush is a poorly known high-desert shrub, favoring the sagebrush country east of the Sierran crest and such high-desert ranges as the White Mountains, in bristlecone pine country. It is an upright shrub with many strict branches, clothed below in dense, deep green, resinously aromatic fernlike leaves, and it is crowned from late summer through fall with spires of white blossoms resembling small single roses. It is an excellent companion to other high-desert shrubs, making a fine foil for desert sagebrush (*Artemisia tridentata*), rabbitbrush (*Chrysothamnus nauseosus*) or antelope brush (*Purshia* spp.).

Fernbush is a good addition at the back of a well-drained rock garden, where its unique foliage and late flowering would be best appreciated. Some may object to the rather strong scent, although its odor is not nearly so penetrating as that of its close relative mountain misery (*Chamaebatia foliolosa*). Fernbush is easy to grow from seed and grows rapidly, but it is especially prone to damping-off (drench starting beds with fungicides). Success in the garden is best achieved with full sun, little winter dampness, and excellent drainage. It is well adapted to hot summers and cold winters.

Chilopsis linearis. Desert Willow. Trumpet vine family (Bignoniaceae)

HT: 6 to 20 feet. LVS: deciduous from midsummer to winter. FLWS: rose or pink-purple trumpets; mid to late spring. SMR WTR: occasional deep watering. PROP: cuttings; seeds. EXP: full sun

Desert willow forms large, multibranched shrubs with a willowlike aspect. Botanically it belongs to the usually tropical trumpet vine family. It is common in lower deserts lining gravelly washes or on the borders of oases, where its willowlike leaves lend grace in spring and summer. In its leafless winter condition, the attractive red-gray bark is highlighted by many elliptical lenticels. Late spring ushers in racemes of highly decorative, pale pink to deep rose-purple flowers. Flared like trumpets, the petal lobes turn out in a two-lipped design sprinkled with darker spots and lines, and the throat is marked yellow. Flower shape recalls that of its relatives the trumpet vines. Flowers are succeeded by long, beanlike pods with numerous flattened brown seeds surrounded by serrated white wings.

Desert willow is a shrub for large spaces and hot climates, not appropriate for wet coastal situations. It is dramatic as a background shrub, as for example against a light-walled building or as a feature around a pond in a desert or xeriscape garden (not so inconsistent an idea as one might suppose!). Its attractive bark and beautiful flowers add a special note, and the latter are attractive to hummingbirds and butterflies. As with other hot-desert plants, seeds and seedlings should be handled with care: excellent drainage and a minimum of wet-cold winter conditions. Expect desert willow to grow rapidly to maturity.

Special note: Hybrids between the desert willow and the cold-hardy catalpa have produced small trees called *Chitalpa*, whose flowers are highly ornamental and whose overall requirements are less exacting than the true desert willow.

Chrysolepis chrysophylla minor. Shrub Chinquapin. Beech family (Fagaceae)

HT: to about 15 feet. LVS: evergreen. FLWS: males in umbrellalike clusters of whitish catkins; female, minute burrs; summer. SMR WTR: occasional deep watering.
PROP: cuttings (use bottom heat); fruits (stratify). EXP: full sun to light shade

Shrub chinquapin is a little-appreciated, tough evergreen shrub with dense foliage, pretty shape, and beautiful leaves. It is the shrub version of the much larger tree chinquapin of coastal forests. The shrub form occurs on rocky outcroppings on forest edges or among coastal chaparral. It appreciates occasional summer fog but tolerates hot temperatures (in the latter case, light shade is beneficial). Though a slow grower, it rewards patience. Both cuttings and seed propagation are slow, and again, patience is required.

Shrub chinquapin has glossy, dark green, ovate leaves, highlighted beneath by their golden scales. Looking up into the branches is the best way to fully appreciate these leaves. Flowers, occurring in late spring, are seldom showy enough to merit comment. The male catkins—when produced in great numbers—provide a short-lived display not unlike the male flowers of chestnuts: masses of tiny, creamy flowers on whorled spikes. Female flowers are borne solitary or in small clusters, and are much more noticeable at summer's end when they mature into large burrs with wickedly interlaced, sharp spines surrounding a few small, edible nuts. Usable nuts are seldom left behind to gather; squirrels find the good ones, and insects lay eggs in the remainder.

Use shrub chinquapin in the back of a woodland garden or clipped into a barrier plant along walks or as a permanent hedge. In the latter capacity it is a welcome change from the humdrum boxwood or privet of so many gardens. Wherever possible, plant chinquapin so that you can look up into the branches.

Chrysolepis sempervirens. Sierra Chinquapin. Beech family (Fagaceae)

HT: 2 to 8 feet. LVS: evergreen. FLWS: like those in shrub chinquapin, above; midsummer. SMR WTR: occasional deep watering. PROP: cuttings (use bottom heat); seeds (stratify). EXP: full sun to light shade

Most of the comments made above for shrub chinquapin apply to Sierra chinquapin. The latter occurs throughout pine woods and rocky openings, in company with montane chaparral at middle elevations of California's mountains, and it is a common sight throughout the Sierra. It grows as a dense, rounded shrub whose leaves are more oblong in shape, the tips rounded rather than pointed, and the undersides a rusty or tawny color.

Sierra chinquapin is an excellent choice as a low-maintenance foundation shrub for homes in the mountains or as a hedge, in combination with huckleberry oak (*Quercus vaccinifolia*). It is a tough plant for droughty situations, very cold winters, and intense sun (give it light shade). It is likely to prove inappropriate for coastal gardens, but there may be replaced by shrub chinquapin.

Chrysothamnus spp. Rabbitbrush. Sunflower family (Asteraceae)

HT: 1½ to 6 feet. LVS: evergreen. FLWS: small bright yellow heads arranged in dense cymes; fall. SMR WTR: none. PROP: cuttings; seeds. EXP: full sun

Rabbitbrush is another nearly ubiquitous member of the Great Basin sagebrush country east of the Sierran crest, also extending through high-desert mountains. It is little known outside its homeland, although some varieties of this particular species range into the dry parts of the high north Coast Ranges. A name so unlovely is unfortunate, for rabbitbrush bursts forth with masses of bright golden flowers in fall, just when other plants are either losing their leaves or going dormant. The species name "nauseosus" is in allusion to the strongly scented leaves and stems, which to many are pleasant, being reminiscent of the high, sage desert country.

Rabbitbrush is a small shrub with many upright branches from its base, the bark shreddy brown, the newer twigs covered with a close felt of gray, white, or green wool. Leaves are bright green, so long and narrow they are nearly linear in shape, and remain on the bush all year. Rabbitbrush is a pleasing plant all year long, needing little water or care. It makes an excellent choice as a filler in the foreground of a desert or xeriscape planting or as a contrast of bright green evergreen foliage in a dry mixed border, where fall color is often in short supply. Its texture and foliage complement desert sagebrush and other grayish shrubs.

Other species of rabbitbrush are shorter; many combine the scent and brilliant masses of yellow flower heads of *C. nauseosus* with a lower, more compact plan of growth. They often occur on the very highest slopes of desert mountains. Species to try include *C. parryi* (Parry's rabbitbrush) and *C. viscidiflorus* (curl-leaf rabbitbrush).

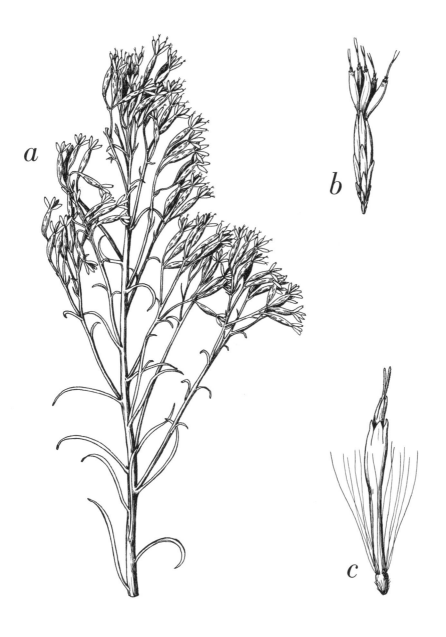

a

b

c

Rabbitbrush (*Chrysothamus* spp.)
a. flowering branches   *b*. flower head detail   *c*. floret detail

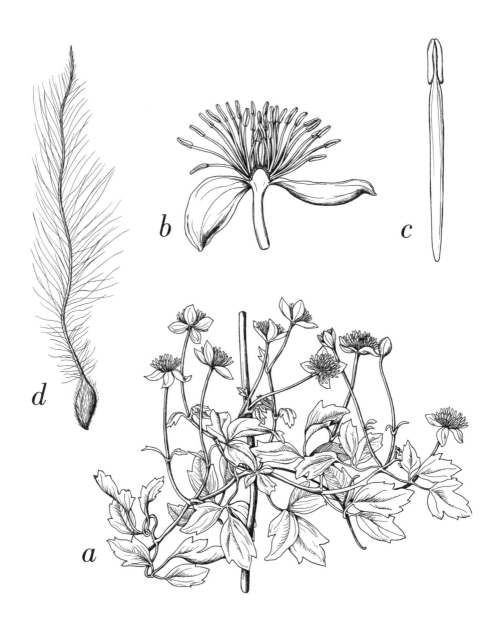

Virgin's Bower (*Clematis lasiantha*)
a. flowering branch   *b*. flower detail   *c*. stamen detail
d. fruit detail

Clematis spp. Virgin's Bower. Buttercup family (Ranunculaceae)

HT: woody vine to 20 or 30 feet. LVS: winter deciduous. FLWS: creamy stars in small clusters or dense masses; spring to summer. SMR WTR: little. PROP: layered stems; seeds (stratify). EXP: full sun to light shade

Clematis is included here because of its woody stems, although it is properly classified as a vine. Blessed with great vigor and rapid growth, clematis is sometimes overwhelming in garden settings; be sure to allow it plenty of space to spread and ample support to climb. It may be started by layering stems or from stratified seed.

Two clematises are frequent throughout California's foothill country: *C. ligusticifolia* as companion to riparian forests, where its great festoons and encircling stems cover lower branches of trees; and *C. lasiantha* as lover of chaparral shrubs in protected canyons. Both have pairs of dissected, toothed, deciduous leaves and swirled masses of feather-tipped, white-plumed fruits in summer and fall (often the most conspicuous phase of the life cycle). *C. lasiantha*, however, is the better of the two for its floral display—usually April to May—since the tight clusters of creamy starlike flowers are very showy. *C. ligusticifolia*, on the other hand, has more open masses of smaller creamy-white stars in summer.

Use clematis to adorn a pergola, archway, or unsightly dead shrub, but be careful of its smothering tendency with living shrubs.

Cneoridium dumosum. Bush Rue or Berry Rue. Rue family (Rutaceae)

HT: 2 to 6 feet. LVS: evergreen. FLWS: small clusters of white four-pointed stars; early spring. SMR WTR: occasional deep watering (none near coast). PROP: cuttings. EXP: full sun

Bush rue is a low, dense, somewhat sprawling shrub with dull green, heavily scented, linear to oblong leaves. Under a lens, the source of the odor is manifested as dark, pointlike glands similar to those seen in citrus. Flowers are borne in small clusters and are individually small, but in full flower there is a profusion of white stars. Flowers are followed by small bronze-red, berrylike fruits.

Bush rue inhabits coastal mountains of southern California, where it gets little summer moisture except for occasional fogs. It is tender and so not appropriate for northern inland or mountain gardens, where it would quickly perish in winter. Use bush rue as a backdrop for a rock garden or planted in masses in front of taller shrubberies. It would be especially attractive interplanted with the contrasting foliage of California sagebrush (*Artemisia californica*) or dune sagebrush (*Artemisia pycnocephala*).

Comarostaphylis diversifolia. Summer Holly. Heather family (Ericaceae)

HT: 6 to 17 feet. LVS: evergreen. FLWS: racemes of white urns; mid-spring.
SMR WTR: none. PROP: cuttings; seeds (stratify). EXP: light shade to full sun

Summer holly is a seldom-used horticultural gem. A close relative to manzanitas, it occurs naturally near the coast or on islands off the southern California coast, often on the edge of live oak or Bishop pine forests. Although it lacks the polished, red-purple bark of manzanitas, its handsome, dense branches are thickly clothed with leathery, dark green, broadly elliptical leaves, finely toothed along their margins and often with edges turned down. These lend an enduring quality through the year; graceful racemes of white, urn-shaped, madronelike blossoms decorate branches in spring and are followed by bright red, bumpy berries in summer and early fall (hence the common name).

Summer holly can be pruned as a tall hedge (try it with toyon, *Heteromeles arbutifolia*, for a long season of bright berries), grown as a shrub at the back of a woodland garden, or displayed as a specimen or foundation shrub. It should be left alone once established and carefully watched for signs of dieback, an indication of fungal root infection due to too much water. It requires excellent drainage and can handle hot summers, but beware cold, overly damp winters.

Coreopsis gigantea. Tree Coreopsis. Sunflower family (Asteraceae)

HT: 3 to 7 feet. LVS: summer deciduous. FLWS: bright yellow daisies in circles; early to mid spring. SMR WTR: minimal. PROP: seeds. EXP: full sun

Tree coreopsis is a unique species and atypical for its genus; most coreopsises are annual or perennial herbs. Growth occurs rapidly from freely germinating seeds; in short order this coreopsis establishes a miniature trunk with a "mop" of feathery, fern-like leaves at the top. Within a couple of seasons plants have reached mature size as single-trunked, miniature trees, with short branches near the top, a green skinlike bark, and a large crown of beautiful leaves decorated with circles of showy, yellow coreopsis flowers. Summer brings dramatic changes; leaves gradually brown and droop, seeds are scattered to the winds, and trunks stand like so many dead poles. This is just a resting period, the way tree coreopsis handles severe water shortage on the rocky cliffs or wind-blown sand dunes it calls home. With fall's first rains healthy new leaves appear, and stems fatten up by absorbing as much water as possible for later use.

Because tree coreopsis is so dramatic—yet ugly in summer—its landscape use should be carefully considered. It makes a dramatic container plant that could be moved out of the way—say to a lath house—when dormant. Or its starkness could be incorporated into a desert-type landscape where its "dead sticks" make a dramatic statement about the harshness of the summer environment. An island of tree coreopsis in such a setting would be entirely appropriate.

Although easy to grow, tree coreopsis is highly vulnerable to damp, cold winters and rots readily when subjected for long periods to freezing temperatures. Drainage should be sharp and watering carefully monitored.

Cornus nuttallii. Flowering Dogwood or Pacific Mountain Dogwood. Dogwood family (Cornaceae)

HT: 12 to 75 feet. LVS: winter deciduous. FLWS: showy white saucers; April and May. SMR WTR: moist soil needed. PROP: cuttings; layering; seeds (stratify). EXP: dappled or light shade

California's flowering dogwood is the counterpart to the renowned eastern dogwood, *Cornus florida*. It may grow as a tree or a multitrunked shrub, with horizontal tiers of branches arrayed in fine fashion. Dogwood is one of our best shrubs for a shaded moist spot in the garden, while in its native haunts it follows stream courses and canyon bottoms in the mountains. There it receives winter chill, which many coastal or lowland gardens lack, so that it seldom adapts fully to such situations. To most inland gardens, however, it is amenable. Dogwood thrives best where winter nights fall below freezing and the requisite shade and moisture are available in summer.

Flowering dogwood is a seasonal plant par excellence. Winter finds beautifully displayed branches with new, red twigs. Early spring brings delicate green canopies of broadly ovate new leaves followed by masses of immense, saucerlike flowers (not flowers at all but tight buttons of tiny greenish flowers surrounded by four white, petallike bracts). Summer is the quiet green season. Fall highlights brightly colored knobs of rose to red fruits succeeded by leaves flushed rose, purple, red, or orange.

Surely flowering dogwood would be the focal point in any wooded garden, along a stream, behind a pond, as a backdrop, or as a large specimen plant. It is elegant planted with other beautiful flowering shrubs, such as spicebush (*Calycanthus occidentalis*), western azalea (*Rhododendron occidentale*), mock orange (*Philadelphus lewisii*), or snowbell bush (*Styrax officinalis*), many of which flower around the same time. All are shorter plants with similar cultural requirements, and they all produce matching white flowers. Propagation could be from layered branches or stratified seeds.

Cornus stolonifera. Creek Dogwood. Dogwood family (Cornaceae)

HT: 6 to 16 feet. LVS: winter deciduous. FLWS: small white stars borne in flat-topped clusters; spring. SMR WTR: moist soil needed. PROP: easily layered; or take cuttings. EXP: light shade

Creek dogwood is the poor relative of its glamorous sister, flowering dogwood, yet has many redeeming qualities of its own. California is actually home to three closely sim-

Creek Dogwood (*Cornus glabrata*)
a. flowering branch   *b*. fruiting branch

ilar species, all followers of permanent streams in wooded areas: *C. stolonifera, C. glabrata,* and *C. occidentalis.* Discriminable only with difficulty, all three are included under the single creek dogwood heading.

Creek dogwood quickly establishes widely branched rounded shrubs, which may sucker from roots or naturally layer themselves when a branch is buried. It is excellent for lining stream sides, as an open hedge, or as a seasonal barrier plant for driveways and paths. Although the flowers are modest, four-pointed white stars arranged in flat-topped clusters (no showy petallike bracts), the handsome leaves, similar to those of flowering dogwood, turn fine shades of red and purple in autumn. The bright red twigs add beautiful color in the drab winter season. These colors make creek dogwood a fortuitous choice in front of a white wall.

The chief differences among the various creek dogwoods are as follows: *C. glabrata* has hairless leaves and bluish fruits; *C. stolonifera* has very small flowers, white fruits, and leaves covered beneath with fine hairs; *C. occidentalis* has slightly larger flowers, white fruits, and leaves with shaggy hairs beneath. Of the three, *C. stolonifera* occurs over the widest range of altitudes and is the best choice for mountain gardens.

Corylus cornuta californica. California Hazelnut. Birch family (Betulaceae)

HT: 6 to 20 feet. LVS: winter deciduous. FLWS: dangling male catkins, late winter; female flowers insignificant. SMR WTR: periodic deep watering. PROP: layering; nuts (stratify). EXP: shade

California hazelnut may be regarded as either a small tree or large shrub; it is amenable to training either way. To keep one or a few trunks, prune out the suckers. Hazel sends out long tiers of horizontal branches, giving it an effect much like that of flowering dogwood but with a very different leaf pattern. Hazel's deep green leaves are soft, broadly heart shaped, with jagged fine and coarse teeth along the margins. The light coming through the canopy in summer is a beautiful sight, for one sees layer upon layer, tier upon tier of green. Although bare in winter, by winter's end hazel's branches wear long dangling chains of male flowers waving in the breezes and (look hard) tiny female flowers, the three feathery, red stigmas extended to receive pollen. Soon new leaves follow, but you must wait until summer's end for mature nuts. Unfortunately, most hazels bear a sparing crop of nuts, and most of the sound ones are quickly gathered by squirrels; if you want a good nut crop for the garden plant the European filbert instead.

California hazelnut grows along the margins of wet forests from the coast redwoods up into the yellow pine belt of the Sierra. A fast grower, it thrives where it has consistent summer water and light filtering through the fringes of tall trees. Plant it in the background of your woodland garden for a beautiful green wall, or along a stream or

California Hazelnut (*Corylus cornuta californica*)
leaves and nut detail

behind a pond with shrubs of similar requirements: western azalea (*Rhododendron occidentale*), rosebay (*Rhododendron macrophyllum*), huckleberries (*Vaccinium* spp.), or thimbleberry (*Rubus parviflorus*).

Cowania mexicana. Cliff Rose. Rose family (Rosaceae)

HT: 1½ to 10 feet. LVS: evergreen. FLWS: single white roselike flowers; late spring to early summer. SMR WTR: none. PROP: cuttings; seeds (stratify). EXP: full sun

Cliff rose is a finely branched shrub, often springing from one or just a few trunks, with long, shreddy brown bark. The ends of branches are covered in late spring or early summer with showy, single white roselike flowers, then small clusters of white, plumelike fruits. Because of its beautiful trunks and evergreen leaves (small three- to five-pinnately lobed, leathery leaves covered with sticky glands), this commanding plant may be the star of the desert garden, combining seasonal color with sturdy drought tolerance and love of hot summers. It comes from the higher elevations of desert mountains on rocky banks, where it often overlooks sagebrush and antelope brush.

Use cliff rose toward the back of a sunny rock garden, or combine it with other desert shrubs whose flowers occur at other times or whose leaves are more dramatic (for example, fernbush, *Chamaebatiaria millefolium*; desert sagebrush, *Artemisia tridentata*; or rabbitbrush, *Chrysothamnus nauseosus*).

Crataegus douglasii. Native Hawthorn. Rose family (Rosaceae)

HT: 6 to 30 feet. LVS: winter deciduous. FLWS: small white single roses in terminal flat-topped clusters; late spring. SMR WTR: occasional deep watering. PROP: suckers; layering. EXP: full sun to light shade

Our native hawthorn will never compete with the many well-established cultivated forms of European hawthorn. But when judged on its own merits native hawthorn is an attractive, easy to grow small tree or large shrub. It suckers readily, but these can be removed to form a single zigzaggy trunk; from these suckers new plants can be easily propagated. Hawthorn has many horizontal, angular branches lined with stout thorns, which are not to be taken lightly, and a reddish skin on new twigs. The thin leaves are of typical hawthorn shape, with irregular lobes, teeth, or both, and with flowers, modest by themselves, that transform the tree when borne in great numbers in late spring.

Native hawthorn occurs in wet meadows or borders of forest in California's north, nowhere common but succeeding especially well where grazing pressure is high, because of its staunch defenses. It grows rapidly to full size and makes a plethora of dark purplish-black fruits the birds love. It creates a pretty picture as a backdrop to a woodland garden, especially in combination with such other seasonal bloomers as

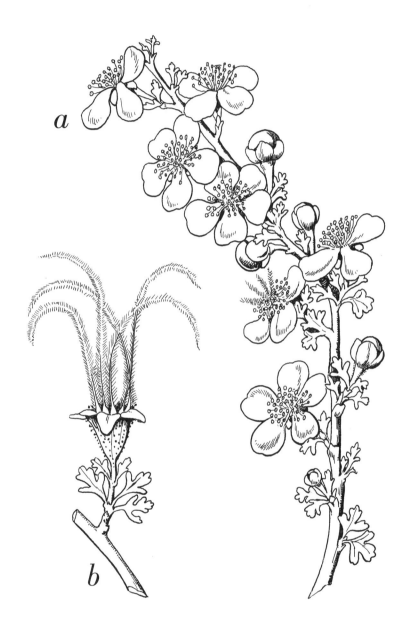

Cliff Rose (*Cowania mexicana*)
a. flowering branch   *b*. leaf and fruit detail

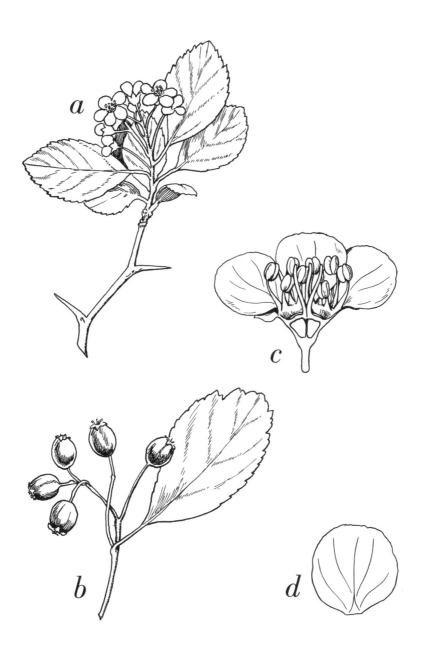

Native Hawthorn (*Crataegus douglasii*)
a. flowering branch   *b.* fruit detail   *c.* flower detail   *d.* petal detail

flowering dogwood and western azalea. If grown to encourage the suckers, you can quickly establish a formidable informal hedge.

Cupressus goveniana. Gowen's Cypress. Cypress family (Cupressaceae)

HT: 15 to 40 feet. LVS: scalelike, evergreen. FLWS: none; instead, tiny pollen cones and globe-shaped, shiny brown seed cones. SMR WTR: little or none. PROP: cuttings (use bottom heat); seeds (stratify). EXP: light shade to full sun

California's cypresses are a fascinating group of trees, ranging from small and bushy, such as Gowen's cypress, to moderately tall, with ample crown. Most are relicts, restricted to unusual or infertile soils. Some, such as Monterey cypress (*Cupressus macrocarpa*), are famous as street and roadside trees. But Gowen's cypress is a tree amenable to shaping as a dense shrub, use as a foundation planting or as barrier or hedge, or pruned to miniature form as a beautiful bonsai subject. Rare in nature—in only two small groves on the Monterey peninsula—Gowen's cypress is easy to grow in the garden, the seeds germinating readily and the plants maturing rapidly in poor but well drained, sandy or loamy soils.

Like all cypresses, Gowen's twigs are closely covered with minute spirally arranged, scalelike leaves with a pleasantly fresh, piny aroma when crushed. In late summer or fall, new branchlets carry myriad minuscule yellow pollen cones and a new crop of seed cones. The seed cones mature in one year but don't open except on very hot days or after fire. The mature cones are knobby, shiny brown globes with shieldlike scales.

Because it is fire adapted, Gowen's cypress is not a plant for use near buildings. Other than that its garden use is excellent for pleasant appearance, easy shaping, rapid growth, and adaptation to shallow, poor soils. One other cypress with potential for use as a bushy treelet or bonsai subject is the closely related pygmy cypress—*Cupressus pygmaea*. It comes from the old marine terraces of the Mendocino coast. Just remember, though, that pygmy cypress is *not* pygmy on fertile soils, where the trunks soar to over eighty feet!

Dalea spp. Indigo Bush. Pea family (Fabaceae)

HT: 3 to 10 feet. LVS: summer deciduous. FLWS: deep, indigo blue or rose-colored peas in short spikes; March to May. SMR WTR: none. PROP: seeds (scarify, stratify, or both). EXP: full sun

The half-dozen or so shrubby species of indigo bush are fairly similar, all being low- to medium-sized shrubs with intricate, spine-tipped branches sprinkled with strongly aromatic, yellowish glands, and with leaves that appear only after rains. Details differ as to color and hairiness of young twigs (green to white and wooly), shape of glands, size of leaves, and arrangement of flowers (heads or loose spikes). Flowers are generally a rich, deep blue or blue-purple—sometimes tinged with rose—and appear in spring. All indigo bushes are lovers of warm deserts, where they thrive in rocky or sandy soils. All are named for the rich color of their pea-shaped flowers. The most common and thus most likely available species are *D. schottii*, with green twigs and tiny simple leaves, and *D. fremontii*, with white-hairy new twigs and pealike leaves.

Indigo bushes lend interest throughout the year according to their form, and the thorny branches make them useful as barriers in desert gardens. Their vivid flowers in spring contrast with the yellows of bush daisies and incienso, the orange of apricot mallow, and the pale blue-purple of desert aster. As to their odor, I find it a plus, but you will have to decide for yourself whether it is pleasant or overpowering.

Dalea spinosa. Smoke Tree. Pea family (Fabaceae)

HT: 3 to 20 feet. LVS: very short lived; deciduous most of the year. FLWS: bright blue-purple, in massed spikes; June and July. SMR WTR: none. PROP: seeds (scarify, stratify, or both). EXP: full sun

Smoke tree is a unique kind of dalea, immediately recognizable and distinctive by its shape, color, and habitat. This small tree often assumes a roughly globular shape, but with myriad interlaced, smoky grayish branchlets that are spine tipped. From a distance the effect is truly like a puff of gray smoke. The leaves are tiny and ephemeral, adding nothing to the overall appearance. For a couple of weeks each year, however, smoke tree's early summer profusion of fine, blue-purple pea flowers transforms it. Smoke tree favors dry, gravelly washes and arroyos, where its province may overlap with desert willow and catclaw acacia. It occurs only in the lower, hotter reaches of our southernmost desert, the Colorado.

Smoke tree would be a fine focal point in any summer dry or desert garden, given gritty soil with excellent drainage. Its unique shape and color recommend it as a specimen, either by itself or contrasted with plants of dramatically different shapes, such as ocotillo, cacti, or elephant tree.

Dendromecon rigida and variety harfordii. Bush or Tree Poppy. Poppy family (Papaveraceae)

HT: 3 to 15 feet. LVS: evergreen. FLWS: showy yellow saucers; peaking mid-spring. SMR WTR: none. PROP: suckers; root divisions; seeds (stratify). EXP: full sun

Bush or tree poppy is a rather open, large shrub with stems going in many directions; oblique, gray-green, willowlike, lance-shaped leaves; and large, bright yellow, saucer-shaped flowers of great beauty. Each flower is the essence of poppy, with its crinkled petals and bunches of yellow stamens in the center. Although flowering peaks around April, bush poppy may produce flowers any season in mild climates. The preferred variety *harfordii* has broader, nearly elliptical leaves and slightly larger flowers than others. This variety comes from the Channel Islands; the common variety is from hot, dry chaparral on the mainland.

Bush poppy grows rapidly; it responds in the garden to extra water, but when given it is short-lived, being vulnerable to fungal root diseases. For best performance it needs full summer sun, ample root run, and good drainage (especially in winter wet and cold conditions). The Channel Island variety is less hardy and should be reserved for coastal gardens with mild winters. Since roots may send out runners to colonize new areas, they offer a naturally easy way to propagate this poppy; seeds prove difficult, with uneven germination, even when stratified or subjected to the burn treatment.

Use bush poppy where it has room to spread. Smaller shrubs in the foreground would help hide the openness of lower branches: try, for example, buckwheats (*Eriogonum*), rockroses (*Cistus* spp.), sunrose (*Helianthemum*), and bush monkey-flowers (*Diplacus* spp.). Other bold shrubs to place near bush poppy could include rose-purple chaparral pea (*Pickeringia montana*), yerba santa (*Eriodictyon* spp.), and various ceanothuses. You could also mingle this poppy with the magnificent white-and-yellow-flowered Matilija poppy (*Romneya coulteri*).

Diplacus spp. Bush Monkeyflowers. Figwort family (Scrophulariaceae)

HT: ½ to 5 feet. LVS: mostly evergreen; sometimes partially summer deciduous. FLWS: showy monkeyflowers with two-lipped petals in warm colors; through summer. SMR WTR: occasional deep watering. PROP: cuttings; seeds. EXP: full sun to light shade

California's bush monkeyflowers are special plants, belonging to a series of closely related species that can be hybridized in the garden. Their stature places them between true shrubs and half-woody perennials; their garden use is best as perennials. Because the several species are closely similar in cultural requirements, uses, and overall appearance, they are treated here as a genus first, then briefly elaborated as species.

Bush monkeyflowers are low, half-decumbent to upright, many-branched shrubs with narrow, lance-shaped, shiny green leaves that are varnished with a sticky gum on hot days. In severe summer drought, many older leaves are sacrificed in order to lower water demands; in the garden, therefore, plants look better with at least occasional thorough watering. Flowers are borne in small clusters at stem tips, are uncommonly large and showy with flared throats and two-lipped petals, and often are marked on the lower lip with contrasting spots or stripes that serve as nectar guides to bees. Although flowers peak in late spring, the season is prolonged by extra water and mild summer temperatures. Under these circumstances life expectancies are shortened, but new plants are readily started from half-ripe cuttings.

Use masses of bush monkeyflowers in a mixed, partially dry border, and use the smaller species toward the back of rock gardens. They are also excellent in front of larger shrubberies, and those with weak stems may even cascade or spill over rock walls. Many hybrids in selected colors (in particular, the Verity hybrids) are available, and these offer exciting color combinations: pure yellow, white, raspberry, and burnt orange, among others. Here are some species:

D. aridus. A low, weak-stemmed species from the far south and therefore more tender; sticky stems and large clear-yellow flowers. Prolific bloomer.

D. aurantiacus. A tall species with smallish but fine orange flowers. Widespread along the coast of central and northern California, and very easy to grow. Occasionally with very pale or yellowish flowers.

D. bifidus. Medium-sized but weak-stemmed shrub from the northern Sierra foothills. Tolerates light shade. Having perhaps the finest flowers of all— uncommonly large, pale buff with deep orange spots—it is known as the azalea-flowered monkeyflower.

D. flemingii. A low shrub tolerating light shade with glossy leaves and rather small deep orange-red flowers. An island species. Tender.

D. longiflorus. More a southern species, but similar to *D. aurantiacus* in most respects, with larger flowers of a paler—often buff—color.

D. puniceus. Similar to *D. flemingii* but taller, with larger flowers. From the southern California mainland.

Dirca occidentalis. Western Leatherwood. Mezereum or daphne family (Thymeleaceae)

HT: 2 to 8 feet. LVS: winter deciduous. FLWS: small clusters of hanging yellow bells; late winter. SMR WTR: some deep watering. PROP: difficult; try suckers. EXP: light shade

Western leatherwood is a shrub as rare as it is distinctive. Endemic to the counties immediately around San Francisco Bay, it inhabits the interface between coastal scrub and mixed-evergreen forests, typically near bay laurel (*Umbellularia californica*), coast live oak (*Quercus agrifolia*), and evergreen huckleberry (*Vaccinium ovatum*). It is an open, multibranched shrub with handsome, tough, leathery bark and very flexible branches. Bare in winter, it sends out small clusters of pendant yellow bells at winter's end before the new leaves unfurl. Leaves are thin, light green, and rather oval, much resembling those of oso berry (*Osmaronia cerasiformis*). Flowers may be followed by small, single-seeded yellow-green berries, but often pollination fails.

Leatherwood makes an imposing shrub that would be an excellent specimen, a fine shrub against a wall or on the edge of the woodland garden where its early flowers can be shown to best advantage. Good companions include canyon gooseberry (*Ribes*

Western Leatherwood (*Dirca occidentalis*)
a. flowering branches   *b.* fruiting branch with leaves
c. flower detail   *d.* fruit detail

menziesii) and flowering currant (*Ribes sanguineum glutinosum*), both also early bloomers. Underplant it with ferns for a beautiful composition.

The biggest problem with leatherwood is that it is exceedingly difficult to propagate; cuttings generally fail and seed germination is poor. The seeds probably have a double dormancy. The most likely method might prove to be by suckers from the base of mature shrubs, but it should be attempted only from nursery stock or other cultivated sources, since this is a rare shrub.

Dyssodia cooperi. Cooper's Dyssodia. Sunflower family (Asteraceae)

HT: 1 to 2 feet. LVS: seasonal; only after rains. FLWS: showy single daisies with orange rays; late spring. SMR WTR: none. PROP: cuttings; seeds. EXP: full sun

Dyssodias are but one of many sunflower relatives adapted to desert heat and drought. Subshrubs woody only at their base, they send up many greenish, wandlike branches that carry small, lance-shaped leaves bordered by spiny teeth, and in late spring, colorful flower heads. A combination of rich yellow and orange, the showy rays persist after pollination. Like so many other desert shrubs, dyssodia is for spring show, planted along a gravelly wash, the back of a rock garden, or among other desert shrubs. It may reward with a second blossoming in fall, after unexpected summer showers or with late summer watering.

Echinocactus triglochidiatus. Mound Cactus (Claret Cup). Cactus family (Cactaceae)

HT: Low mounds to about 8 inches. LVS: none; green, globe-shaped stems have white spines. FLWS: showy, strawberry-red cups; mid to late spring. SMR WTR: none. PROP: stem divisions; seeds (stratify). EXP: full sun

Here is one of the handsomest of native cacti, worthy of a place in any desert garden. Because cacti have unique architecture they may not fit in every landscape, and most require hot summers and low precipitation to do their best, although more winter rain should not be harmful in soils with excellent drainage. To guard against rot at the root crown, dress the soil with coarse pebbles.

Mound cactus grows horizontally to make great clumps of fat, globular stems—old plants may have thirty or more. When these bear myriad handsome claret cups of red flowers, the plant is truly spectacular. The rest of the year rely on the interesting form, which remains green all year and is sprinkled with starbursts of spreading white spines.

Mound cactus is beautiful displayed with other cacti, with yuccas and nolinas, or in front of small junipers or pinyon pines (*Pinus monophylla, quadrifolia,* and *edulis*). It is especially striking draped over granite or sandstone rocks.

Empetrum nigrum. Crowberry. Crowberry family (Empetraceae)

HT: to about 3 inches. LVS: evergreen. FLWS: tiny axillary greenish male and female flowers; spring. SMR WTR: moist soil. PROP: cuttings; layering. EXP: light shade

Crowberry is a rarity in California but well known in the Pacific Northwest and Alaska, where it extends into the tundra. In California we see this sprawling woody ground cover as draperies on rocks along fog-drenched, coastal bluffs in the far north. There it forms attractive, circular mats, with a thick covering of bright green, needle-like leaves that retain their good looks throughout the year. The flowers are totally insignificant, but the shiny black berries add interest in summer.

Crowberry makes an uncommonly neat and pretty ground cover in light shade, flowing over rocks or between stepping-stones. It is not suitable for a summer-hot garden, but it thrives in the cool, moist air of the foggy coast.

Encelia californica. Coast Brittlebush. Sunflower family (Asteraceae)

HT: 1½ to 6 feet. LVS: sometimes summer deciduous. FLWS: single bright yellow daisies with black-purple centers; late winter through spring. SMR WTR: occasional deep watering. PROP: cuttings. EXP: full sun

Coast brittlebush varies from a low, semisprawling shrub to a dense upright shrub, always with a rounded, mounded appearance. Its broad, triangular leaves are dull green and may shrivel in severe summer drought; occasional extra water (especially in hot climes) is recommended to prevent this. Flowering extends over a long period, from late winter through spring, but it finishes sooner inland away from the mediating temperatures of the ocean. Flowers are attractive, large yellow daisies with a dark, almost black center. Deadheading prolongs flowering.

Coast brittlebush tolerates poor, sandy, or rocky soils, so is ideal for the back of a rock garden or in front of much taller shrubberies. It combines well with other low coastal shrubs such as California sagebrush (*Artemisia californica*), various bush monkeyflowers (*Diplacus* spp.), salvias, and low-growing ceanothuses. It is ideal for the coast garden but not the best selection for summer-hot, inland areas. It is also sensitive to long periods of cold and wet in winter.

Encelia farinosa. Desert Brittlebush or Incienso. Sunflower family (Asteraceae)

HT: 1 to 3 feet. LVS: often summer deciduous. FLWS: golden daisies in dense clusters; mid-spring. SMR WTR: none. PROP: cuttings early in year; seeds (stratify). EXP: full sun

Desert brittlebush is a striking shrub of alluvial fans and rocky aprons, forming low, rounded bushes with branches radiating in all directions from the center and covered with broadly elliptical to oval silver-gray leaves. The showy golden daisies are borne in tight clusters in great profusion in mid-spring; they light up areas where they're planted in masses.

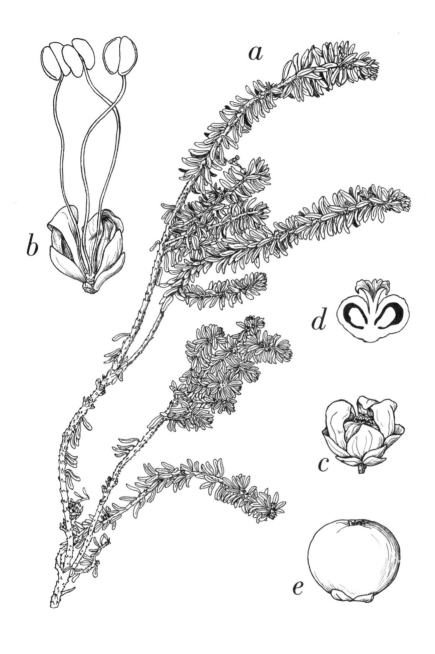

Crowberry (*Empetrum nigrum*)
a. leafy branches   *b*. male flower details   *c*. female flower detail
d. view through ovary   *e*. fruit detail

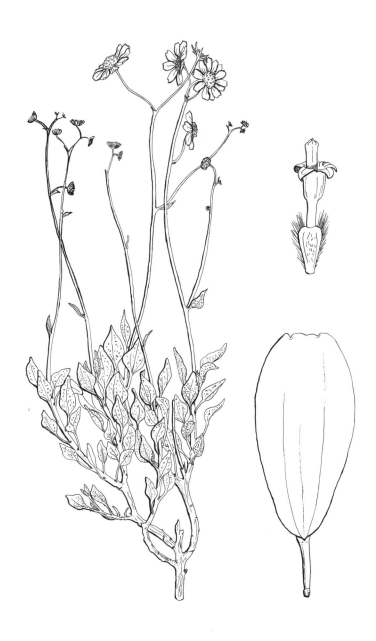

Incienso (*Encelia farinosa*)
left: habit of flowering plant   *lower right*: ray flower detail
upper right: disc floret detail

The biggest problem with this brittlebush is that by summer's end the desert sun has burned off all the leaves, and the branches look like bunches of dead twigs bundled together. Because of this liability, desert brittlebush will have limited appeal in many garden applications. One way around this is to grow it in a tub on castors so that it may be rolled out of sight at spring's end. Another is to plant it with or near plants with interesting summer form—various cacti, for example, in a desert garden. Brittlebush will make the most of its fine floral display planted in drifts; it can complement other low spring-flowering desert shrubs such as desert senna (*Cassia armata*), various salvias, paperbag bush (*Salazaria mexicana*), and apricot mallow (*Sphaeralcea ambigua*). It is recommended only for gardens where summers are hot and winters fairly dry. (If planted elsewhere, be sure to give very good drainage with extra crushed rock.)

Ephedra spp. Mormon Tea. Ephedra family (Ephedraceae)

HT: 1 to 4 feet. LVS: minute scales. FLWS: tiny yellow pollen cones on male plants; tiny whitish to greenish seed cones on female plants. SMR WTR: none. PROP: root divisions; seeds (stratify). EXP: full sun

Where most green-twigged desert shrubs look shabby or drab in summer and fall, ephedras make bold statements that enhance the scene. These strange gymnosperms have reduced their leaves to minute brown, gray, or black scales and have placed all their chlorophyll in the numerous, finely branched twigs; lower branches develop bark and wood. Because bare-appearing branches are neat and tidy, with a pattern all their own, ephedras are dramatic all year. Only in spring and early summer do they appear in another guise. Then, the male plants bear dozens of tiny yellow pollen cones that soon wither. The female plants make similarly shaped greenish seed cones, which gradually turn white while one or two terminal black seeds ripen and protrude from their tips.

Ephedras favor sandy places or rocky hillsides where drainage is perfect, and ask no more than scattered rains to be "happy." In the garden, this translates to no additional water lest they rot or slowly decline. They grow in a variety of desert situations from low, hot deserts to the high pinyon pine and sagebrush country. Their use in gardens should be in the back of a rock garden, or as a specimen in gravelly soil. They would be a good choice with smaller shrubs that fade into the background as summer approaches.

Of California's seven different species, two of the best are *E. californica* for lower elevations and *E. viridis* for higher altitudes with cold winters. Both have vivid green twigs, the former with older twigs turning a deeper green, the latter maintaining a vivid color all year. Other species are more drably colored.

Eriodictyon spp. Yerba Santa. Waterleaf family (Hydrophyllaceae)

HT: 2 to 10 feet. LVS: evergreen. FLWS: small, white to purple, in open cymes; late spring. SMR WTR: none. PROP: root cuttings. EXP: full sun

"Yerba santa" is Spanish for holy herb, and it has been used as well as a medicinal herb. Crush a leaf: a minty and refreshing odor is released, one of the charms of these shrubs. All species have many characteristics in common: wide, open branches with wandering roots, sending up new shoots here and there as they go; leaves that are lance-shaped to oval, shiny and sticky in some, wooly and gray in others. Flowers are produced in profusion above the leaves in open, intricately branched cymes. Individual flowers are tubular with flared petals, and attract butterflies.

Yerba santas usually live along the chaparral's edge where their shorter stature doesn't cause them to be shaded out. They are opportunists that quickly claim new ground along road cuts or after fires. Because they wander by roots they have the potential to become invasive, but they are easy to control in garden situations. They are, however, sensitive to excessive winter wet and cold conditions, and those with shiny green leaves are prone to a disfiguring black, sooty fungus; the gray, wooly-leafed kinds don't suffer this problem.

Use yerba santas where they can freely naturalize, on rocky embankments, for example. Planted in drifts they make fetching combinations with bush poppy (*Dendromecon rigida*) and chaparral pea (*Pickeringia montana*), flowering toward the end of spring. Here are three recommended species:

> *E. californicum*. California yerba santa. A shrub seldom reaching over six feet, with pale purple flowers, upper leaf surface a shiny dark green, and lower surface pale, with a netlike, whitish pattern. North and central California.

> *E. crassifolium*. Wooly yerba santa. The best of the wooly kinds, with broad, densely white-felted leaves. From far southern California. Grows the largest of all, with clear, pale purple flowers.

> *E. trichocalyx*. Southern yerba santa. Similar to the first, but with fuzzy hairs on the flowers. From southern California.

Eriogonum spp. Wild Buckwheat. Buckwheat family (Polygonaceae)

HT: ½ to 6 feet. LVS: evergreen. FLWS: mostly in tight heads or umbels; summer to fall. SMR WTR: little or none. PROP: cuttings; seeds. EXP: most, full sun

The wild buckwheats constitute a large and varied group in California's flora, but most species don't qualify as true shrubs, although many have woody crowns. In nature they seek out sandy or rocky slopes where there's little competition; they're distributed throughout California, however, from coastal sand dunes across the moun-

Yerba Santa (*Eriodictyon californicum*)
a. flowering branches   *b*. cut-away flower detail

tains and into the alpine regions of the Sierra Nevada, and throughout the deserts. Few species are discussed here; for more, refer to the sister volume: *Complete Garden Guide to the Native Perennials of California*.

The larger buckwheats have varied leaves, but all are drought tolerant and display masses of tiny white to pinkish flowers in broad, umbrellalike clusters. Because they flower late in the season, they're ideal for giving late summer and fall color. Use them in dry mixed borders, in front of taller shrubberies, or in desert gardens. Not only do their attractive flowers last long in the garden, they can also be cut and dried for beautiful arrangements, either when actually in flower or afterward, when they've dried to tones of bronze and rust. The boldness of St. Catherine's lace recommends it for a place where its shape can be admired all year, but bear in mind that the two island buckwheats are frost tender. Here are six shrubby buckwheats:

E. arborescens. Santa Cruz Island buckwheat. Endemic to that island, this buckwheat is a low shrub that forms dense clumps and has dull to gray-green, narrow leaves (again curled under) and delightful broad fans of white or pink flowers that fade to a burnished rusty red-brown.

E. × blisseanum. A hybrid between Santa Cruz Island buckwheat and St. Catherine's lace, with intermediate stature and leaves; flowers much like those of *E. giganteum*.

E. fasciculatum. Flat-top buckwheat. A widely variable species from the southern seashore and across the coast ranges into desert mountains. Leaves are dull or bright green, needlelike (actually the margins turn under and give the impression that they're this narrow), and borne in close bunches. Flat-topped clusters of white to deep pink flowers. Adapted to hot climates, and an excellent bee and honey plant.

E. giganteum. St. Catherine's lace. The giant of the genus, up to six or more feet high, from Catalina Island. Broad, spoon-shaped gray leaves; shreddy bark on old trunks; and exceptionally broad umbrellas of pale pink flowers, with a lacy appearance.

E. heermannii. Dichotomous buckwheat. Unusual compact high-desert shrub to two feet, with intricate, equally divided, greenish twigs all year, and leaves seasonally. The branching pattern is noteworthy. Smothered in late summer to fall by masses of white blossoms. Excellent for seasonal interest in a desert garden or rockery. Tolerates high temperatures without extra water.

E. umbellatum. Sulfur buckwheat. A woody, matted subshrub, but so useful in a drought garden it's included here. Low mounds of dark green to whitish silver, spoon-shaped leaves, bearing open umbels of intensely yellow flowers in sum-

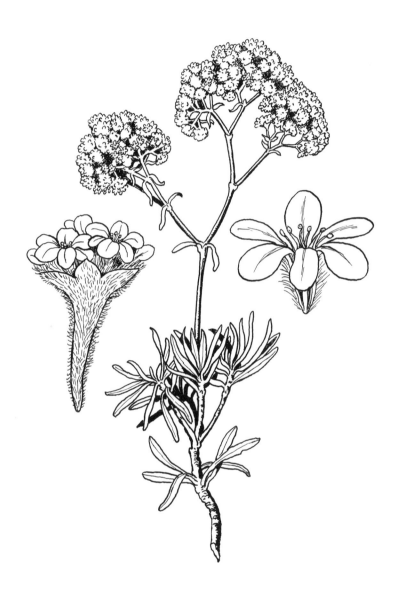

Santa Cruz Island Buckwheat (*Eriogonum arborescens*)
middle left: flowering branch, with details of flower cluster
middle right: flower

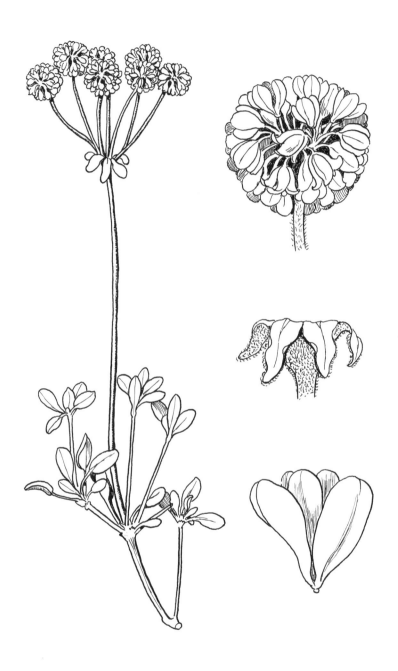

Sulfur Buckwheat (*Eriogonum umbellatum*)
lower right: flowering branch from base, with details of flower
middle right: floral bract   *upper right*: flower cluster

mer. Flowers fade reddish. Ideal for rockeries, in front of tall shrubs, or in the front of the chaparral garden.

Eriophyllum spp. Lizard Tail and Golden Yarrow. Sunflower family (Asteraceae)

HT: to 2½ feet. LVS: evergreen most of year. FLWS: flat-topped clusters of small, bright yellow daisies; late spring to summer. SMR WTR: little or none. PROP: half-ripened cuttings; seeds. EXP: full sun in most situations

Eriophyllums represent the gamut from low, bushy subshrubs to perennials (such as the wooly sunflower *E. lanatum*) and tiny desert annuals (*E. pringlei* and *E. wallacei*). California's two bushy species—*E. stachaedifolium* and *E. confertiflorum*—are excellent in the garden, being easy and fast to grow, with little need for extra water once established (although their leaves prosper better in summer-hot regions with occasional supplemental water). *E. stachaedifolium*—lizard tail—is a mounded, coastal subshrub from bluffs overlooking the ocean, where the winds often prune it into a shapely form as though a gardener were carefully pruning a rounded topiary. The numerous leaves are deeply pinnately cleft—green above and wooly white beneath—and good looking most of the year. In June, a profusion and succession of flat-topped clusters of small, bright yellow daisies appears, each head with tiny rays surrounding many starlike disc flowers.

E. confertiflorum, in contrast, is a miniature shrublet—usually of rocky places away from the immediate coast, where it can bask in hot summer sun. Its leaves are miniaturized versions of lizard tail, often with tinier leaves clustered in the angles between leaf and stem. The flat-topped clusters of small yellow daisies, of closely similar design, are held a bit higher above the stem leaves, giving a tidy appearance.

Use these two eriophyllums for the foreground of a rock garden, massed in front of taller shrubs, or in the front of a droughty mixed border. Their trim shape and burst of colorful flowers is an endearing combination. They make good contrast with orange diplacuses and blue penstemons. Note that the branches of both eriophyllums become leggy unless pinched back, especially if shaded.

Eucnide urens. Desert Nettle. Blazing star family (Loasaceae)

HT: 1 to 2 feet. LVS: partially summer deciduous. FLWS: showy, cream-colored vases; late spring. SMR WTR: none. PROP: perhaps stem divisions; seeds (stratify). EXP: full sun

Desert nettle sounds forbidding, and it is if you accidentally touch the stinging hairs lining young stems and leaves. This lining also guarantees a measure of protection from chewing critters. But the real virtue is in the lovely, creamy flowers, closely resembling those of the related, annual blazing stars in the genus *Mentzelia*. Unlike the latter, which require frequent resowing of seed, desert nettle lives for several years, becoming a low subshrub with ever-expanding branches close to the roots.

Adapted to very hot deserts in rocky soils, desert nettle is an excellent candidate for a low-profile, natural desert garden. It should be planted near taller plants that retain handsome twigs or leaves through the summer, including the ephedras, daleas, and some bush daisies. By itself, its drabness for more than half the year, with bedraggled leaves awaiting the rejuvenation of winter rains, is more notable.

Euonymus occidentalis. Western Burning-bush. Staff tree family (Celastraceae)

HT: 6 to 20 feet. LVS: winter deciduous. FLWS: small maroon-brown stars; late spring. SMR WTR: some deep watering. PROP: cuttings; seeds (stratify). EXP: shade

Western burning-bush is related to the well-known Asiatic euonymuses often used as shrubs and hedges in California gardens. It lacks the variegated foliage of some; the leaves are a rather ordinary green, of ovate shape with pointed tips and serrated edges, borne in pairs. Nor are the flowers particularly noteworthy, produced in small clusters, colored brownish maroon, and often hidden among leafy branches. The special feature here is the wonderful late-summer fruits, capsules that split open into three sections to display jet black seeds capped by bright red arils. These seeds are sought by birds and give the shade garden a splash of color when little else is happening there.

Since western burning-bush comes from canyons and stream sides in north coastal forests, it needs summer water to remain healthy. Fitting companions include twinberry honeysuckle (*Lonicera involucrata*), western azalea (*Rhododendron occidentale*), and western spicebush (*Calycanthus occidentalis*). Use it for informal hedges in a shade garden, or in the background.

Euphorbia misera. Shrub Spurge. Spurge family (Euphorbiaceae)

HT: up to 3 feet. LVS: summer and drought deciduous. FLWS: single, tiny cups rimmed by dark purple and white petallike glands; spring and summer. SMR WTR: none. PROP: cuttings; seeds (scarify). EXP: full sun

Shrub spurge is an odd little-known shrublet, typical of Baja California's deserts, and barely entering California along the southernmost San Diego coast. Adapted to rocky, sandy soils, where moisture is scant most of the year, it defoliates readily to reduce its water loss in the scorching sun. Like its relatives (the genus *Euphorbia* is enormous), it is protected internally with a copious milky sap, which is poisonous. The flowers proclaim its relationship with other spurges; the minute male and female flowers (consisting each of a single stamen or pistil) are borne inside tiny green cups, surrounded by curious petallike, nectar-secreting glands, white trimmed with dark purple.

Shrub spurge is not for the average garden. Its often contorted branches, leafless most of the year, add interest in a garden of unusual desert plants, including small cacti, ephedras, dudleyas, echeverias, and perhaps the desert milkweeds. Needing practically no care, it is often naturally decorated with yellow, orange, or pale gray-green lichens that live on the older bark, especially along the foggy coastline.

Fagonia californica. California Pagoda Bush. Caltrops family (Zygophyllaceae)

HT: 3 to 16 inches. LVS: often summer deciduous. FLWS: pink-purple in small flat-topped clusters; spring and winter. SMR WTR: none. PROP: seeds; perhaps cuttings from half-ripe wood. EXP: full sun

The pagoda bush is an unusual miniature, half-woody shrublet, with tiers of horizontal, greenish branches thinly clothed with bright green, sticky leaves divided fanwise into threes. The pretty flowers, shaped like those of the familiar desert creosote bush (*Larrea tridentata*), are pink-purple and appear after late winter or fall rains, adding winter color in a bleak landscape. Pagoda bush seeks out loose scree or shaley slopes in the warm deserts of far southern California, where it finds perfect drainage year-round.

Pagoda bush would be interesting in a desert rock garden growing happily between rocks. With its unique growth habit, it lends special character throughout the year.

Fallugia paradoxa. Apache Plume. Rose family (Rosaceae)

HT: 1 to 5 feet. LVS: winter deciduous. FLWS: showy white single roses in small clusters; late spring. SMR WTR: none. PROP: cuttings; seeds (stratify). EXP: full sun

Apache plume is a close sister to cliff rose (*Cowania mexicana*) and is a similar match for the garden. Living on rocky banks in high deserts, it is a low, rounded shrub with attractive shreddy bark, small leaves slashed into pinnate divisions like feathers, and small bunches of white, single roselike flowers. After flowering, apache plume ripens its fruits into bunches of achenes, each achene adorned by a long, beautiful, feathery pink plume. When seen in late afternoon, these lovely feathers glow.

For best effect plant several apache plumes in the foreground of a desert garden in front of sagebrushes and other larger shrubs, or in little islands by themselves, or tucked next to cacti for contrast. These lovely shrubs must have summer heat, excellent drainage, and well-spaced winter rains for best performance.

Ferocactus acanthodes. Barrel Cactus. Cactus family (Cactaceae)

HT: to about 6 feet with time. LVS: none; green stems are covered with spines. FLWS: circles of bright yellow multirayed stars; mid to late spring. SMR WTR: none. PROP: seeds (stratify). EXP: full sun

Although California also has some smaller barrel cacti, this is *the* barrel cactus par excellence. Slow growing, it begins life as a fat green globe, then gradually stretches into a massive, spine-encrusted cylinder. Spines are recurved, are imprinted with a fascinating crosshatch pattern, and vary from white to rosy red. Individual flowers

Pagoda Bush (*Fagonia californica*)
a. flowering branches   *b*. flower detail   *c*. seed pod detail

are fairly small but borne in circles near the stem top, wreathing the plant in luminous color. Later, fleshy fruits develop if bees have pollinated.

Barrel cactus is one of the instantly recognizable symbols of the desert, and it is fetching for a desert garden where summers are long and hot. It can serve as a bold specimen—especially when fully mature—or blend with smaller cacti and other spiny plants, such as agaves and yuccas. It should have super drainage, and it is most attractive when surrounded by coarse pebbles or various small rocks. It is also an excellent plant for a large, colorful pot.

Barrel cacti should always be started from seeds, even though the process is slow. If you're purchasing one from a succulent or cactus nursery, be sure to ask if the plant has been raised at the nursery—not collected in the wild. All too frequently, cacti are simply gathered from their natural habitats because they require many years to mature. If you can't wait—the process of growing cacti from seeds is fascinating—don't try this plant in your garden!

Forestiera neomexicana. Desert Olive. Olive family (Oleaceae)

HT: 5 to 10 feet. LVS: winter deciduous. FLWS: greenish, unisexual, inconspicuous in small bunches; early spring. SMR WTR: occasional deep watering. PROP: layering; suckers. EXP: full sun

Desert olive is an unusual and uncommon shrub in California. It naturally grows into dense hedges along stony watercourses that are dry most of the year yet maintain a higher water table than in adjoining habitats. Adapted to searingly hot summers, it also tolerates cold winters.

Although the flowers are totally inconsequential, desert olive has several traits to recommend it for hot-climate gardens: attractive, smooth gray bark in winter; thorn-tipped branches, which make it a superior barrier plant; and attractive bright green spoon-shaped to elliptical leaves, which thickly clothe the shrub. Desert olive is most useful planted in groups for lining a walk, as an effective barrier or as an informal hedge. It could also serve to separate parts of a garden.

Fouquieria splendens. Ocotillo. Candlewood family (Fouquieriaceae)

HT: 6 to 25 feet. LVS: present only after rains. FLWS: bright scarlet tubes borne in racemes; spring to early summer. SMR WTR: none. PROP: cuttings; seeds. EXP: full sun

Ocotillo is one of California's most bizarre and spectacular shrubs and serves as a special symbol of the Sonoran desert. Often mistaken for a cactus, it belongs to its own special family. From its trunklike base, several exceedingly long, wandlike branches carry two kinds of leaves in season—primary leaves on the canes, and secondary leaves in spine axils. The primary leaves, produced in abundance after spring or winter rains, are stalked, with the blade oval and light green; when shed, the stalk remains

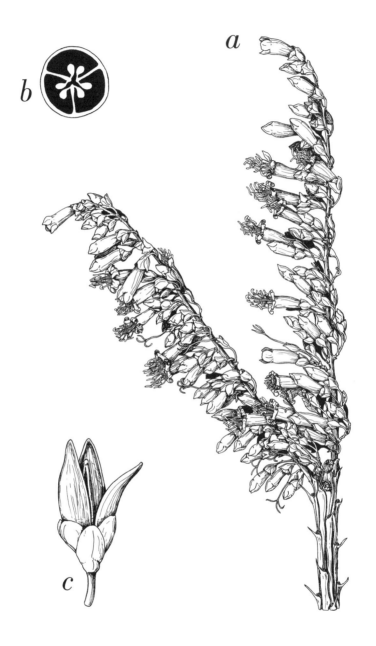

Ocotillo (*Fouquieria splendens*)
a. flowering branches   *b.* cross section, ovary   *c.* seed pod detail

behind as a stout spine to protect the cane. Even when leafless ocotillo is able to make food, through the strips of green bark carrying chlorophyllous cells.

From spring through early summer the stems are crowned by a succession of racemes of spectacular flowers. Flowers are long, satiny red tubes tipped by recurved petals and protruding red stamens, carrying golden pollen. These flowers are perfectly designed to attract hummingbirds from nearby oases.

Ocotillo demands the hottest, sunniest garden setting in California foothills, and it is perhaps truly at home only in the desert itself. It resents poor drainage, excessive moisture near the crown, and leaden skies. Give it an honored place as a specimen, perhaps standing all by itself; or for spectacular color contrasts grow it with palo verde (*Cercidium floridum*), whose golden flowers add an explosion of color in spring. Other fitting companions are the smaller cacti, arrayed close to the base of the trunks.

Fraxinus dipetala. Flowering Ash. Olive family (Oleaceae)

HT: 6 to 25 feet. LVS: winter deciduous. FLWS: white, in racemes; mid-spring. SMR WTR: some deep watering. PROP: cuttings; seeds. EXP: sun to light shade

Flowering ash, a large shrub or multitrunked tree, is our only native ash with showy flowers—white petals grace the floral racemes in April and May. Flowering ash follows ravines and edges of watercourses in the hot interior foothill country, where it may lose leaves early during heavy droughts. Leaves are pinnately divided in the manner of other ashes but generally with only three to five broad, obovate leaflets. The flowers are followed by single-winged fruits called samaras, which lend grace in late spring and summer.

Flowering ash is an excellent garden candidate where you need a large shrub that grows quickly and appreciates some summer water. Its rounded, light green crown makes it an excellent choice with other stream followers or by itself.

Fremontodendron spp. Fremontia or Flannel Bush. Cacao family (Sterculiaceae)

HT: 6 to 25 feet. LVS: evergreen. FLWS: large yellow-orange saucers or open bells; spring. SMR WTR: none. PROP: cuttings; seeds (stratify). EXP: full sun

Fremontias are one of the truly magnificent flowering shrubs of California. Although the number of species is in dispute, there are several varieties and at least two major species: *F. californica*, widely distributed in chaparral or on forest borders throughout central and southern California, has two-inch broad, shallow, saucerlike flowers; *F. mexicana* occurs only in the extreme south and has three-inch open, bell-shaped flowers. An additional rare fremontia is often named separately: *F. decumbens*, from the central Sierra foothills, has widely spreading stems and smaller, shallow, pink-orange flowers. For the gardener these species distinctions are often meaningless, since many nurseries offer superior, named cultivars of hybrid origin. Among these

'California Glory' is particularly outstanding, with large flowers produced in great profusion and rapid growth (see Appendix D for cultivar details).

Fremontias are all large shrubs that can be pruned to develop single trunks; some old specimens have become trees in the wild. The slippery bark makes the removal of branches a hassle; if you prune, be sure to have sharp shears so that cuts are clean. Leaves are more or less round in outline, with several palmate lobes varying from shallow to deep. Leaves are dark green above, pale beneath. The undersides (and the large capsular fruits) are covered with bristly hairs that may cause skin rashes—they're capable of penetrating the skin on contact—so be sure to wear gloves to avoid direct contact.

Fremontias are notoriously difficult to propagate, but stratification of two months or more should improve seed germination. Once the seedlings have vigorous roots they should be moved into the garden as swiftly as possible, in order to establish deep roots before the summer drought. It's better not to water fremontias during summer as they're prone to fungal root rot. The symptoms of this rot may manifest themselves suddenly as branches start to die one by one. Fremontias thrive on lots of heat in summer and full sun.

Because fremontias put on such a spectacular floral show through the spring months—April through June—they deserve an honored place in the garden. They are superb planted next to shrubs with complementary flower colors, such as the blues and purples of ceanothuses, the yellows of bush poppies, or the whites of Matilija poppies. They can be espaliered against a southern wall, grown as a large specimen with trunk, or, in the case of *F. decumbens*, used as a woody ground cover in a rock garden. They also are excellent as a backdrop for a dry mixed border.

Galvezia speciosa. Island Snapdragon. Figwort family (Scrophulariaceae)

HT: to 3 feet. LVS: evergreen. FLWS: dense racemes of red snapdragons; through spring. SMR WTR: little or none. PROP: semihardwood cuttings. EXP: full sun to light shade (inland)

Island snapdragon is a small shrub with wide, open branching, the branches with whorls of three elliptical to ovate, leathery leaves. Green all year, the bush is highlighted by the succession of tight clusters of showy red, snapdragonlike flowers, and is favored by hummingbirds.

Since island snapdragon finds its home on coastal bluffs of the Channel Islands, it is adapted to frost-free winters and requires excellent drainage. In hot inland areas, light shade will help protect it from excessively hot air and sun. Because of its attractive flowers, island snapdragon is excellent in the middle part of a mixed border, in front of tall chaparral shrubs, or even as a small specimen shrub.

Garrya spp. Silk-tassel Bush or Garrya. Garrya family (Garryaceae)

HT: up to 25 feet. LVS: evergreen. FLWS: male in long dangling catkins; female in shorter catkins; midwinter to early spring. SMR WTR: occasional deep watering. PROP: cuttings (use bottom heat). EXP: full sun to light shade

Our native garryas share many characteristics: they're tough-limbed shrubs or small trees with attractive brown bark, have thick, leathery, broadly elliptical leaves, and bear male and female flowers in dangling catkins on separate plants. Flowers sometimes appear by midwinter or early spring when little else is happening in the garden. Male shrubs are grown most often, since their catkins are longer and more decorative than the female's, although the latter ripen into grapelike, red-purple berries later. Propagation is by cuttings in order to assure the sex of the plants; seeds will yield both male and female plants.

California's garryas are rugged, drought-tolerant plants whose habitats range from the margins of coastal forests (where they grow cheek by jowl with closed-cone pines) to the high deserts, most often in company with other rock-inhabiting chaparral shrubs. Consequently, their demands in gardens are minimal, and growth rate is often rapid. Because of their dense branches garryas can be pruned into handsome hedges or screens, but under such circumstances they would lose much of the appeal afforded by more open branches in displaying to best advantage the soft, fuzzy, whitish green male catkins. Garryas can also be used as specimen plants, for foundation plantings, and for their foliage contrast with such fine-textured foliage plants as ironwood (*Lyonothamnus*), artemisias, and chamise (*Adenostoma fasciculatum*). Here are five garryas for consideration:

G. buxifolia. Boxleaf silk-tassel. A smaller shrub than the often-planted coast silk-tassel, tolerant of heavy winter rains and hot summers. Handsome, dark green leaves like large boxwoods with edges curled under.

G. congdoni. Chaparral silk-tassel. A moderate-sized shrub with particularly thick, leathery leaves, dark green above and pale beneath, the surfaces often wavy. Tolerates plenty of summer heat.

G. elliptica. Coast silk-tassel. This is the species most widely planted; it has handsome, dark green, wavy leaves, and especially long catkins, and grows the tallest of all. Coastal conditions are best. Tolerates sandy soils. Named cultivars with especially decorative, extra-long tassels include 'James Roof,' a very prolific bloomer.

G. flavescens. Desert silk-tassel. Tall shrub, to twelve feet, with yellowish green leaves, covered with dense hairs underneath. The typical form is from the high

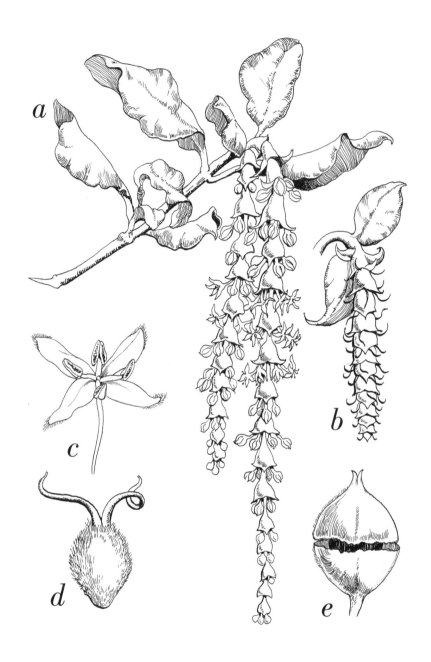

Silk-tassel Bush (*Garrya elliptica*)
a. male-flowering branch   *b.* female flower catkin detail   *c.* male flower detail
d. female flower detail   *e.* fruit detail

eastern Mojave and is particularly showy in flower, in mid to late spring. Good companion to Mexican manzanita, *Arctostaphylos pungens.*

G. fremontii. Fremont silk-tassel. This is a smaller shrub for summer-hot areas; leaves are flat, yellow-green, and manzanitalike. The leaves look closely similar to those of green-leaf manzanita and may achieve the same effect in the garden.

Gaultheria shallon. Salal. Heather family (Ericaceae)

HT: 1½ to 6 feet. LVS: evergreen. FLWS: racemes of white or pale pink urns; mid to late spring. SMR WTR: at least some deep watering. PROP: divisions; layering. EXP: shade

Salal is an uncommonly handsome, evergreen shrub of the heather family. It favors ravines and hills in wet, coastal forests, where it often grows as a dense, almost impenetrable hedge along the forest edge. Plants grow from creeping roots, which gradually colonize and appropriate entire areas with their intricate, zigzaggy stems. The large, ovate, dark green, leathery leaves are beautifully veined with a fine interconnecting network. The foliage keeps well when picked, and it is often incorporated into Christmas greens. Racemes of nodding, urnlike flowers appear over the course of several weeks in spring. Details include rose-pink sepals and white to pale pink petals. In fall, flowers are replaced by fat, near-black berries of good flavor. Thus, salal is a fine shrub three ways: for foliage, flowers, and fruits.

Because of its preference for areas of high rainfall and foggy summers, salal is a plant for coastal gardens and requires at least some supplemental summer water. Like many other members of its family, salal is slow to establish itself in a new home (roots need the right mycorrhizal fungi for healthy growth) and should have acidic soils. A thick layer of pine, fir, redwood, or other conifer needles improves the soil immeasurably for this and other acid-loving plants. Once settled in, salal increases readily by wandering roots, so room should be made to accommodate it.

Use salal as a superior hedge for a shaded situation, or in combination with other shrubs of similar requirements: western azalea (*Rhododendron occidentale*), thimbleberry (*Rubus parviflorus*), and huckleberry (*Vaccinium* spp.). Salal is also an ideal choice for a coarse woody ground cover in a shaded spot and can be pruned to stay low. And, of course, salal is an integral component of a natural redwood forest in company with many of the perennials found there: redwood sorrel (*Oxalis oregana*), vancouverias, redwood violet (*Viola sempervirens*), and wild ginger (*Asarum caudatum*).

Grindelia spp. Gumweed. Sunflower family (Asteraceae)

HT: 2 to 4 feet. LVS: evergreen. FLWS: large bright yellow daisies; summer to early fall. SMR WTR: little or none. PROP: cuttings (take half-ripened wood); seeds. EXP: full sun

Gumweeds do not appeal by name, nor do their habitats—road sides, rocky fields, and edges of salt marshes—call up particularly fond associations. Yet these are tough plants with pleasing features: thick, dark green, scented leaves with fluted or serrated edges (often spoon-shaped), and myriad daisy flowers, which are white gummy in bud but open to showy flowers with yellow rays and yellow centers. They flower late in the season when many shrubs are sleeping, awaiting the return of the rains. Gumweeds are often considered herbaceous perennials, but a few are half-woody to fully woody at the base.

Since these are relatively low-growing plants (often with several stems to the same height), they are excellent for the dry mixed border (in the middle zone) or in front of taller chaparral shrubs. They are also without peer for salty soils, or to stabilize sand dunes near the coast. Three species are closely similar: one, *G. humilis*, is a shrub to four or five feet; the other two, *G. maritima* and *G. robusta*, are merely woody at the root crown. A fourth should receive brief mention: *G. stricta venulosa*, a subwoody, creeping ground cover from coastal bluffs, easy of culture and with beautiful leaves and flowers. It is excellent on coastal sand dunes or in a coastal rock garden cascading over rocks.

Gutierrezia spp. Matchstick. Sunflower family (Asteraceae)

HT: 1 to 2 feet. LVS: sometimes summer deciduous. FLWS: tiny yellow daisy flower heads, often borne in masses; summer and early fall. SMR WTR: occasional for best appearance. PROP: seeds (stratify). EXP: full sun

Matchstick is a small genus of miniature shrublets, all closely similar, with densely branched, fine twiglets producing a rounded shape; tiny, linear leaves (shed when it's very dry); and a profusion of minute yellow daisies in summer or fall. By themselves they're unimposing out of flower, and are best used in front of or between somewhat larger shrubs, such as various penstemons, buckwheats, or bush daisies. The greatest pluses are the tidy, trim shape and the bright splashes of color late in the season. Both *Gutierrezia sarothrae* and *G. microcephala* hail from the driest deserts; *G. californica* is from the dry foothills and sandy soils of the Delta. You would do best to match geographical range with that of your garden; foothill gardeners use *G. californica*; desert gardeners, the other two.

Gumweed (*Grindelia camphorum*)
a. flowering branch   *b*. leaf detail   *c*. floret detail

Haplopappus arborescens. Golden Fleece. Sunflower family (Asteraceae)

HT: 2 to 7 feet. LVS: evergreen. FLWS: many small golden heads in terminal flat-topped clusters; fall. SMR WTR: none. PROP: cuttings; seeds. EXP: full sun

Golden fleece is a handsome chaparral shrub from the foothills, where it grows on rocky slopes baked by the harsh summer sun. Although it is not a tall shrub, it may assume the form of a miniature tree: single-trunked specimens make rounded canopies composed of numerous slender, upright branches clothed with narrow, linear, bright green leaves with a resinous fragrance redolent of the chaparral. Just when it seems that golden fleece will never flower, it bursts into color, with many small, rayless heads of golden flowers creating a bright splash because they're massed together.

Golden fleece makes an excellent, low-maintenance shrub; it looks good all year, requires no water, and adds color at a slow time. Use it as a large container plant or in a shrubbery; or, for a novel effect, use a row of the plants as an informal hedge.

Haplopappus ericoides. Mock Heather. Sunflower family (Asteraceae)

HT: 1 to 5 feet. LVS: evergreen. FLWS: small yellow heads in dense panicles; fall. SMR WTR: little or none. PROP: cuttings; seeds. EXP: full sun

Mock heather is well named for its heatherlike appearance out of flower. You find mock heather on sand hills and dunes overlooking the ocean, where fogs cool the long summer days and winds are relentless. Thus it adapts well to coastal gardens, thriving in sandy soils. It is not, however, particularly amenable to hot inland gardens.

Mock heather is a low, mounded shrub with peculiar, comblike clusters of needle leaves; they resemble and have a fragrance reminiscent of pine needles. It is a tidy shrub most of the year, and like its relative golden fleece, waits until late to flower. Individual flower heads are small, with tiny, raggedy ray flowers around the periphery, but they may manage to put on a modest display through sheer numbers. Showier are the fruits, the single-seeded achenes covered with long tawny hairs, borne in great masses before their release to the winds.

Mock heather is perfect to help stabilize sandy beach soils, and when pruned, makes a low compact shrub well suited to the back of a rock garden or to be a very low hedge.

Haplopappus linearifolius. Bush Sunflower. Sunflower family (Asteraceae)

HT: 2 to 5 feet. LVS: evergreen. FLWS: showy golden daisies in profusion; spring. SMR WTR: none. PROP: cuttings; seeds. EXP: full sun or light shade

Bush sunflower has the showiest flowers of the three haplopappuses discussed here. Note that there are other shrubby species; those included here were selected for hav-

a

b

Mock Heather (*Haplopappus ericoides*)
a. flowering branches and leaves   *b*. disc floret detail

Bush Sunflower (*Haplopappus linearifolius*)
flowering branches with leaves

ing the greatest horticultural potential. Bush sunflower is widely distributed through our summer-hot, interior foothills as well as through parts of our deserts. Thus, it represents one of the best-adapted shrubs for a true xeriscape garden design.

Bush sunflower is an open, multibranched shrub, with leaves markedly less dense than in the other haplopappuses. Leaves are long and linear, with a resinous odor. The best feature of this shrub is the spring display of showy yellow daisies with conspicuous ray flowers. Like mock heather it is also showy in its fruiting phase, with puffs of fluffy, pure white pappus hairs, beautiful when backlit in the afternoon sun.

Use bush sunflower in front of taller shrubs of complementary flower colors: ceanothuses with blue flowers for a gold and blue theme, or bush poppies (*Dendromecon*) and fremontias (*Fremontodendron*) for an all-gold theme. They also light up the edges of oak woodlands, where the summer dry conditions needed for oaks fit well with their thrifty use of water.

Four other haplopappuses for garden use are:

H. cuneatus. Wedge-leaf goldenbush. A low, rounded shrublet to a foot tall, with resinous, shiny, short, wedge-shaped evergreen leaves and modest buttons of rayless, golden flower heads. Good rock garden plant, well adapted to hot climates; from high deserts.

H. detonsus. Santa Cruz Island goldenbush. An unusual shrub to two or three feet. It has a few upright wooly branches, tufts of broad, basal, silvery leaves, and scapes carrying several curious heads of rayless yellow flowers, bordered by shinglelike silver, scaly bracts. Pretty shrub for coastal rock gardens. Winter tender.

H. pinifolius. Pine-leaf bush sunflower. Substantial shrub to eight feet or more, with one-and-one-half-inch-long, linear, pinelike leaves (also with piny scent). Leaves are vivid green and last all year. Flower heads are scattered in spring, often more numerous and clustered in fall. Individual heads have yellow rays and disc flowers, followed by tufts of reddish-brown hairs. Excellent for the back of the rock garden, or with coarsely textured chaparral shrubs, or used for its foliage to hide shrubs with summer-deciduous leaves. Tolerant of hot, dry summers.

H. venetus sedoides. Sand dune goldenbush. A low, decumbent subshrub, with fleshy, sticky, green elliptical leaves and modest heads of small yellow, rayed daisy flowers. Ideal for the front of a coastal rock garden or to help bind sandy soils.

Helianthemum scoparium. Rushrose, Sunrose. Rockrose family (Cistaceae)

HT: 1 to 2 feet. LVS: sometimes summer deciduous. FLWS: bright yellow saucers; late spring to early summer. SMR WTR: little or none. PROP: perhaps cuttings; seeds (stratify or use burn treatment). EXP: full sun

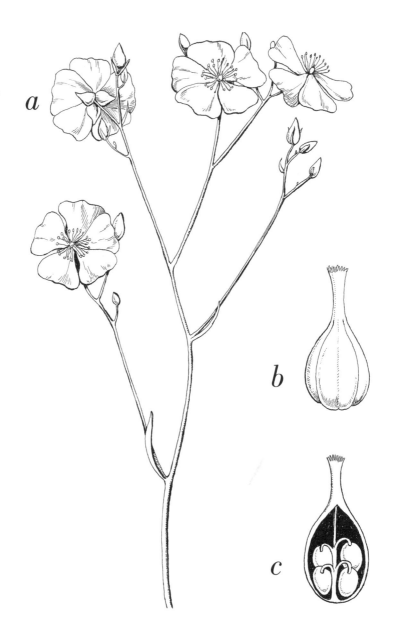

a

b

c

Rushrose (*Helianthemum scoparium*)
a. group of flowers   *b.* ovary detail outside   *c.* ovary detail inside

Rushroses are charming miniatures to the usual garden rockroses, their Old World cousins. Some Mediterranean helianthemums are grown in California, but our own native species is seldom seen. Rushroses are most abundant following fires, when hundreds of shrubs quickly grow on the newly fertilized ashy soils. Otherwise, look for them on the margins of mature chaparral. Out of blossom, rushrose looks like a dense bunch of green twigs; the leaves are rather inconspicuous and may be lost during summer droughts. But in bloom, each bushlet is transformed by the myriad jaunty yellow saucers whose centers are filled with numerous stamens of matching hue.

Rushroses would make a fine adjunct to a rock garden or look well planted with their European relatives the helianthemums and rockroses (genus *Cistus*). Or use them next to other low shrubs, such as monardellas, penstemons, and bush monkeyflowers.

Hemizonia clementina and minthornii. Shrub Tarweeds. Sunflower family (Asteraceae)

HT: 1 to 3 feet. LVS: mostly evergreen. FLWS: bright yellow daisies in open clusters; summer to fall. SMR WTR: none. PROP: cuttings; seeds. EXP: full sun

The shrub tarweeds are unusual for their group; most tarweeds are summer-blooming annuals of dry grasslands and road sides, where they flower and fruit during scorchingly hot, bone-dry times of the year. The unkind name tarweed is misleading; the blossoms on many are among our showiest, prettiest yellow daisies, and the heavy scent—a deterrent to chewing insects and browsing animals—is redolent of droughty conditions, and at least to me is very pleasing if sometimes a bit overpowering. Shrub tarweeds differ in habit, being low, sprawling shrublets that live for several years. Our two species come from milder climates—the Santa Susana Mountains of near-coastal Los Angeles County and the bluffs of San Clemente Island off the southern California coast. The two are closely similar, with bright green, narrow leaves lushly produced along the stems and clusters of smaller leaves in leaf axils. Flowering in late summer or fall, shrub tarweeds brighten an often drab, flowerless scene, where summer water is never needed.

Use shrub tarweeds in the forefront of a garden built on stabilized sands, among rocks, or even to edge a droughty mixed border. The cheerful yellow daisies could accompany the taller wands of golden-flowered goldenrods or contrast with the vivid scarlet trumpets of hummingbird fuchsias.

Heteromeles arbutifolia. Toyon or California Holly. Rose family (Rosaceae)

HT: 7 to 35 feet. LVS: evergreen. FLWS: tiny white single roses in flat-topped clusters; early summer. SMR WTR: little or none. PROP: seeds (stratify). EXP: full sun to light shade

Toyon is one of California's classic shrubs, typical of hot chaparral or deep canyons. It is also one of the most enduring for horticultural purposes: stiff, leathery, deep green hollylike leaves last all year; flat-topped clusters of lacy white flowers bloom in early summer; and spectacular bunches of orange-red berries last late in the year (and hence can be used for Christmas greens in place of true holly). An especially handsome winter floral arrangement consists of toyon leaves and berries with manzanita flowers.

Toyon lives long, and under ideal conditions—little summer water but a water table high enough for penetrating roots to reach—grows into a tree. Some specimens on Santa Cruz Island resemble live oaks in shape, size, and habitat, although such dimensions are unlikely to be attained in the garden in any one person's lifetime; toyon grows at a moderate pace.

Use toyon as a spectacular foundation planting, as a hedge, as a very large specimen, or at the back of an oak woodland. If you're particularly fond of birds, be sure to plant one where you can watch them feast on the berries in fall.

Hibiscus denudatus. Desert Rock Hibiscus. Mallow family (Malvaceae)

HT: 1 to 2 feet. LVS: semideciduous in summer. FLWS: pink-lavender to white mallows with red base; through spring. SMR WTR: none. PROP: seeds (stratify or scarify). EXP: full sun

The gaudy tropical hibiscuses have gained such notoriety that we're seldom aware of less flamboyant species, which are pretty plants on their own merits. California has two decidedly different kinds: *H. californicus*, a bold annual from marshlands of the Delta, and the subshrubby desert rock hibiscus featured here. The latter has attractive, yellowish green ovate leaves on a low, multibranched frame, plus attractive hollyhocklike, open blossoms of palest lavender or white with a central red splotch at the base.

Desert rock hibiscus would be a good choice massed in the middle of a droughty rock garden, interspersed with plants of different form, such as small cacti and fleshy succulents. The latter would serve to draw the eye from the hibiscus during its long summer slumber, when leaves are often shed and branches bare. In form, life cycle, and habitat, the hibiscus also complements desert nettle.

Toyon (*Heteromeles arbutifolia*)
fruiting branches with leaves

Creambush (*Holodiscus discolor*)
flowering clusters with leaves

Holodiscus discolor. Creambush or Ocean Spray. Rose family (Rosaceae)

HT: 5 to 20 feet. LVS: winter deciduous. FLWS: tiny cream-colored single roses in dense sprays; summer. SMR WTR: occasional deep waterings. PROP: layering; suckers; seeds. EXP: light to moderate shade

Creambush deserves to be better known. It is a large, vigorous, fast-growing shrub with great arching branches, which often bow gracefully over the surrounding terrain. Dramatic natural settings include perches on wooded promontories within sight and sound of surf or, inland, along openings of mixed evergreen woods. The twigs, winter bare, continue to carry last year's flowers, which have turned to deep brown. Some may find this untidy, but others will appreciate it as added design in a bare winter landscape. The leaves are small and oval, with irregular lobes and teeth and velvety soft texture, and they are delightfully scented with the aroma of fruit when crushed. Great panicles of creamy flowers appear in early summer in the manner of spiraeas. Flowers are delightful to watch change; they're pink in bud, opening creamy white, then finally fade brown.

Creambush thrives with some protection from the direct hot summer sun and will grow much faster with some summer water. Pruning will help to shape it to the needs of garden and gardener, for otherwise it may become lank and scraggly. It should be planted so that its flowering shows to best advantage, such as behind a pond, along a stream (but not next to it), or as the backdrop for an open woodland glade.

> *H. boursieri.* Mountain creambush. This species needs mention as a scaled-down version of its common cousin. In most particulars it closely resembles *H. discolor*, but it grows to only a few feet tall, has a much more compact habit, and favors fully exposed situations among rocks. It is excellent in the mountain garden, particularly toward the back of a rock garden. One final species— *H. microphyllus*—is closely similar to the last but favors hot, rocky canyons high in desert mountains; it would be the best choice for use as a small, drought-tolerant shrub in summer-hot gardens.

Horsfordia alata. Desert Mallow. Mallow family (Malvaceae)

HT: 3 to 10 feet. LVS: partly summer deciduous. FLWS: pink mallows in small clusters; spring and late fall. SMR WTR: none. PROP: perhaps cuttings; seeds (stratify or scarify) EXP: full sun

Horsfordias are unusual desert mallows, with long, straight, wandlike stems covered with densely felted hairs and sparse, ovate leaves with a heart-shaped base. The attractive, hollyhocklike flowers are borne in small clusters along the upper stems, pink when fully opened, then fading pale blue. In areas with mild winters blooming occurs twice—in midspring as days turn warm and again in late fall, when temperatures are mild and there have been one or two rains. California's other horsfordia, *H. newberryi*, is a similar shrub but less garden worthy; although its striking yellowish, felted hairs give it an unusual color all year, the yellow flowers are small and disappointing.

Use desert mallow in the back or middle of a planting of shorter or squatter desert shrubs—matchstick, buckwheats, trixis, desert asters—for contrast in shape and form. The interesting stem pattern could also contrast with other stark shapes of desert plants, including cacti, elephant tree, and burro bush.

Hymenoclea salsola. Cheesebush. Sunflower family (Asteraceae)

HT: 1½ to 4 feet. LVS: summer deciduous. FLWS: male, in tiny yellow-green heads in short spikes; female, with conspicuous white petallike membranes, at base of male; through spring. SMR WTR: none. PROP: perhaps cuttings; seeds (stratify). EXP: full sun

Cheesebush is named for its rather odd odor—leaves and twigs are suggestive of strong cheese or old socks! Although this feature is unlikely to endear it to anyone, the shrub itself is an interesting and striking feature of a desert landscape in midspring, when the peculiar flower heads cover the ends of twigs. The male flower heads, small and greenish, are unlikely to elicit attention, but the female heads, borne just beneath the males, are showy because of their multiple petallike, papery white bracts. Female flowers could also be used for dried bouquets like strawflowers.

Out of flower, cheesebush is "just" another low, desert shrub adapted to dry, sandy soils. Its tiny, linear leaves may be jettisoned in summer, but its branchlets remain green through the year. Cheesebush is neither eye-catching nor unattractive during this time and so can blend in seamlessly with shrubs of more character. Pinch back its new growth to keep a compact shape.

Hyptis emoryi. Desert Lavender. Mint family (Lamiaceae)

HT: 3 to 10 feet. LVS: partly summer deciduous. FLWS: small, pale purple two-lipped flowers in open panicles; through spring. SMR WTR: none. PROP: cuttings; perhaps seeds. EXP: full sun

The tall, wandlike branches of desert lavender lend it a graceful aspect that is lacking in most desert shrubs. Favoring desert washes in gravelly or sandy soils, it grows vigorously. Its pretty pairs of fragrant, broadly ovate leaves have scalloped margins. At the ends of the branches in airy panicles are white wooly flowers (at close inspection, the wooly sepals surround petals of delicate pale lavender), with the heavenly scent of French or Spanish lavender. Although desert lavender is but distantly related to the lavenders of the Old World, they both belong to the mint family. *Hyptis* takes plenty of heat and summer drought, but leaves may be lost then; occasional water in the garden should improve overall appearance during that critical time.

Desert lavender is an unusual shrub deserving garden attention in hot climates, especially as a specimen for seasonal show, along the edge of a dry streambed leading to an oasis setting, or toward the back of an herb garden for its lovely fragrance.

Isomeris arborea. Bladderpod. Caper family (Capparaceae)

HT: 2 to 7 feet. LVS: evergreen. FLWS: yellow and mustardlike, in dense racemes; most of the year. SMR WTR: little or none. PROP: seeds; cuttings. EXP: full sun

Bladderpod is a small desert shrub of sandy soils that tolerates alkaline conditions. Tender in cold climates, and susceptible to poor drainage or excessive winter moisture, bladderpod grows rapidly and flowers profusely under heat and sun. Leaves are divided into three elliptical, bluish green leaflets, which are folded in the hottest weather. Colorful racemes of yellow flowers may appear at any time of the year, but peak flowering generally is in mid-spring. Flowers are followed by large, bladderlike green seed pods, sure to attract attention. These inflated balloons hold pea-size seeds.

Bladderpod is easy to grow from seed, although tender new growth is a special inducement to snails and slugs. It also grows to maturity within a short time. It is equally at home near the coast—in the absence of excessive moisture—or in deserts. Shrubs can serve as a seasonal focal point in a desert setting or be a part of a low shrub border with other seasonally colorful shrubs, such as apricot mallow (*Sphaeralcea ambigua*), desert aster (*Machaeranthera tortifolia*), and desert alyssum (*Lepidium fremontii*).

Jamesia americana. Jamesia. Mock orange family (Philadelphaceae)

HT: 1 to 3 feet. LVS: winter deciduous. FLWS: rose-pink in racemes, like currant flowers; summer. SMR WTR: occasional deep watering. PROP: cuttings. EXP: light shade

Jamesia is a not-so-distant relative of currants and gooseberries but recognizable by its own special attributes: semidecumbent stems, leaves in pairs with coarse, irregular teeth, and dry, capsular fruits. Despite these differentiations, jamesia's shreddy, brown bark and attractive tight racemes of rosy pink flowers are quite reminiscent of currants. Jamesia inhabits some of the most picturesque territory in the state: open, subalpine forests of lodgepole pines, mountain hemlocks, and red firs, where its stems lie plastered against granite boulders or sprout between splits in rocks.

Such beautiful surroundings as jamesia typically inhabits suggest evocative use in the garden: train by appropriate pruning to flow over a granite boulder in the rock garden; fringe a small, rock-bound pond with it; or try to create a low hedge. Since jamesia is seldom grown, experimentation is in order. It can be said safely to be immune to winter cold, but it may possibly languish in climates that are both cold *and* wet.

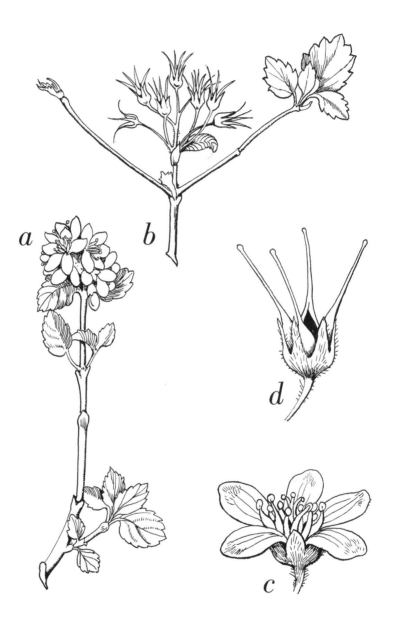

Jamesia (*Jamesia americana*)
a. flowering branch   *b.* fruiting branch   *c.* flower detail   *d.* fruit detail

Juglans californica. California Walnut. Walnut family (Juglandaceae)

HT: 10 to 30 feet. LVS: winter deciduous. FLWS: greenish male flowers in dangling chains, single female flowers with reddish stigmas; early spring. SMR WTR: occasional deep watering. PROP: cuttings (use bottom heat); suckers; fruits (stratify). EXP: light shade

Few are acquainted with California's second native walnut, for the northern species (*J. hindsii*) is the black walnut used commercially as rootstock for grafting on the English walnut. California walnut is a multitrunked small tree, trainable as a large shrub, from canyon bottoms of oak woodlands along the southern California coast. There it accompanies sycamore (*Platanus racemosa*), white alder (*Alnus rhombifolia*), California bay laurel, and coast live oak (*Quercus agrifolia*) where the water table stands high, even though streams may stop running by end of spring.

California walnut has seasonal interest: chunky branches with fissured grayish bark in winter; dangling chains of pollen-bearing male flowers in early spring; and pretty leaf canopies of pinnately compound leaves composed of several elongated lance-shaped, serrated, fragrant leaflets in summer. Fall brings a crop of "nuts," actually fleshy, one-seeded fruits that may create a mess. Don't plant this walnut where fruits might stain concrete paths or sidewalks. The edible nuts are hard-shelled, and the nutmeats are difficult to extract. Better to leave them alone.

California walnut would be a perfect accompaniment to a naturally wooded area along a stream or a small pond where its interesting leaves could contrast with shrubs and trees of other patterns: oaks, bay laurel, alder, maples, and buckeye. Underplantings could include gooseberries, vine honeysuckle, snowberry, and canyon sunflower (*Venegasia carpesioides*).

Juniperus californica. California Juniper. Cypress family (Cupressaceae)

HT: 4 to 20 feet. LVS: evergreen scales. FLWS: minute yellow male pollen cones and fleshy red-brown seed cones. SMR WTR: none. PROP: seeds (stratify); cuttings (take newer growth). EXP: full sun

California juniper may justifiably be considered a large, multitrunked shrub rather than a true tree, unlike its magnificent high Sierran brother *J. occidentalis*. It favors the hot foothills of the interior or climbs into the high mountains in the Mojave desert, where it accompanies pinyon pine (*Pinus monophylla*). In the foothills, frequent companions include California buckeye (*Aesculus californica*), digger pine (*Pinus sabiniana*), and blue and interior live oaks (*Quercus douglasii* and *wislezenii*). California juniper is a tough, miniature tree with lots of visual character: beautiful long strips of brownish bark on old trunks and muted green, scale-covered branches, often decorated with the berrylike, red-brown seed cones. These actually change color throughout their development, starting a green to pale bluish (from a powder that later rubs off) and becoming red-brown. If you like this feature be sure to get a female tree, as there is a strong tendency in the junipers for male and female cones to occur on separate plants. (Take cuttings from a known tree.) California juniper can be shaped into a striking specimen as a focal point in the hot inland or desert garden, where it should be planted alone. Or try pruning and shaping a young shrub into a hedge or a bonsai subject. If you're propagating it from cuttings, be sure to use the newer growth or the juvenile sprouts that arise occasionally near the base (these sprouts bear needles rather than scales); older branches lose their ability to initiate new growth.

Juniperus communis saxatilis. Mat Juniper. Cypress family (Cupressaceae)

HT: 1 to 2 feet. LVS: evergreen needles. FLWS: none; has blue berrylike cones. SMR WTR: little or none. PROP: cuttings. EXP: full sun to light shade

Mat juniper is one of the most attractive of the low-growing junipers and offers a refreshing alternative to tam and pfitzer junipers, which have become horticultural cliches. It seldom exceeds a foot in height. The trailing stems—with their short side branches—are thickly clothed with needles, dark green above and silvery beneath. Both sides are visible from different angles, lending a pleasing color contrast and composition. Branches root as they grow, so that mat juniper provides excellent stabilization for steep banks and sand dunes. Main branches are easily trained in different directions to fit a site. Although there are no flowers, blue "berries" (actually fleshy cones) are powdered with a whitish bloom, adding seasonal interest.

Mat juniper is a tough, drought resistant, woody ground cover, but with a slow growth rate. Imaginative uses find it dripping over rocky banks in the forefront of a rock garden, or spilling over brick walls. The main necessities for vigorous growth are excellent drainage and plenty of winter light. The best forms of this juniper for the lowland garden come from the rugged Siskiyou Mountains along the California-Oregon border, where plants grow at less than three thousand feet elevation.

Kalmia polifolia microphylla. Mountain or Bog Laurel. Heather family (Ericaceae)

HT: 3 to 5 inches. LVS: evergreen. FLWS: short racemes of rose-purple saucers; midsummer. SMR WTR: moist soil. PROP: cuttings; layering; seeds (stratify). EXP: full sun to light shade

California's mountain laurel is closely related to the famed mountain laurel of the eastern United States, but instead of being a large shrub it grows as a creeping ground cover in highland meadows. Up there, you hear the sound of rushing brooks, breathe pure air, and see the clean colors of alpine flowers; mountain laurel is companion to red heather (*Phyllodoce* spp.), white heather (*Cassiope mertensiana*), and dwarf willows, and it blooms just after snowbanks release their waters to create soggy soils. The leaves of California's mountain laurel are hardly laurellike; instead they curl under, making tidy spots of pale green along the earthbound branches. The flowers are miniature replicas of the eastern laurel, with a wonderful, wheellike design in bud, including five tiny, puckered pockets around the periphery that mark nectar glands on the inside. As the saucer-shaped flowers open, two stamens are held under tension in each pocket, each stamen awaiting its turn to spring loose as a visiting pollinator makes contact.

All this beauty is impossible to recreate in the typical lowland garden; short growing seasons and severe winter cold have shaped these wonderful plants over the eons, and while they may survive in the lowlands for a time, they'll slowly give up the struggle without ever flourishing. However, like their companions white and red heather they can be coaxed along in the mountain garden, where a boggy spot or the edge of a pond would create a perfect setting, perhaps rimmed by granite rocks over which the plants may spill. To complete the grouping, include one of the alpine willows (*Salix nivalis* or *S. antiplasta anglorum*).

Larrea divaricata. Creosote Bush. Caltrops family (Zygophyllaceae)

HT: 3 to 15 feet. LVS: evergreen. FLWS: bright yellow and solitary but sometimes produced in abundance, pinwheellike; spring. SMR WTR: none. PROP: perhaps cuttings; seeds (stratify). EXP: full sun

Creosote bush is the essence of California's warm and hot deserts. Covering hundreds of square miles, the shrubs look as though they've been carefully planted, since each shrub's roots fan out the same distance to absorb any all-important surface water during infrequent rains. Despite these shallow roots, creosote bush also has roots that grow deep in well-aerated soils to seek permanent water, far beneath the bone-dry surface. Creosote bush looks carefully tended in the way its branches are tidy and open-trending, and it keeps its good looks through the summer with its varnished, green, aromatic leaves. (The name is derived from the creosotelike odor associated with these leaves.) The suite of characters with which creosote bush has adapted to its environment is highly successful, for ancient rings of these shrubs have been estimated to have an age of eight thousand years! Creosote bush also adds the bonus of seasonal interest: bright yellow, pinwheellike flowers sprinkled liberally over the bush through spring, and sporadically at other times of the year, and tiny, shaggy, white ball-shaped seed pods. Use it as the backdrop in a desert or droughty garden, to set off smaller shrubs or those with grayish, whitish, or bluish green leaves and twigs. A natural combination might include a sprinkling of burro bushes set just in front, much as they might be interspersed in nature, and with both set off by finely textured brown gravel.

Lavatera assurgentiflora. Malva Rosa or Mission Mallow. Mallow family (Malvaceae)

HT: 3 to 14 feet. LVS: evergreen. FLWS: showy hollyhocklike rose-purple flowers; spring to fall. SMR WTR: occasional deep watering. PROP: seeds. EXP: full sun

This tall, striking shrub carries innumerable branches in many directions, creating an open architecture. The bark is green and leaves maplelike and evergreen, but the life span of any individual leaf is short. Fast growing, malva rosa is ready to flower its first year and bears a profusion of handsome rose-purple mallow flowers carried singly. Each is striped with deep purple lines and an explosion of cream-colored stamens in the center. Flowers often appear all year in mild coastal climates.

Because of its unique growth habit, malva rosa may not appeal to everyone; some will find it coarse and leggy, but its beautiful flowers make it worthy of gardens with ample room. It can be placed in back of shorter, compact plantings for best effect, or trained against a warm wall by itself. Plants grow readily from seed but are prone to damping-off and to the ravages of slugs and snails. Malva rosa is not likely to tolerate long periods of freezing temperatures and is best suited to coastal gardens.

Ledum glandulosum. Labrador Tea. Heather family (Ericaceae)

HT: 2 to 10 feet. LVS: evergreen. FLWS: open clusters of small, white azalealike flowers; late spring and summer. SMR WTR: moist at all times. PROP: cuttings; layering. EXP: light shade

Labrador tea is closely related to azaleas, and out of flower is indeed a close fit: the leathery, elliptical leaves are handsome, shiny, dark green, and covered with a soft white down beneath, and have their margins turned under. Leaves carry the deep, sweet fragrance of lemon balm. Although they were purportedly used for an herbal tea by early explorers, they're known to contain a poisonous alkaloid like the toxic principle found in rhododendrons. Therefore, Labrador tea is not recommended for gardens where children are present.

Ledum bears a plethora of small, white flowers that rather resemble tiny, wide-open azalea blossoms. The rest of the year the shrub creates a fine backdrop for other plants. Since it naturally inhabits shady bogs and stream sides, it requires moist soil and light shade for healthy growth. Like its ericaceous relatives, it thrives where soils are decidedly acid. In the garden, Labrador tea creates a lovely border around ponds or behind smaller herbaceous plants in a wet meadow. It can also serve as a focal point in a forest glade.

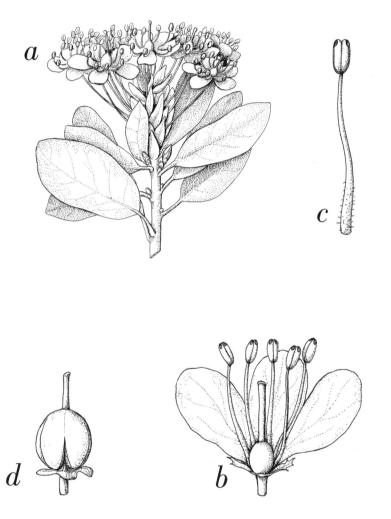

Labrador Tea (*Ledum glandulosum*)
a. flowering branch   *b.* flower detail   *c.* stamen detail   *d.* fruit detail

Lepechinia spp. Pitcher Sage. Mint family (Lamiaceae)

HT: 1½ to 5 feet. LVS: evergreen. FLWS: large glove-shaped flowers with two-lipped petals in racemes; spring. SMR WTR: none. PROP: cuttings; seeds. EXP: full sun

Pitcher sage is a distinctive mint relative found in openings in chaparral, where competition with taller shrubs is minimized. It is a lank, horizontally trending shrub bearing triangular gray-green leaves with soft, quilted surfaces, and has a strong, penetrating odor all its own. Some people find the smell repellent, while others equate it with the aroma of strong sage. Horizontally held racemes of flowers appear in spring, followed by curious fruits. The sepals, prettily veined in a netted pattern, enlarge around the fruits and become inflated, ultimately looking like pitchers hung upside down.

Pitcher sage is unlikely to become a prized ornamental; its shape is too rangy. But its virtues include easy culture, rapid growth in nutrient-poor, rocky soils, and flowers that are both attractive and unusual. You might include it in a native herb garden with salvias and wooly blue curls. Here are two closely similar species:

L. calycina. Common pitcher sage. A widespread species with white to pale purple flowers.

L. fragrans. Island pitcher sage. From Santa Cruz Island comes a prettier but hard-to-find species, with lovely purple flowers and upright, more compact habit. Expect it to be winter tender.

Lepidium fremontii. Desert Alyssum. Mustard family (Brassicaceae)

HT: 1 to 3 feet. LVS: summer deciduous. FLWS: borne in open panicles, white and alyssumlike; spring. SMR WTR: none. PROP: cuttings (take with some wood); seeds. EXP: full sun

Desert alyssum is a half-hearted, "suffrutescent" shrub, with woody base. Half-woody branches are produced in profusion from this base, arching outwards, and are covered with nearly linear leaves, which are shed in hot summers. Expect desert alyssum to look like many other desert shrubs in summer: masses of greenish stems without much character. In spring, however, the shrub is smothered in fragrant white blossoms, beloved by bees and shaped like those of the familiar sweet alyssum (*Lobularia maritima*).

Because of its summer dormancy, desert alyssum can be tucked into a desert garden, between other shrubs that retain their foliage, or grown as a specimen to be moved out of sight during its dormancy. Its profusion of bloom complements other small desert shrubs: desert senna (*Cassia armata*) with golden flowers, desert aster (*Machaeranthera tortifolia*) with blue-purple flowers, and apricot mallow (*Sphaeral-*

cea ambigua) with apricot-orange flowers. It is likely to be short-lived under garden conditions.

Lepidospartum squamatum. Scale Broom. Sunflower family (Asteraceae)

HT: 3 to 6 feet. LVS: summer deciduous. FLWS: heads of tubular, yellow discs arranged in panicles; late summer and into fall. SMR WTR: occasional deep watering. PROP: seeds. EXP: full sun

Scale broom belongs to that fraternity of shrubs that look so similar out of flower: long, broomlike branches with green bark. From dry, stony watercourses in summer-hot southern California, it has appeal in late summer when it unexpectedly bursts into colorful bloom. Individually the flower heads are small, but they're borne in large numbers in airy, branched panicles and are a rich nectar source; count on these to keep the bees going when few other flowers are available.

The common name refers to the fact that the broomlike branches show only tiny, scalelike leaves scattered along their length. However, the new spring growth briefly displays broader leaves on white-hairy twigs.

Use scale broom for a low-maintenance, partly open screen, in the background of a desert oasis, or at the back of a rockery. Once the roots are thoroughly established they usually can tap into sufficient water to keep them going, but an occasional deep drink would probably improve performance.

Leptodactylon californicum. Prickly Phlox. Phlox family (Polemoniaceae)

HT: 1 to 4 feet. LVS: evergreen. FLWS: in crowded terminal clusters; rose-purple, pink, or white, and phloxlike; through spring. SMR WTR: none. PROP: perhaps cuttings; seeds (stratify). EXP: full sun

Prickly phlox is a low, semidecumbent shrub that hunkers between hot sandstone rocks in southern California, along the edges of chaparral. It is smothered in spring with large, showy, phloxlike flowers in shades of brilliant rose-purple to white. Underneath this beautiful exterior it is formidable, owing to close clusters of wickedly spiny leaves splayed into fingerlike segments.

Prickly phlox is so showy and prolific of blossom that it deserves an honored place in any summer-hot, droughty garden. Use it as a container plant (it needs excellent drainage), in front of taller shrubberies, or at the back of a rock garden. Prickly phlox and yellow to orangy-brown sandstone create an unusual and lovely color combination. Look for problems where winters are cold and wet, and take special care to use only sterile soil for seedlings to prevent damping-off. Good companion plants include blue witch (*Solanum xantii*), bush poppy (*Dendromecon rigida*), bush monkeyflowers (*Diplacus* spp.), and sages (*Salvia* spp.).

Leucothoe davisae. Sierra Laurel. Heather family (Ericaceae)

HT: 2 to 5 feet. LVS: evergreen. FLWS: upright racemes of nodding white urns; through summer. SMR WTR: moisture all summer. PROP: cuttings; layering. EXP: shade

Sierra laurel is a fine but little recognized member of the heather family. It grows as a low, sprawling shrub with shiny, leathery, laurellike leaves that are deep green—and evergreen— sometimes with finely serrated edges. For these qualities alone it deserves a special place in the garden. Add to this the masses of pure white, urn-shaped blossoms in summer, and you have a real winner.

Like others in the heather family, including its relative Labrador tea (*Ledum glandulosum*), Sierra laurel appreciates cool, moist, acid soils. Although it grows in parts of our northern mountains where summer temperatures soar, the combination of shade from coniferous trees and constant moisture assure healthy growth. In the garden, Sierra laurel is splendid behind a pond, along a stream, in a shaded corner of a summer-wet meadow, or in a container. It grows at moderate speed and adapts reasonably well to low-elevation gardens.

Lithocarpus densiflorus var. echinoides. Shrub Tan Oak. Beech family (Fagaceae)

HT: to 10 feet. LVS: evergreen. FLWS: male whitish, in umbrellalike catkins, summer; female inconspicuous. SMR WTR: occasional deep watering. PROP: acorns. EXP: full sun to very light shade

Shrub tan oak is common across the mountains of California's far north, most often growing fully exposed to the searingly hot summer sun and deluged with rain, snow, or both in winter. It is an integral part of that peculiar version of chaparral exclusive to the north, with such companions as shrub bay laurel (*Umbellularia californica*), coffee berry (*Rhamnus californica*), boxleaf silk-tassel bush (*Garrya buxifolia*), and tobacco brush ceanothus (*Ceanothus velutinus*). It grows into a tough, compact, densely branched shrub whose leaves are scarcely toothed (a difference from the tree version), but it produces the same upright clusters of cream-colored male catkins and the same acorn cups adorned with fringed scales holding large acorns.

Shrub tan oak deserves a place in every summer-hot garden for its good looks: handsome, broadly elliptical, deep green leaves with a distinctive, "impressed" featherlike vein pattern. It grows at a moderate rate, but it can be pruned into a dense hedge or barrier plant or can serve as a permanent backdrop to seasonal lower-growing plants. It would also be excellent as a neutral background to a mixed border. The acorns germinate readily if they're planted soon after falling to the ground; otherwise they slowly shrivel. Plant acorns horizontally, with the upper third exposed.

Lonicera hispidula and ciliosa. Vine Honeysuckles. Honeysuckle family (Caprifoliaceae)

HT: vines to 30 or 40 feet. LVS: winter deciduous. FLWS: two-lipped white, pink, or scarlet tubes; late spring to summer. SMR WTR: occasional deep watering. PROP: layered stems; root divisions. EXP: light shade

Vine honeysuckles are rapidly growing, woody vines whose stems become cablelike in age. Starting life on the ground, they clamber up any support to reach sunlight, where they flower and fruit. Hair-covered leaves are paired, and the pair just behind the flower clusters are joined together around the stem. Flowers are pale pink to white for *L. hispidula*, and not particularly showy; choose *L. ciliosa*, for its scarlet flowers attractive to hummingbirds. Both produce luminous scarlet berries in late summer; the berries have a strikingly bitter aftertaste, but birds seem fond of them.

Vine honeysuckles are among the easiest of native vines to grow, but be warned that they become invasive if allowed to spread. Be sure to provide support so they can climb rather than scramble along the ground. *L. ciliosa* is the better choice where winter rains are substantial; *L. hispidula* is for areas with low rainfall.

Lonicera involucrata. Twinberry Honeysuckle. Honeysuckle family (Caprifoliaceae)

HT: 3 to 10 feet. LVS: winter deciduous. FLWS: yellow tubes flushed with red, borne in pairs; through spring. SMR WTR: several deep waterings. PROP: cuttings; layering; seeds (stratify). EXP: light shade

If you're used to the Japanese honeysuckle, twinberry honeysuckle comes as a real surprise. It's a neatly branched, moderately tall shrub, with shreddy brown bark, broad, ovate leaves, and odorless flowers borne in pairs within pairs of bright red bracts. The flowers themselves are only slightly irregular (not the usual shape for garden honeysuckles) and are tubular with a short, flared row of petals colored yellow or pale orange. These floral tubes are hummingbird favorites in spring. Still, the best feature of this shrub is the pairs of shiny black fruits set inside those red bracts: a fine lure to birds.

Twinberry honeysuckle is easy to grow, maturing rapidly when supplied with deep summer water (in nature it grows by springs, at seeps, and along streams). One problem I've experienced is a disfiguring reddish viral infection of the leaves. Remove all infected parts immediately and burn them; if you catch it in time, next year's growth should return to normal.

Use twinberry honeysuckle behind a pond or along a stream in a woodland garden, and be sure to place it where those beautiful fruits can be seen. Good companions include spicebush (*Calycanthus occidentalis*), western azalea (*Rhododendron occidentale*), and red elderberry (*Sambucus callicarpa*).

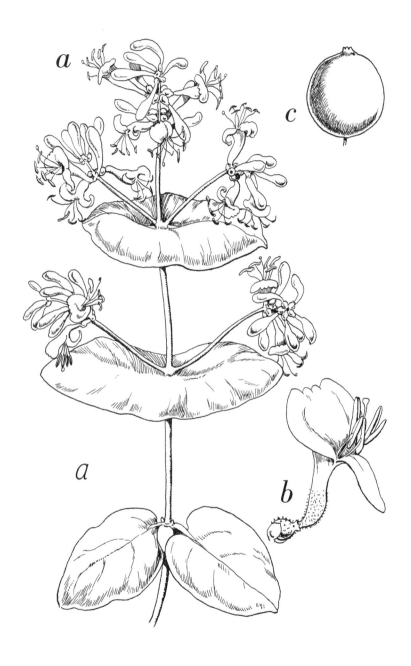

Vine Honeysuckle (*Lonicera hispidula*)
a. flowering branch showing leaves   *b*. flower detail   *c*. fruit detail

Twinberry Honeysuckle (*Lonicera involucrata*)
flowering and fruiting branch

One other shrubby honeysuckle deserves brief mention: *Lonicera conjugialis* (twin or Sierra honeysuckle), from the middle elevations of the Sierra. This low shrub seldom exceeds three feet, favors damp places in partial shade, and has rather ordinary looking, broadly elliptical, paired leaves. The tiny maroon flowers are hardly noticed, but the bright orange berries—joined together most of their length—are pleasing punctuations of color in late summer. Consider this one for the mountain garden.

Lotus scoparius and dendroideus. Deerbroom Lotus. Pea family (Fabaceae)

HT: 1 to 3 feet. LVS: summer deciduous. FLWS: umbels of yellow pea flowers; spring and summer. SMR WTR: little or none. PROP: cuttings; seeds (soak). EXP: full sun

Deerbroom lotus is a lax, decumbent or sprawling, half-woody shrublet with green twigs. The small leaves consist of three leaflets (like reduced pea leaves); they are sacrificed during summer drought. The masses of seasonal yellow pea flowers make this a striking plant, especially when cascading over rocks, and the flowers extend their beauty by turning red as they dry. In its natural environment, deerbroom is a short-lived opportunist that moves into chaparral after fire, grows rapidly, flowers and seeds prolifically, then dies. If it is treated similarly—or especially if the life cycle is speeded up by extra summer water (with lengthened flowering)—deerbroom will last only one or two seasons in the garden.

Obviously deerbroom lotus is not for a long-term landscape design, but it is easily started over. It might be considered for a place in a rock garden or among dune plants (there's an especially low form from the dunes of the central coast) in company with dune sagebrush (*Artemisia pycnocephala*), seaside daisy (*Erigeron glaucus*), and sea-thrift (*Armeria maritima*). It can also be used as a specimen if moved out of sight during its summer leafless condition.

Lotus dendroideus from the Channel Islands deserves special mention. It is a slender, upright shrub growing with broomlike appearance, up to six feet tall but similar to *L. scoparius* in its flowers and leaves. If you're looking for an alternative to the invasive European brooms, here's a native that fills the bill. This species is winter tender.

Lupinus spp. Lupines. Pea family (Fabaceae)

HT: 6 inches to 6 feet. LVS: evergreen. FLWS: spikes of blue, purple or yellow pea flowers; spring to early summer. SMR WTR: reduced or occasional waterings. PROP: cuttings; seeds (use immediately or break dormancy). EXP: full sun

The lupines compose one of California's largest genera, but the majority of species are nonwoody. All lupines, regardless of habit, have palmately compound leaves—the leaflets suggest the fingers of a hand—and showy spikes of pealike flowers, arranged in tiers or spirals. All start readily from fresh seed; when seed is stored they

Deerbroom Lotus (*Lotus scoparius*)
a. flowering branches   *b.* flower detail   *c.* fruit detail

develop a dormancy, which must be broken by soaking, stratification, or both. All lupines grow rapidly, have nitrogen-fixing nodules on their roots that help enrich the soil with nitrogen, and are vulnerable to damping-off and to predation by slugs and snails.

California bush lupines vary from prostrate, mat-forming kinds to multibranched, upright shrubs. Most flower from mid to late spring with a great flourish of showy, often perfumed spikes (the scent often intensifies in the afternoon). Seed pods twist suddenly to eject seeds, by season's end. At this point lupines need a rest; too much water will induce fungal rot. All lupines favor sandy soils and require no fertilizer.

Feature lupines in tubs as container plants (a good way to provide excellent drainage), in rock gardens, in mixed borders, or in front of other shrubberies. Here are four garden-worthy species:

L. albifrons. White-leaf bush lupine. The beautiful montane variety *collinus* is semiprostrate; the main species grows to three feet. Leaves are covered with white to silvery hairs; flowers are intense blue-purple, with a white spot on the banner. Fragrant. A close relative, *L. excubitus* (southern white-leaf bush lupine), is tolerant of very hot, dry summers.

L. arboreus. Yellow bush or tree lupine. Well adapted to coastal areas with cool summers, and excellent for beaches. Candles of pale yellow flowers in late spring; green leaves. Fragrant. Hybridizes with mat lupine.

L. chamissonis. Beach lupine. A beautiful, mounding shrub to three feet, with silvery leaves and blue-purple flowers. Excellent for beaches and sand dunes.

L. variicolor. Mat lupine. Sprawling plant for cool coastal areas and rocky soils. Flowers are held above leaves and come in various shades of blue, purple, and white. Hybridizes with yellow bush lupine; the offspring are often intermediate in height and combine the flower colors of both parents.

Lycium pallidum. Pale Boxthorn. Nightshade family (Solanaceae)

HT: 3 to 6 feet. LVS: summer deciduous. FLWS: semipendent tubular, white or pale purple trumpets along leafy stems; spring. SMR WTR: none. PROP: cuttings (use bottom heat); seeds (scarify or stratify). EXP: full sun

The eight or so boxthorns are small shrubs with intricate greenish, thorn-tipped branchlets and tiny leaves, which sometimes are shed during the dry season. All are characterized by trumpet-shaped spring blossoms of white, purple, or greenish and tiny miniature-tomato-like fruits, sometimes orange or red, other times purple to green. Of these, *Lycium pallidum* is the showiest, its young twigs lined with myriad pale purple, trumpet-shaped blooms in midspring. The purplish-green fruits that follow are unexceptional. Another boxthorn to try is *L. californicum*, from sandy places near the coast, with curious tiny, fleshy, bright green leaves and small purple flowers followed by miniature red fruits.

Boxthorns are like so many other desert shrubs out of flower, small and unimposing, although the greenish twigs look good through the summer. They are ideal for garden areas calling for shrubs adapted to rocky soils with no water, and they could blend in with such other similar shrubs as paperbag bush, ephedras, and desert alyssum.

Lyonothamnus floribundus. Island Ironwood. Rose family (Rosaceae)

HT: 15 to 50 feet. LVS: evergreen. FLWS: tiny white single roses in flat-topped clusters; late spring. SMR WTR: occasional deep watering. PROP: cuttings; suckers; seeds (stratify). EXP: full sun to light shade

Island ironwood is really a small tree, but because of its size it could be pruned into a shrub. There are two varieties, both from the Channel Islands: variety *floribundus* from Santa Catalina Island has narrowly lance-shaped leaves, while variety *asplenifolius*—the Santa Cruz Island ironwood—has fernlike, pinnately divided leaves of great beauty. Only the latter variety is widely cultivated.

Island ironwood has many interesting qualities—gorgeous stringy brown bark, peeling in long strips year-round, and masses of white flowers in flat-topped cymes at spring's end. Given time, it forms groves from wandering roots that sucker and sprout. Its one drawback, other than the space needed to display it to advantage, is that the faded, brown flower clusters persist for several seasons.

Island ironwood makes a dramatic backdrop for any garden, especially when allowed ample space. Its thirsty roots, however, eliminate most understory plants. It would also make a spectacular specimen for a large container, or it could be pruned into an unusual dense screen or hedge. With ample space, a single planting could also grow into a miniature grove or copse. It is best propagated from cuttings or suckers; seeds are unreliable and uneven in germination.

Machaeranthera tortifolia. Desert Aster. Sunflower family (Asteraceae)

HT: 1 to 3 feet. LVS: partly deciduous in summer. FLWS: showy purple and yellow daisies; spring. SMR WTR: none. PROP: cuttings or suckers; seeds. EXP: full sun

Desert aster differs from other asters by growing as a bush, which is woody at the base. Although there are several species, *M. tortifolia* is the only reasonably common well-known species. Native to the hot deserts of southern California, it is well adapted to hot, dry summers, but like other such shrubs it defoliates, resulting in unsightly twigs at the height of summer drought. It is partial to sandy soils and demands good drainage.

Catalina Island Ironwood (*Lyonothamnus floribundus floribundus*)
a. flowering branch with simple leaves

Santa Cruz Island Ironwood (*Lyonothamnus floribundus asplenifolius*)
b. leaf detail showing divided leaf   *c.* flower detail

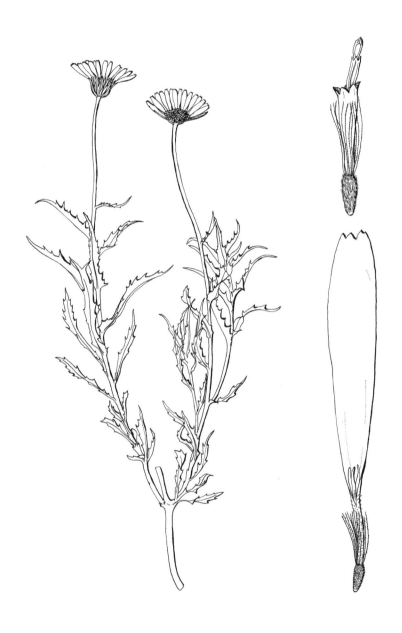

Desert Aster (*Machaeranthera tortifolia*)
left: flowering branches with leaves   *lower right:* ray floret detail
upper right: disc floret detail

Desert aster is useful as a small shrub for the foreground of a sunny rock or desert garden, best intermixed with other plants whose foliage remains summer green. Its glory in spring is the prolific production of large, showy daisies with blue-purple ray flowers and golden centers. This color combination complements the gold daisies of desert brittlebush (*Encelia farinosa*), the orange cups of apricot mallow (*Sphaeralcea ambigua*), and the white blossoms of desert alyssum (*Lepidium fremontii*).

Mahonia (Berberis) spp. Holly Grape or Barberry. Barberry family (Berberidaceae)

HT: 1 to 40 feet. LVS: evergreen. FLWS: small and yellow, forming branched racemes; spring. SMR WTR: varies. PROP: divisions; cuttings; layering. EXP: varies

The barberries are a variable group, but with many features in common: all grow into widely wandering shrubs—easily propagated from creeping rootstocks—and bear stiff, evergreen, pinnately compound leaves, the leaflets hollylike and lined with prickly teeth. The flowers are borne in compound spikes, pale to bright yellow, the petals arrayed in several rows. The fruits are attractive and edible purple, blue, red, or black berries resembling grapes. Species vary in habit and habitat and thus in their garden uses. All are tough once established, but most take a year or two to settle in (during which time they scarcely grow). All have handsome evergreen foliage, pretty flowers, and decorative berries, which make excellent preserves. They also share bright yellow inner bark, which is used as a natural dye. All are easy to propagate by divisions of the rootstocks. Here are eight of California's species:

M. *aquifolium*. Oregon grape (state flower of Oregon). A tall shrub with shiny, dark green leaves, from shaded forests. Moderately drought tolerant. Woodland gardens. Fine, long-lasting foliage for bouquets.

M. *dictyota*. Veined holly grape. Shrub to about six feet with decorative stiff, gray-green, wavy leaves bearing stout spines. Handsome compound clusters of flowers. Excellent for full sun and no summer water.

M. *haematocarpa*. Desert holly grape. Tall, treelike shrub may develop well-defined trunk with age. Gray-green, rather wavy leaves. Fine for hot summers; no water. Specimen plant.

M. *nervosa*. Northern holly grape. A very fine species with especially long, leathery, deep green glossy leaves, from moist forests. Wanders widely. Most forms grow to about one foot, but one variety reaches three or more feet. Some summer water. Woodland garden. Fine foliage for bouquets.

M. *nevinii*. From the hot chaparral of southern California, a tall, dense shrub with small, flat, grayish prickly leaves. Not so showy in flower but good as a barrier or hedge plant. No summer water.

M. pinnata. California holly grape. A modest shrub of rocky coastal promontories, tolerant of wind and summer fog. Occasional summer water. Beautiful bronze new foliage and glossy green leaves, the leaflets closely overlapping. For rock gardens or at the back of a mixed border.

M. pumila. Dwarf holly grape. A miniature shrub to one foot high, from dry chaparral slopes on California's northwestern mountains. Dull, blue-green, veined leaves turn purple or red at season's end; attractive blue-purple fruits. Drought and heat tolerant. Good choice for rock gardens.

M. repens. Creeping holly grape. Low, sprawling ground cover, often less than one foot high. Polished green leaves turn red-purple in fall. Excellent for low-maintenance ground cover or a large rock garden; little summer water.

Malacothamnus spp. Bush Mallows. Mallow family (Malvaceae)

HT: 3 to 15 feet. LVS: evergreen. FLWS: white, pink, or purple hollyhocks in heads or spikes; mid-spring to early summer. SMR WTR: little or none. PROP: suckers; cuttings; seeds (stratify). EXP: full sun

The bush mallows constitute a group of half-woody shrubs from the edges of chaparral, occurring in abundance after fires. Their many wandlike stems wear green bark and have an open pattern of secondary branches. Leaves are rounded to palmately lobed, are often maplelike, and vary from pale green to silvery white, most often with a dense felt of soft, thick hairs. Flowers are borne in profusion on slender branches, in midspring and early summer. Individual flowers are cup-shaped, hollyhock-like blossoms with numerous yellow or orange stamens offset by purple to rosy hairlike stigmas.

The several bush mallows native to California differ mostly in small details not especially important to the gardener. They grow rapidly, appreciate well-lit, warm situations, are drought tolerant, and quickly fill their space but tend toward legginess. Prune out old growth and pinch back new growth to maintain a bushier shape. Division of the basal suckers may provide a means of increasing your stock. One liability is that shrubs have short life spans of only a few years and are vulnerable to wet winters.

Use bush mallows for informal barriers or background shrubberies, or feature well-shaped ones behind a dry mixed border or as specimen plants, displayed in a prominent place while they are in flower. Here are four common species:

M. fasciculatus. Southern bush mallow. Tall, open shrub with vigorous growth, greenish, shallowly lobed leaves, and pink flowers in whorled spikes on wandlike branches.

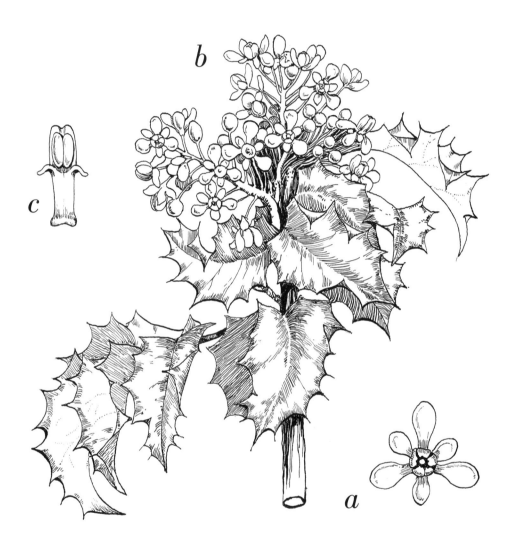

California Barberry (*Mahonia pinnata*)
a. flower detail *b.* flowering branches and leaves *c.* stamen detail

M. fremontii. Fremont bush mallow. A small shrub from mountains around the Central Valley; leaves silver-white, flowers pale lavender.

M. palmeri. Palmer bush mallow. Medium-tall shrub from the Monterey mountains. Leaves greenish and scarcely lobed, flowers in dense heads, palest pink-purple or white. Rather rounded, dense shape for shrubs.

M. rotundifolius. Round-leaf bush mallow. Low shrub to three feet, with soft, pale green, rounded leaves and numerous wands of pale lilac flowers in summer. From the east side of the southern Sierra; drought and heat tolerant. Feature it in a mountain rock garden.

Malacothrix saxatilis. Bush Chicory. Sunflower family (Asteraceae)

HT: to around 3 feet. LVS: evergreen, or in droughts summer deciduous. FLWS: showy chicorylike heads of white flowers, striped pink; summer and fall. SMR WTR: none near coast. PROP: half-woody cuttings; seeds. EXP: full sun near coast

Bush chicory is California's only chicory relative with a bushy appearance. Actually a subshrub with green, widely spreading branchlets, bush chicory is quite attractive in summer or early fall, when the white, chicorylike flower heads are sprinkled over the bush. At close inspection, each tongue-shaped ray flower has pinkish stripes, a handsome color combination. The fleshy, narrowly spoon-shaped leaves are undistinguished but not unattractive.

Bush chicory is a tender shrub, favoring coastal areas where the proximity to the ocean keeps frosts away most years. It also needs good drainage, for otherwise it's prone to root rot. Use it in an informal planting with other low shrubs, such as coast brittlebush, blue witch, redberry buckthorn, and bush mallow, or use it for an informal backdrop to a rock garden. The variety *arachnoidea* is an interesting variant: its branches and leaves are covered with close, spider-web-like white hairs.

Malus fusca. Native Crabapple. Rose family (Rosaceae)

HT: 15 to 30 feet. LVS: winter deciduous. FLWS: white, applelike, flat-topped clusters; late spring. SMR WTR: some. PROP: cuttings (use bottom heat); suckers; seeds (stratify). EXP: light shade

Native crabapple is a small tree trainable as a large shrub with multiple branches. It favors the edge of northern conifer forests, often with Sitka spruce (*Picea sitchensis*), Douglas fir (*Pseudotsuga menziesii*), or coast hemlock (*Tsuga heterophylla*). There it matures at a moderate growth rate into a pretty but unexceptional treelet. Deciduous, dull green, applelike leaves have finely serrated edges. In late spring, the pretty clusters of white apple blossoms set it off; later, some of these ripen into small ovoid, red-purple crabapples of no value for food. The leaf shape, although typical of apples, differs from other kinds by an occasional mittenlike lobe on one or both sides of the leaf.

Use crabapple as a pleasing background shrub for the watered woodland garden or toward the back of a pond, in light shade. Companion shrubs could include native hawthorn, western azalea, and service berry.

Menziesia ferruginea. Rustyleaf Menziesia or Mock Azalea. Heather family (Ericaceae)

HT: 3 to 12 feet. LVS: winter deciduous. FLWS: tiny yellow-pink urns in small clusters; early summer. SMR WTR: some deep watering. PROP: cuttings; layering. EXP: shade

Mock azalea is a fitting name for this shrub, for out of flower it looks remarkably similar to western azalea (*Rhododendron occidentale*), but on closer inspection the branching pattern is subtly different, and leaf details don't quite fit. Branches grow in horizontal layers, and leaves are somewhat smaller than those of the azalea, with scattered rusty hairs beneath and tiny serrations along the margins. The small bunches of diminutive blossoms are pretty, close up—pale yellow urns marked with red or orange—but hardly showy. Mock azalea is a pretty but not exciting shrub for the coastal garden where there's plenty of shade and summer moisture. It grows in our northern redwood forests not far from the sound of the surf.

Use mock azalea as a fast-growing, acid-loving shrub for the background of a wooded garden or behind a pond, where a filling of attractive foliage is wanted (without the need for the color of showy blossoms). It could also create an informal hedge, where the blossoms could be enjoyed at close range.

Monardella spp. Coyote Mint, Western Pennyroyal. Mint family (Lamiaceae)

HT: 4 to 18 inches. LVS: usually evergreen. FLWS: long tubes clustered together as dense heads; summer. SMR WTR: little or none. PROP: cuttings; seeds. EXP: full sun

The monardellas are miniature shrublets with great possibilities for the droughty garden. They not only require little extra water and are happy in full sun and heat, but they flower during the summer months, sometimes into early fall. Occasional water will prolong the blooming season and give greater vigor, but may shorten the life span.

Monardellas are rather open, multibranched plants with small, fuzzy to shiny oval leaves that carry a strong fragrance somewhere between minty and sagey. The flowers, although individually small, are massed together in showy heads; they range from white to purple to orange-red. Hummingbirds seek out the red-flowered kinds, while bumblebees and butterflies are fond of the others. Living on the edge of chaparral or other brushy plant communities, monardellas frequently grow on rocky outcrops. For this reason they need perfect drainage in the garden.

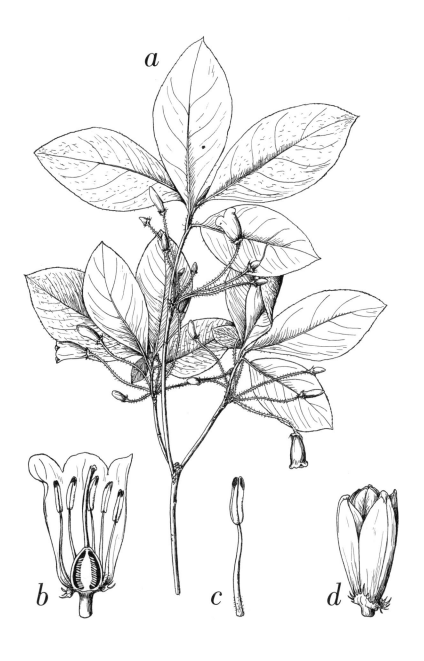

Mock Azalea (*Menziesia ferruginea*)
a. leafy branches with flowers   *b.* flower detail   *c.* stamen detail
d. flower bud detail

Use monardellas in a rock garden, massed in front of taller shrubs, or as container plants for seasonal color. They go nicely with bush monkeyflowers, zauschnerias, penstemons, and rushrose. Here are a few species for consideration:

M. linoides. Desert coyote mint. Bushy plants to eighteen inches tall, with narrow leaves covered with silvery hairs. Flowers pale pink-purple. Good for desert gardens.

M. macrantha. Hummingbird mint. Low sprawling to creeping plants with dark green, shiny leaves and large, loose heads of vivid scarlet or red-orange tubular flowers. Excellent for coastal rock gardens.

M. odoratissima. Mountain pennyroyal. Multibranched bush to around one foot tall, with pale, very strongly scented leaves. Profusion of white to blue-purple flower heads through summer. Excellent for rock and mountain gardens.

M. purpurea. Del Norte coyote mint. Low, intricately branched bushlet, with glossy green leaves and rose-purple flowers. Excellent for the front of a summer-hot rock garden.

M. villosa. Common coyote mint. Variable shrublet to eight inches, with pale green leaves and long-lasting heads of purple flowers. Good all-around plant for the front of a droughty border or rock garden.

M. viridis. Interior coyote mint. Low, creeping subwoody plant, with green leaves curled under and closely covered with whitish hairs beneath; showy heads of rose-purple flowers. Excellent for a rock garden in summer-hot situations.

Myrica californica. California Wax Myrtle or Bayberry. Bayberry family (Myricaceae)

HT: 6 to 35 feet. LVS: evergreen. FLWS: insignificant and greenish to purplish, in catkins; March and April. SMR WTR: frequent deep waterings are best. PROP: cuttings; seeds (stratify). EXP: shade

California bayberry can grow as a dense shrub or, with stump sprouts removed, as a small tree. Except along the immediate coast, it needs the shade of taller shrubs or trees. Bayberry is a decidedly handsome plant: its best features include the neat, compact branches and thick evergreen leaves. Leaves are long and narrow, frequently curled under, and lined with tiny sawlike teeth. Shiny and deep green, they have a spicy aroma that is enhanced on warm days or when leaves are dried. Unlike the true bay (*Umbellularia californica*), bayberry leaves are not overpowering when used to flavor stews and sauces. The flowers are altogether unremarkable; the greenish male catkins are borne between leaves toward the bases of branches, the purplish female catkins between leaves near branch tips. The female catkins later turn into waxy,

Hummingbird Mint (*Monardella macrantha*)
a. leafy branches with flower head   *b*. sepal detail

Common Coyote Mint (*Monardella villosa*)
a. flowering stem with head of flowers   *b.* flower detail   *c.* sepal detail

California Bayberry (*Myrica californica*)
center: branch with female flowers   *lower left:* male flower detail
lower right: female flower detail

bumpy, purplish berries. Although the fragrant wax on the berries may be used for scented candles as with the eastern bayberry, the wax content is too scant for serious consideration.

Bayberry grows at a moderate rate, requires some summer irrigation—especially inland—and prefers cool, damp summers near the coast. Under these conditions it persists for a long time and is perfectly amenable to pruning to maintain shape and keep branches dense. Its handsome leaves make it ideal for a foundation shrub, for a hedge or barrier, or for use behind a pond or in a woodland setting. It deserves widespread use in the landscape.

Nolina parryi. Parry Nolina or Beargrass. Agave family (Agavaceae)

HT: 1 to 4 feet. LVS: evergreen. FLWS: small creamy flowers in huge open panicles; spring. SMR WTR: none. PROP: pups; cuttings; seeds. EXP: full sun

Parry nolina is a yucca look-alike with great presence and drama. From the hot chaparral or desert edge in far southern California, it is a slow-growing plant with a short, branched trunk, each arm carrying thick bunches of long, straplike, lance-shaped flexible leaves. Unlike the yucca, whose dagger-tipped leaves are dangerous at close range, nolina's leaves are soft and forgiving. When mature, plants send up huge open panicles of innumerable small, creamy flowers, the stalks often reaching four or more feet above the leaves. A second show comes in summer, when the fruits develop into lovely three-winged, papery seed pods of enduring beauty.

Parry nolina deserves special treatment in the garden: a place to itself to heighten drama, excellent drainage (sandy soils are best), and lots of sun and heat. It is fine for a desert garden, in a large container, or at the back of a rock or herb garden. Coastal gardens and foggy conditions are to be avoided.

Opuntia spp. Prickly Pears. Cactus family (Cactaceae)

HT: to 6 feet, often much lower. LVS: none; flattened, pancakelike, jointed green stems have spines. FLWS: large, showy, roselike flowers in yellow or pink; spring. SMR WTR: none. PROP: stem sections or pads; seeds (stratify). EXP: full sun

Prickly pears are among California's representative cacti, both for their notable form—series of circular, flattened, jointed pads covered with long spines and with minute, sneaky, barbed spines—and for their multiple uses. The stems are skinned and cooked as the vegetable nopales, and the fleshy, juicy, sweet fruits called tunas are made into confections and preserves. Of the dozens of kinds throughout the Southwest and Mexico, California has several that are appropriate to dry landscapes, particularly desert gardens. All are truly drought-tolerant plants (and form larger colonies over time), and all are dramatic in their form and beautiful in flower.

Prickly pears are easily started from individual pads, which are easily severed with a sharp knife. But use caution in handling them: good sturdy gloves are in order, since those tiny barbed spines can work their way into skin and prove difficult to extract. Larger species can serve as specimens; the smaller kinds blend nicely with other cacti, such as the mound cactus and various hedgehogs (*Echinocereus* spp.) and fish-hook cacti (*Mamillaria* spp.). They remain good looking all year, unless attacked by aggressive pests, which can disfigure them. Here are three possibilities:

O. basilaris. Beavertail cactus. Grows into large clumps that seldom exceed a foot in height. Pads are pale gray-green, seemingly spineless (but watch out for those tiny barbs!). In spring, a long succession of blossoms lines the tops of pads, with gorgeous pink to rose-colored, waterlilylike blossoms of great beauty.

O. chlorotica. Pancake cactus. Sizeable shrubberies of bright green pads to six or more feet tall. Long spines and barbs. In late spring it has bright yellow blossoms, similar in shape to those of beavertail. Excellent for an informal fence or barrier plant.

O. erinacea ursina. Old man prickly pear. Grows in fashion similar to beavertail, but the green pads are densely covered with white spines and shaggy white hairs—beautiful when back lit. Pretty yellow flowers, fading red, in late spring. Excellent accent plant; good in rock gardens.

Osmaronia cerasiformis. Oso Berry. Rose family (Rosaceae)

HT: 2 to 15 feet. LVS: winter deciduous. FLWS: small white applelike blossoms in nodding racemes; early spring. SMR WTR: occasional deep watering. PROP: suckers; layering; cuttings. EXP: light shade

Oso berry grows as a small, wind-pruned shrub on coastal bluffs, while inland on forest edges it becomes a large shrub. Out of flower, its oblong, dull greenish, smooth leaves match the shape of several other shrubs, especially the rhamnuses and prunuses, and so may help fill out their pattern when conditions call for similar leaf shape and texture. The smooth gray to reddish bark is pretty in winter, and the modest, pendant racemes of fragrant, white, applelike flowers add special charm in early spring, just as new leaves are beginning to expand. The fruits are single-seeded drupes rather than berries, which turn deep black-purple when ripe. They were said to have been dried and mixed with other fruits by Native Americans, although they are somewhat bitter.

Oso berry is not a bold or unusual shrub, but it is altogether modest and pleasant. It grows rapidly at first, then slows, and may be rooted by layering. Use it in a natural forest or woodland border, or as an informal shade-loving barrier. Its presence will encourage birds in late summer as fruits ripen.

Paxistima myrsinites. Oregon Boxwood or Mountain Lover. Staff-tree family (Celastraceae)

HT: 1 to 3 feet. LVS: evergreen. FLWS: inconspicuous, dull maroon, hidden under branches; late spring. SMR WTR: moist soil. PROP: layering; cuttings. EXP: shade

Oregon boxwood is a poorly known shrub in California; its main homeland lies in the Pacific Northwest, where it grows happily under moisture-loving conifers, often on mossy, rocky banks in company with saxifrages, twinflower (*Linnaea borealis*), and vanilla leaf (*Achlys triphylla*). Still, it deserves a trial in gardens, for its compact, low, semiprostrate habit makes it a handsome evergreen ground cover that likes shade. Leaves are leathery deep green above and elliptical to obovate, with minutely serrate edges. The tiny flowers are four-pointed, maroon stars, which are nearly invisible, since they hide beneath leaves. Because Oregon boxwood grows slowly and transplants with difficulty, it should be installed in one place and not further disturbed.

Oregon boxwood is an excellent miniature shrub for the forefront of a shade garden or to have scramble over rocks near a streambed or around a shaded pond. It requires some summer water and at least partial shade, but it will tolerate hot summers and cold winters with good looks the year-round. With ample summer water it will grow up to two or three feet tall. Grow it with some of its natural companions, such as those mentioned above or *Anemone deltoidea*, *Clintonia uniflora*, and *Phlox adsurgens*.

Penstemon spp. Penstemon or Beardtongue. Figwort family (Scrophulariaceae)

HT: 4 inches to 5 or more feet. LVS: mostly evergreen, sometimes dying back in winter. FLWS: showy, two-lipped snapdragons in rose, purple, blue, red, or yellow; late spring through summer. SMR WTR: occasional deep watering. PROP: cuttings (take fairly new wood); seeds. EXP: mostly full sun, sometimes light shade

Our penstemons include some of the showiest and most colorful of wildflowers and are generously represented in the western states, mostly in open, rocky places. Their growth habit is most often that of a half-shrub or perennial, yet there are several true shrubs as well. It is impossible to draw a distinct line between different kinds of habit; included here are shrubs and a few subshrubs.

Since penstemons range from the low foothills up to the alpine, and from openings in redwood forest to dry, hot deserts, their culture and uses must be treated separately, species by species. Most penstemons are multistemmed plants that strike root readily from new or half-ripe wood and that germinate readily from seeds (but are susceptible to damping-off). Their foliage frequently complements their flowers, the leaves ranging from small and scalelike to large and elliptical, and from bright green to blue- or gray-green. Wands of showy flowers appear from late spring through summer. Flowering is extended by summer water, but at the expense of shortening the life span. Short life under cultivation is not a particular problem, since penstemons are easy to

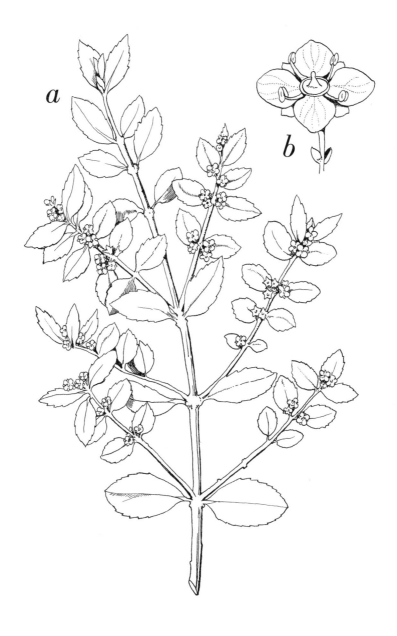

Oregon Boxwood (*Paxistima myrsinites*)
a. flowering branches with leaves   *b*. flower detail

propagate. Flowers consist of an expanded tube, which flares into two-lipped petals; the lower lip is often marked by splotches and lines of contrasting color leading into the throat. Many bear a long, bearded "tongue," a sterile stamen lined with dense yellow to whitish hairs. Here are several of the best species for garden purposes:

P. (Keckiella) antirrhinoides. Bush snapdragon. Small, modest bush of rounded shape, with small, narrowly triangular, light green leaves and close, showy racemes of bright yellow snapdragons with open "mouths," appearing in late spring. Fine as a specimen or for dry mixed borders. Full sun and hot summers.

P. bridgesii. Bridge's penstemon. A woody-based, low-growing perennial from the dry parts of high mountains on rocky outcroppings. Cold winters and warm summers; little water. Narrowly spoon-shaped, pale green leaves and long wands of scarlet red, wide-mouthed flowers in summer. For rock gardens.

P. centranthifolius. Scarlet bugler. Low mounds of broadly spoon-shaped, gray leaves and tall wands of long, tubular, scarlet flowers in late spring to summer. Takes hot, dry conditions in full sun. Fine for hummingbirds. For rock gardens or the mixed dry border.

P. (Keckiella) cordifolius. Climbing penstemon. Half-climbing, green-woody shrub to five or more feet. Grows up through chaparral shrubs such as ceanothuses and scrub oaks. Takes hot, dry summers; mild winters. Deciduous in winter. Small triangular, toothed leaves; short racemes of wide-mouthed scarlet to yellow flowers appreciated by hummingbirds.

P. (Keckiella) corymbosus. Red-flowered rock penstemon. Sprawling to upright low, densely branched shrub from rocky cliffs near chaparral or forest in north Coast Ranges. Will take intense sun and heat and plentiful winter rain, with good drainage. Close clusters of scarlet flowers are much like those of *P. cordifolius.* For rock gardens or dry mixed borders.

P. eatonii. Eaton's firecracker. Small, upright subshrub, with narrow leaves and long wands of scarlet, two-lipped, tubular flowers. From high deserts; tolerant of summer heat and drought.

P. grinnellii scrophularioides. Inflated penstemon. Similar in most details to *P. palmeri* but only two to three feet tall. The inflated flowers are pale purple, the lower lip sometimes with darker purple tracings. From the inner south Coast Ranges, and possibly more adaptable to coastal or lowland gardens.

P. newberryi. Mountain pride. Low, matlike, half-woody shrublet four or five inches tall with numerous elliptical, blue-green leaves and startling racemes of rose-purple to pink-purple flowers in summer. Superb in rock gardens and visited by many pollinators. Variety *sonomensis* is best for gardens because it occurs as low as two thousand feet; other varieties grow at mid to high elevations.

P. palmeri. Palmer's penstemon. Spectacular half-shrub of deserts. Give full sun and heat; sandy soils. Close clusters of narrowly elliptical, toothed, bluish green leaves and wands (to six feet) of inflated, fragrant, white to purple flowers have great beauty. The detail of lines and the showy "bearded tongue" lend extra interest close up.

Petrophytum caespitosum. Rock Spiraea. Rose family (Rosaceae)

HT: 2 to 4 inches. LVS: evergreen. FLWS: white, spiraealike in dense spikes; late spring through summer. SMR WTR: none. PROP: layering; cuttings. EXP: full sun to light shade

Rock spiraea is a plant unlikely to be mistaken for any other. Its thick, carpetlike mats hug the ground, or more accurately they drape down talus slopes or over limestone boulders in the high, rare air of dry mountains. It is not unusual to see rock spiraea in company with other lime lovers, such as the famous bristlecone pines (*Pinus longaeva*), as in California's White Mountains. The modest flower spikes add interest and different texture after snows have departed. Up close, the mats consist of thickly overlapping, velvet-textured, long, narrowly spoon-shaped leaves.

Since rock spiraea has such a specialized habitat, it should not be expected to perform well in the average garden. Mountain gardens with low precipitation might host this plant—a natural for the front of a rock garden—but bear in mind that limestone is on the alkaline side of the pH scale, while most mountain settings are in or near forests with acid soils. This can be remedied by deliberately building a bed of crushed limestone or other similar rock (for example, dolomite).

Peucephyllum schottii. Pygmy Cedar. Sunflower family (Asteraceae)

HT: 2 to 8 feet. LVS: evergreen. FLWS: small pale yellow rayless heads; mostly in spring. SMR WTR: none. PROP: seeds. EXP: sun

As belies its common name, pygmy cedar mimics a dwarf conifer, yet the truth is that it's a member of the sunflower family, not a conifer at all. The handsome habit of this plant includes a short trunk, shreddy strips of bark, and open branches covered with sticky, needlelike, pleasantly aromatic (essence of pine) leaves, making it worthy of a spot in gardens with hot, dry summers. The flower heads are modest, pale yellow, and rayless.

Use pygmy cedar for an informal hedge, at the back of a rock garden, or around some of the desert shrubs with beautiful spring blossoms but twiggy, nondescript branches in summer. The foliage remains attractive throughout the year without the need of extra water.

Philadelphus lewisii. California Mock Orange. Mock orange family. (Philadelphaceae)

HT: 3 to 10 feet. LVS: winter deciduous. FLWS: white single-rose-like, highly fragrant flowers; late spring to early summer. SMR WTR: occasional deep watering. PROP: cuttings; suckers. EXP: light shade

Whether it's called mock orange, philadelphus, or even syringa, this lovely, medium-sized shrub has many winning attributes: densely branched, narrow twigs showing shreddy, brown bark in winter; handsome ovate, light green, opposite leaves in spring and summer; and myriad dense racemes of deliciously fragrant white blossoms in late spring or early summer. Each flower is an open saucer filled with numerous pale, creamy stamens and a single green pistil.

Mock orange follows canyon bottoms and forest edges of the lower yellow pine belt in the Sierra and the mixed woodlands of the north Coast Ranges, filling narrow glades with fragrant bloom. A moderately fast grower, it creates dense clumps of fine twigs excellent for a barrier in spring and summer. Or use it behind lower shrubs in a lightly shaded situation, behind a pond, along a stream, or at the back of a woodland, but preferably where the fine flowers are easily seen. Fitting companions include bush anemone (*Carpenteria californica*), western spicebush (*Calycanthus occidentalis*), and snowbell bush (*Styrax officinalis*).

Phyllodoce spp. Red Heather. Heather family (Ericaceae)

HT: 4 inches to 2 feet. LVS: evergreen. FLWS: rose-purple bells in umbrellalike clusters; midsummer. SMR WTR: moist soil. PROP: cuttings; seeds (stratify). EXP: full sun to light shade

Red heathers are among our most beautiful high mountain shrubs; they make sprawling, rounded mounds covered with narrow, bright green needlelike leaves. As the last snows recede they burst into flower, becoming smothered in vivid rose-purple bells. Frequent companions include the smaller bells of white heather (*Cassiope mertensiana*), the open rosy saucers of mountain laurel (*Kalmia polifolia microphylla*), or the creamy clusters of Labrador tea (*Ledum glandulosum*), often juxtaposed with brilliantly colored, perennial wildflowers. Red heathers favor boggy places, where they "run" between granite boulders or fringe the edges of glacial tarns.

As with most of its companions, red heather seems nearly impossible to maintain in lowland gardens. It's always better to start with seeds, so that plants are acclimated as much as possible to these totally different surroundings, but still full vigor is only assured in mountain gardens. Red heather is a very beautiful alpine shrub for fringing a pond or for a boggy spot in the rock garden, interplanted with its alpine associates.

California Mock Orange (*Philadelphus lewisii*)
a. flowering branch with leaves   *b.* fruit detail

Physocarpus capitatus. Ninebark. Rose family (Rosaceae)

HT: 3 to 8 feet. LVS: winter deciduous. FLWS: small white single roses from headlike clusters; late spring. SMR WTR: some deep watering. PROP: cuttings; seeds. EXP: shade

Ninebark is a fine yet little used shrub, favoring wooded streams throughout the lower elevations of mountains. It remains attractive all year: in winter the numerous branches show shreddy strips of brownish bark and newer reddish twigs; in spring and summer twigs bear attractive, rounded leaves with deep slashes and coarse teeth; in mid to late spring branches are lined with balls of white flowers; and in early summer red, capsular fruits replace the flowers. The beauty of the flowering pageant, from rose-pink buds through white flowers to red fruits, heightens interest over more than a month each year.

Ninebark grows vigorously and rapidly, and may need some restraint so as not to develop into an ungainly, leggy shrub; pruning helps keep it bushy. Both stump sprouts and layered lower branches are easy ways to propagate new shrubs. Use ninebark for an informal seasonal hedge or barrier, behind a pond, or along the edge of a woodland garden. Its distinctive leaves contrast well with those of oso berry (*Osmaronia cerasiformis*), bush anemone (*Carpenteria californica*), and California bayberry (*Myrica californica*).

Pickeringia montana. Chaparral Pea. Pea family (Fabaceae)

HT: 3 to 8 feet. LVS: evergreen. FLWS: single large, showy, rose-purple pea flowers; late spring. SMR WTR: none. PROP: root cuttings; suckers. EXP: full sun

Chaparral pea is a typical border shrub in hot, dry chaparral, and it is especially abundant on road cuts, after burns, or on markedly rocky slopes. Its branches spread in all directions and are easily recognized by the sharp thorny tips. Other features include small, oblanceolate leaflets in threes and masses of gorgeous, rose-purple pea flowers in late spring, sometimes so dense they make the whole bush glow. Seed pods are rarely formed, so plants depend mostly upon vegetative reproduction. This is good news for gardeners, since they can use rooted sprouts or divisions of the running underground roots and stems, which send up new plantlets some distance from the parent shrub. Expect reluctant growth at first until the new plantlets are well established.

Chaparral pea is not a beautiful shrub out of flower, but once established it is tough, drought tolerant, and accepting of heat and rocky, nutrient-poor soils. In flower, however, there are few rivals for its hue and overall brilliance. For these reasons, you could use chaparral pea in a large movable container to display as a specimen in season, use it as a formidable barrier, or plant it to blend with other chaparral shrubs in a background planting, where lusher leaves of other shrubs offset its thorny personality. Good companion shrubs include ceanothuses, manzanitas (*Arctostaphylos* spp.), bush poppy (*Dendromecon rigida*), and yerba santa (*Erio-dictyon* spp.).

Pinus contorta bolanderi. Bolander or Pygmy Pine. Pine family (Pinaceae)

HT: in nature, to 8 feet. LVS: evergreen needles. FLWS: pollen cones in spring; seed cones ripen in fall. SMR WTR: some, deep. PROP: seeds. EXP: full sun on coast

Bolander pine probably represents a genetic dwarfing of the normally much taller beach pine *Pinus contorta*. It codominates the pygmy forests on the ancient, leached sea terraces of the Mendocino coast, where soils are ash-white, bereft of nutrients, and underlain by a cementlike hardpan. There it grows with the equally dwarfed pygmy cypress and various shrubby members of the heather family, such as salal, evergreen huckleberry, Fort Bragg manzanita, and Labrador tea.

The shrublike appearance, the dwarf size, and the already small seed cones make this the perfect pine for small-scale gardens. Use it in a large planter by itself, much as the well-known mugo pine (*Pinus mugo*) is grown—for a handsome specimen or bonsai—or plant it toward the back of a coastal rock garden as a backdrop.

Populus tremuloides. Quaking Aspen. Willow family (Salicaceae)

HT: 9 to 50 feet. LVS: winter deciduous. FLWS: short spikelike clusters of tiny, petalless flowers, male and female on separate plants; mid to late spring. SMR WTR: some deep watering. PROP: suckers. EXP: light shade to full sun

Although quaking aspen is normally considered a small tree, it can be pruned into a bushier shape or sculpted as a large container plant. Anyone familiar with the high Sierra in autumn knows this tree as one of California's most beautiful, with seasonal interest through the rest of the year as well. In fall, the constantly quaking leaves (twisting in the wind because of their flexible, flattened petiole) turn burnished gold, coloring whole mountainsides and stream margins for one to two weeks. The bare branches and trunk are tidy through winter, the older bark appearing smooth and white or pale green according to the angle of light and time of year.

The new leaves appear in early summer (earlier at low elevations), and their shiny surfaces cause the light to dance as they flutter about. Leaves are broad and shaped like rounded triangles, with smooth margins. The flowers are produced sparingly: tiny clusters of green pistils for the female, later shedding white, cotton-covered seeds; and small spikes of pale yellow stamens for the male. Quaking aspen usually skips blossoming altogether. Most trees reproduce locally by vegetative means, since the widely spreading roots throw up suckers some distance from the parent plant, eventually establishing a whole copse of trees.

Quaking aspen grows quickly, but is very thirsty and a serious competitor for any available water. Use it only where there is ample space for its wandering ways (unless you containerize it), and where little is expected to grow beneath. Pruned to stay short, a colony of these lovely trees creates a beautiful green light when the summer sun shines through and a golden haze in autumn. But be warned that although they grow well at low elevations, the leaves seldom color well there.

Potentilla fruticosa. Shrub Cinquefoil. Rose family (Rosaceae)

HT: to around 3 feet. LVS: sometimes winter deciduous. FLWS: bright yellow single roses; summer. SMR WTR: some. PROP: cuttings; seeds (stratify). EXP: full sun

Shrub cinquefoil is one of several circumboreal plants, that is, plants native to the northern reaches of the northern hemisphere and distributed across North America, Europe, and Asia. As such it has long been cultivated in varied forms, although few nurseries carrying it are aware that it is native to the high Sierra of California. Doubtless the simplest way to grow this pretty shrub is to select from already existing cultivars long in cultivation, but it would be fun to try races of native stock.

Look for shrub cinquefoil near timberline, in gravelly places on the borders of lush meadows or on scree with underground irrigation from snow melt. Out of flower, it's unexceptional: a densely branched, rounded bush with small, deeply pinnately cleft leaves shed in winter. But around midsummer it is smothered in bright golden blossoms resembling small, single roses. Use it toward the back of a rock garden, in the middle of a mixed border, or as a specimen; be sure to give it at least some water, since its most active growth and reproduction is during our drought months.

Primula suffrutescens. Sierra Primrose. Primrose family (Primulaceae)

HT: 2 to 4 inches. LVS: evergreen. FLWS: bright magenta primroses with yellow center in umbels; mid to late summer. SMR WTR: some water, but excellent drainage required. PROP: divisions; layering; seeds (stratify). EXP: full sun

Our Sierra primrose is at once arresting in flower and unusual for its genus, living in highly specialized niches in the alpine zone of high mountains. Unlike our familiar garden primroses, this species is a creeping shrub with numerous short branches bearing close tufts of shiny, dark green, spoon-shaped leaves, prettily serrated with coarse teeth at their ends. As the branches grow, they send down deep adventitious roots that work their way through loose scree to water trickling down from some melting snow patch above. Thus, they require the unusual combination of super drainage and moisture beneath.

After snowbanks have melted, plants are covered in myriad naked flowering stalks, bearing crowded umbels of short, brilliantly colored primrose blossoms: magenta petals with a yellow-green throat. In hue, these match such other high-mountain flowers as red heathers (*Phyllodoce* spp.); rock-fringe (*Epilobium obcordatum*), a sprawling perennial; and mountain pride penstemon (*Penstemon newberryi*). Each kind selects a slightly different habitat, yet all should be amenable to a high-mountain, rock garden setting.

Unfortunately, only rock-fringe and mountain pride appear adaptable to lowland gardens. Like the red heathers, Sierra primrose seems easy to start (rooted sections move well at first), but gradually vigor diminishes, and death follows. Better to leave this stunning beauty for a mountain garden or enjoy it in its own habitat.

Prosopis juliflora. Mesquite. Pea family (Fabaceae)

HT: 8 to 24 feet. LVS: summer deciduous. FLWS: long slender spikes of pale yellow acacialike blossoms; mid to late spring. SMR WTR: little or none. PROP: suckers; seeds (scarify, stratify, or both). EXP: full

Mesquite is reputed for the quality of the charcoal made from its wood. Its other attributes are less well known. A large, widely branched shrub or small tree flourishing in desert heat, where the water table stands high, it has a spring flush of pretty light green, pealike leaves at the same time that copious cream-colored flowers mass in long, cylindrical spikes, with a honeyed perfume. These are followed by an abundance of long, pealike seed pods. In summer, the green twigs take over photosynthesis while the leaves are shed; then the pairs of green spines along branches are evident. Mesquite flowers are reminiscent of certain acacias in size and arrangement. The bees are fond of them for making honey, and the seed pods and seeds were an important staple food for Native Americans.

Mesquite is probably not appropriate for the average garden: it needs plenty of room to spread sideways, lots of summer heat, and a water table accessible to the deeply probing roots. Use it in the background of a desert garden, interplanted perhaps with desert willow, smoke tree, or palo verde, and fronted by chuparosa and hummingbird fuchsia.

Prunus. Deciduous spp. Wild Plums or Cherries. Rose family (Rosaceae)

HT: 3 to 20 feet. LVS: deciduous. FLWS: white to rose, in clusters or racemes; late spring to summer. SMR WTR: most, occasional deep watering. PROP: cuttings; suckers; layering; seeds (scarify and stratify). EXP: full sun to light shade

The native plums and cherries compose a varied group of useful, ornamental shrubs. Several attain small-tree status if stump sprouts and suckers are removed; all have handsome, shiny bark, characteristically marked by bands of linear to elliptical, whitish lenticels. Without pruning, native plums send branches out in all directions, resulting in bushes or hedges of impenetrable branches. Leaves vary from narrow and toothless to broadly oblong and toothed, and branches may end in sharp spines or not. All bear small, plumlike flowers either in short clusters or in long, terminal racemes. Fruits are typical plumlike drupes, usually with thin, bitter flesh.

California's native plums vary; each is described below in order to ensure best garden usage.

P. andersonii. Desert peach. A low, intricately branched, spine-tipped shrub with grayish bark. Small, narrowly oblanceolate, nearly smooth-margined leaves are borne in close clusters. Masses of rose to pink flowers in midspring. Fruits, with dry brownish pulp, are inedible; the best feature is the flowers. Excellent for desert gardens. No summer water.

P. emarginata. Bitter cherry. Tall shrub with many erect branches; forms hedges. New bark is red; older bark is shiny silver. Narrowly wedge-shaped, smooth leaves and masses of white flowers in late spring. Exceedingly bitter red fruits are loved by birds. Excellent as a barrier or hedge plant or pruned as a single specimen.

P. subcordata. Sierra plum. Tall shrub or small tree with branchlets spine tipped; leaves ovate to round with saw teeth; small clusters of white to pink flowers in spring; and purple plumlike fruits with bitter flesh (excellent for preserves). Pretty for light shade in woodlands or as a specimen. Summer water.

P. virginiana var. *demissa.* Choke cherry. Tall shrub or small tree with handsome red-purple bark and broad, rounded to elliptical leaves with saw teeth. Showy racemes of white flowers bloom in late spring to early summer; dark red fruits are very bitter (but excellent for preserves). Feature it as a specimen tree, along a stream, or behind a pond or at the forest edge. Summer water.

Prunus. Evergreen spp. Chaparral Cherries or Islay. Rose family (Rosaceae)

HT: 3 to 50 feet. LVS: evergreen, shiny. FLWS: in dense racemes, white; late spring. SMR WTR: occasional deep watering. PROP: cuttings (use bottom heat); seeds (stratify briefly). EXP: full sun

Our two evergreen cherries are closely similar; each is a densely branched shrub, which may be pruned to a single trunk to create a modest-sized tree of great beauty. The reddish to gray bark is complemented by shiny, leathery hollylike or smooth-edged leaves. Indeed, the holly-leaf cherry (*P. ilicifolia*), with its spine-lined leaves, makes an excellent substitute for holly as decorations. The other species, the island cherry (*P. lyonii*), has smooth-edged but otherwise similar leaves and may grow a bit taller. Both produce showy racemes of plumlike flowers followed by uncommonly large, red-purple "cherries" with exceptionally large stones. Although the pulp is sweet and tasty, it's much too thin for use as food; birds, however, love to feed on them.

Plant the evergreen cherries where they can be trained into handsome trees by themselves or, as smaller versions, in large containers, or clump them together as

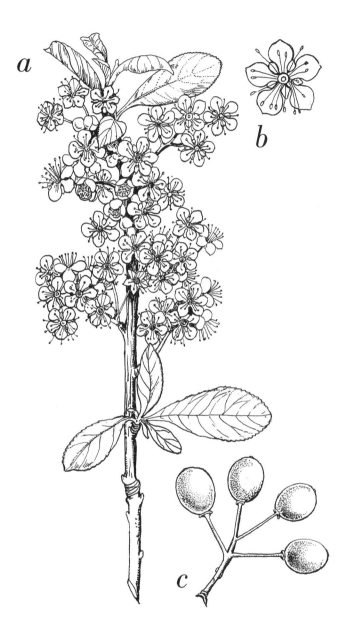

Bitter Cherry (*Prunus emarginata*)
a. flowering branches   *b.* flower detail   *c.* fruit detail

dense, handsome hedges. If they're pruned to stay low they can be used to hide taller chaparral shrubs in foundation plantings, where their attractive foliage focuses the eye when other shrubs are semidormant. They need little special care, and they grow slowly and steadily to maturity. Their roots are vulnerable to gophers just as are those of the edible cherries and plums.

Ptelea crenulata. Hopbush. Rue family (Rutaceae)

HT: 6 to 18 feet. LVS: winter deciduous. FLWS: small white flowers in flat-topped clusters; mid-spring. SMR WTR: occasional deep watering. PROP: suckers; cuttings; seeds (stratify). EXP: full sun to light shade

Hopbush is not related to hops, although its fruits, bordered by circular wings, may look a bit like them. Actually hopbush is a large shrub to small tree with ornamental qualities throughout the year: bare, red-purple young branches sprinkled with round white lenticels in winter; beanlike trifoliate, rue-scented leaves in spring and summer; pretty clusters of white, citruslike flowers in mid-spring; and decorative circular, winged fruits from summer through fall. The latter often stay on the branches after leaves have fallen.

Hopbush favors canyon bottoms with high water tables, growing most often between live oaks, digger pines, or buckeyes in California's hot interior foothills. It thrives with lots of heat but grows best with some supplemental summer water. Don't expect hopbush to grow fast; it plods along, but in time rewards with a lovely shape. Use it for an informal screen, mixed with other chaparral shrubs, or especially as a specimen. Hopbush deserves wider use in the summer-hot garden.

Purshia spp. Antelope Brush. Rose family (Rosaceae)

HT: 1 to 12 feet. LVS: evergreen. FLWS: single but scattered all over, pale yellow; late spring to early summer. SMR WTR: none. PROP: layering; cuttings (use bottom heat); seeds (stratify). EXP: full sun

Antelope brush is one of those "taken-for-granted" shrubs, a common sight in the sagebrush country of high deserts and along the east side of the Sierra. There it forms dense, rounded or strict, spire-shaped shrubs covered with small, tough, dark green aromatic leaves, the smell resinous and reflecting the essence of the high desert. Details of leaves and hairs determine the difference between California's two species, *P. glandulosa* and *P. tridentata*, but are of trifling importance to the gardener. Besides the singular toughness and pleasing all-year appearance, the best feature is the masses of pale yellow, roselike blossoms from late spring to early summer. Unobtrusive fruits follow, which are attractive to various small rodents.

Antelope brush has handsome grayish bark, which gives it status as a small specimen tree in desert gardens. Or plant it in groups for an effective barrier. Its leaves complement other high desert shrubs, especially the grays of sagebrush (*Artemisia tridentata*) and the bright green of rabbitbrush (*Chrysothamnus nauseosus*). With hard pruning, you can train antelope brush as an espalier on a warm wall, as a low-creeping woody ground cover, or to spill over a rock face in an informal rock garden, for which it's ideal. Best performance will be in winter-cold areas; expect relatively slow growth but long life.

Quercus spp. Scrub Oaks. Beech family (Fagaceae)

HT: 3 to 20 feet. LVS: deciduous or evergreen. FLWS: male in dangling catkins, spring; female inconspicuous. SMR WTR: little or none for most. PROP: cuttings (use bottom heat); acorns. EXP: full sun

California's oaks are one of the truly characteristic elements in its landscapes. Most people are familiar with the beautiful shapes of oaks, but often our gardens don't have room to accommodate them. Try instead some of the "miniature" scrub oaks. Some are shrubby versions of oaks that normally grow as trees; others are species unique unto themselves.

Scrub oaks vary considerably in detail of leaf design, height, and origin, but they share the following traits: dense branches, dangling chains (catkins) of yellowish to pinkish male flowers (mostly in early spring), and inconspicuous female flowers that later become acorns held in scaly cups. They also share drought tolerance. Few oaks—once thoroughly established—need coaxing through summers with extra water. In fact, many oaks are susceptible to oak-root fungus (*Armariella* spp.) and slowly die when wet and warm conditions occur in summer. For this reason, considerable care needs to be exercised in choosing appropriate companions. Such companions could include other chaparral shrubs, or for underplanting, drought-tolerant ferns (common wood fern, *Dryopteris arguta*, and common sword fern, *Polystichum munitum*), low-growing currants and gooseberries (*Ribes*), yerba buena (*Satureja douglasii*), vancouverias, California fescue (*Festuca californica*), melic grasses (*Melica* spp.), and hummingbird sage (*Salvia spathacea*).

In general, oaks grow readily from fresh acorns gathered in autumn; plant them on their sides half-submerged and they should germinate rapidly after the first rains. Don't store acorns for long, however; they shrivel and lose vigor. Oaks vary in their growth rate but usually qualify as moderate growers: neither rapid nor slow. Once acorns have sprouted in pots, set them out as soon as possible, for they quickly send down long taproots; delay will make transplanting more difficult. It's this taproot that helps find deep water during long, hot summers when soil surfaces are bone dry.

Scrub oaks make excellent barrier or hedge plants, although the deciduous kinds may be seasonally less attractive. Other uses include shaping through judicious pruning into specimen plants, either in large tubs or directly in the ground; many will develop one or a few trunks if suckers are pruned out. The smallest kinds can be used as coarse, woody ground cover or in the back of rock gardens. Here are seven kinds worthy of trial:

Q. dumosa. Scrub oak. The largest and toughest, up to twenty or more feet tall and often developing a miniature multitrunked tree shape. Leathery, evergreen leaves with saw-tooth margins, paler underneath. Scrub oak is highly heat and drought tolerant.

Q. durata. Leather oak. A dense shrub to ten feet tall, favoring serpentine soils in the wild. Aspect similar to that of smaller forms of scrub oak, except the often-curled leaves look dusty and gray-green. This is due to a close covering of minute, white, starlike hairs. Good shrub for poor soils in summer-hot climates. Use as barrier or hedge.

Q. garryana breweri. Brewer oak. A medium-sized shrub with winter deciduous leaves, the leaves oblong and deeply pinnately lobed, the lobes rounded. New leaves are a beautiful pinkish red as they emerge in spring. Excellent as a bonsai subject, specimen, or trained as ground cover to spill over rocks.

Q. garryana semota. Dwarf Garry oak. A medium-sized, densely branched shrub, with leaves similar to those of Brewer oak. Good as a barrier or hedge plant in hot, summer-dry climates.

Q. parvula. Dwarf interior live oak. A medium-sized to large shrub, but prunable to a low, semidecumbent, sprawling shape. Attractive leathery, bright green leaves with serrated margins last all year. Some forms have lovely rose-colored male catkins in spring—especially attractive with blue-flowered ceanothuses. Another good choice for hot, dry summers.

Q. sadleriana. Sadler oak. Unusual handsome, evergreen species to eight feet tall with large, leathery, dark green coarsely toothed leaves, imprinted with a featherlike vein pattern. Fine as a specimen or for the edge of woodland gardens. Tolerates light shade, lots of winter rain, and hot summer temperatures.

Q. vaccinifolia. Huckleberry oak. Particularly fine small, evergreen oak, well adapted to mountain gardens with very cold winters and warm, sunny summers. Tight branches are covered with shiny, huckleberry-shaped leaves, paler beneath. New leaves are bronze or bright red on some forms. Adaptable but slow growing in lowland gardens; superior as a small barrier or hedge.

Rhamnus spp. Buckthorns. Buckthorn family (Rhamnaceae)

HT: 3 to 40 feet. LVS: evergreen or deciduous. FLWS: tiny greenish stars in dense clusters; time varies. SMR WTR: none to occasional deep watering. PROP: cuttings; seeds (stratify). EXP: full sun to shade

Physically, the rhamnuses have many features in common: angular, flexible branches, often with reddish new growth; obovate to broadly elliptical leaves with pinnate veins, which swoop out in looplike curves to leaf margins; tiny teeth along leaf edges; small clusters of inconspicuous greenish to yellow, starlike flowers; and berries with few, large coffee-bean-shaped seeds. Habit varies from tall with many open branches to low and matted with tight, dense branching. Height varies from sprawling ground covers less than three feet tall to small trees with one or a few trunks.

Habitats include wind-swept coastal bluffs; hot, sun-kissed, rocky slopes; cool coastal forests or bog margins; and granite slopes in montane chaparral. Thus, there is some kind of buckthorn for every garden. Uses include as fine evergreen hedges, small specimen trees, borders for woodland gardens, and informal, low-maintenance ground covers. All the buckthorns are noted for attractive leaves and pretty new bark; all bear fruits that are attractive to birds but that act as laxatives for humans. Among them, here are five species in detail:

R. californica. Coffee berry. Choose for the garden according to cultivar or growth form; some, like 'Eve Case,' are low and compact; others grow to ten feet. Some have deep green leaves; others, like variety *tomentella*, bear dusty-looking, gray-green leaves. All are evergreen and drought tolerant. All require full sun for best growth, grow at a moderate rate, and produce dark purple berries. Excellent for woody ground cover, hedge, or barrier, in a mixture with deciduous shrubs, or to complement chaparral shrubs with showy flowers.

R. crocea. Redberry buckthorn. This variable species can create a sprawling, woody ground cover with tiny, glossy, smooth-edged leaves; or it can be a small, upright tree with glossy leaves edged with hollylike teeth. The former is excellent in coastal gardens with summer fog, the latter in hot inland situations as a foundation shrub or barrier plant. All make bright red berries in fall and have evergreen leaves. In order to pick the right form for the garden, inquire from your local nursery as to growth habits of the particular plants they're selling. Drought tolerant and slow growing.

R. pirifolia. Island buckthorn. A large shrub on the Channel Islands, with fine, bright green, broadly elliptical leaves edged with fine teeth. Evergreen leaves and red berries like the last species'. Tough in hot, dry summers, but should have mild winter temperatures. Fine specimen shrub or barrier plant.

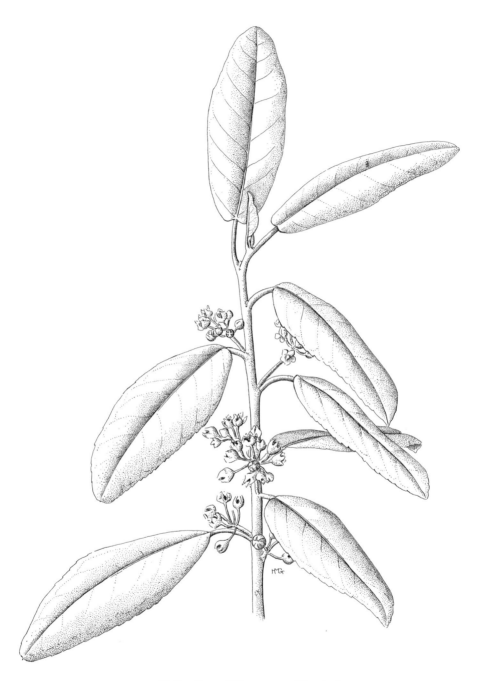

Coffee Berry (*Rhamnus californica*)
flowering branch with leaves

R. purshiana. Cascara sagrada. This plant with "holy bark" is a tall, open shrub or small tree to thirty or more feet with especially long, broadly elliptical leaves that are of pleasing design but winter deciduous. It is fast growing, needs shade and some summer water, and is tolerant of temporarily soggy soils. Dark purple berries in fall. Excellent for the background of woodland gardens, by a pond, or as a specimen tree for shade.

R. rubra. Redbark buckthorn. Similar to coffee berry except leaves are winter deciduous—otherwise always a fine, lively green—and new growth is a striking red, showing to excellent advantage at winter's end. Smaller stature, to a maximum of about five feet. Excellent for the back of rock gardens, especially in the mountains, where it's tolerant of low winter temperatures. Occasional deep summer watering.

Rhododendron macrophyllum. California Rosebay. Heather family (Ericaceae)

HT: 3 to 20 feet. LVS: evergreen. FLWS: clusters of showy rose-purple trumpets; late spring. SMR WTR: moist soil. PROP: cuttings (use bottom heat). EXP: shade

Rosebay rhododendron is a magnificent counterpart to western azalea, a "true" rhododendron-type shrub with firm, leathery, deep green leaves whose edges curl under in sunny situations. Unlike its cousin, however, it is much more demanding both of its native home—the margins of cool coastal forests that are fog swept in summer and rain pelted in winter—and its establishment in the garden. Although it is capable of rapid growth, it may languish for several years if conditions are not to its liking, and transplanting causes setback, probably because of disturbance of the delicate fungal web of mycorrhizae associated with the fine roots. In any event, rosebay is for the shaded coastal garden, where it establishes best as a small seedling or newly rooted cutting. It thrives on undisturbed, acid soil (because of shallow roots) and summer moisture and humidity.

When all is said and done, California rosebay is a truly outstanding shade shrub and can be trained into a small tree. The typical rhododendron leaves make this an attractive plant all year, but the real show is in late May to early June when masses of pale pink to rose-purple flowers cover the branch tips; flowers are as large as those of most cultivated rhododendrons. An added bonus is the pretty, red, velvety-haired seed pods that follow, later splitting into five-pointed stars to spill the tiny seeds. Seeds can be grown on sphagnum under sterile conditions, but it takes much longer for plants to reach flowering size this way. Be careful not to prune behind the old flowers, because this is where next year's flower buds are initiated.

Rosebay can be used in any wooded setting, and it is beautiful when set off by large ferns (lady fern, sword fern, chain fern) or surrounded by mounds of ground covers (redwood sorrel, wild ginger, redwood violet, piggy-back plant, woodland anemone).

Rhododendron occidentale. Western Azalea. Heather family (Ericaceae)

HT: 3 to 15 feet. LVS: winter deciduous. FLWS: close clusters of showy white to pink trumpets, marked yellow; late spring to early summer. SMR WTR: frequent watering. PROP: cuttings; layering. EXP: some shade

Western azalea is one of our most beautiful native shrubs and is well worth any effort to grow it in the garden. In winter, the open branches bear umbrellalike clusters of branchlets. In spring, bright green leaves usher in the awakening of other flowers; late spring sees massive displays of glorious large, fragrant azalea flowers. Fall is the time for leaves to turn burnished bronze or flame orange (with chilly fall nights). The profusion, aroma, and color of the flowers is at once arresting and satisfying. Several named varieties are now available, especially from the Stage Coach Hill area of the northern redwood country, where flowers may be pure white or pale to deep rose pink and be single or double, most of them marked with an upper patch of yellow or orange. These varieties must be propagated exclusively by vegetative means; cuttings strike root readily with rooting hormone and bottom heat; layering is a dependable but slower way.

Although western azalea ranges through a broad band of elevations and exposures—from sea level to six thousand feet in the south, and from the edge of deeply shaded redwood forests to the brilliant sun of serpentine seeps—it performs best in partial shade and luxuriates in cool coastal or midmontane gardens. A rapid grower, it reaches quickly for sun in a shady place, but deep shade will limit flowering.

Western azalea can be used in just about every conceivable wooded niche of the garden; it is outstanding as a specimen, behind a pond, or along a stream. It complements other shade lovers such as bush anemone (*Carpenteria californica*), spicebush (*Calycanthus occidentalis*), or ninebark (*Physocarpus capitatus*), and can have an underpinning of lower shrubs such as mahonias or salal (*Gaultheria shallon*), as well as ferns, bleeding heart, or wild ginger. Since it has shallow roots it should be planted away from foot traffic. It also needs a rather acid soil; enrich the topsoil with pine or redwood needles for best results.

Rhus spp. Sumacs. Sumac family (Anacardiaceae)

HT: 3 to 15 feet. LVS: evergreen. FLWS: in dense panicles, white to pinkish; spring. SMR WTR: none. PROP: cuttings; seeds (stratify). EXP: full sun

California's native sumacs are nothing like the eastern kinds; for in place of large, pinnately compound leaves, ours have simple, leathery, evergreen, oblong to elliptical leaves. So handsome and durable are these leaves that California's rhuses should be grown for their leaves alone. Sumacs also produce a profusion of long-lasting bloom from mid to late spring, in close clusters or panicles. Flowers are pretty even in bud, being rosy tinted and open to tiny bowls of white or white blushed pink. Colorful fruits on two species replace flowers by summer's end, and can be used to make drinks (soaked, they create a lemonade-flavored concoction).

Since all sumacs favor the hot, rocky slopes of chaparral in southern California, they are excellent subjects for inland and desert gardens, where they need little or no summer water. Relatively slow of growth, they mature into handsome foundation shrubs or can be used for informal hedges and barriers. Their fine leaves can be used in combination with deciduous shrubs, and their deep green color is a good foil to gray-leafed kinds. Laurel sumac is also trainable as a small tree and excellent for a large container. Here are details on the three species:

R. integrifolia. Lemonade berry. A small shrub to about six feet, with broadly elliptical, flat leaves, usually finely toothed along the edges. Sticky, reddish fruits can make a lemonade substitute. Somewhat winter tender.

R. laurina. Laurel sumac. The largest of all, and prunable into tree form. Leaves are a beautiful bronze-red when new, later becoming bright green, and are folded; flower clusters are airier than in the others; fruits a whitish green. Foliage is pleasantly lemon scented. Winter tender.

R. ovata. Sugar bush. Similar to lemonade berry, but the leaves are folded and the margins smooth. Fruits similar in appearance and use. The hardiest in winter.

Rhus trilobata. Squaw Bush or Sourberry. Sumac family (Anacardiaceae)

HT: 2 to 5 feet. LVS: winter deciduous. FLWS: in small racemes, pale yellow; early to mid-spring. SMR WTR: little or none. PROP: cuttings; layering. EXP: full sun to light shade

Squaw bush is such a distinctive shrub, it's treated separately here. On first glance it might be mistaken for its cousin poison oak (*Toxicodendron diversilobum*), but there are many differences. The low branches of squaw bush arch outwards, drooping at their tips, lending a special pattern to this shrub. The leaves, composed of three smallish, elliptical leaflets, are dark green, slightly fuzzy, and with crenated margins. The bark, strongly astringent, is palpably fragrant on hot summer days. The pretty, modest, bell-shaped flowers are pale yellow and borne in profusion at branch tips early in the year. These are followed by sticky reddish fruits reminiscent of California's other sumacs. Altogether, squaw bush is an interesting shrub that combines traits not matched by any other, but that may not easily fit into many landscapes because of these same characteristics. Its chief charms are its ease of culture and natural look in an informal woodland setting.

Squaw bush is one of the most widely distributed western shrubs, finding a home near canyon bottoms or lightly shaded slopes in the drier parts of mountains or high deserts. Here, it forms nearly impenetrable colonies with dispatch. Its use in the garden is dictated by these facts. Use it for a low, informal hedge or near a watercourse with other rambling plants, such as the wild roses (particularly *Rosa californica*), mugwort (*Artemisia douglasiana*), currants (*Ribes* spp.), and redberry buckthorn (*Rhamnus crocea*). It is drought tolerant, easy to propagate by layered branches, and forgiving of hot summers and cold winters.

Ribes spp. Currants. Gooseberry family (Grossulariaceae)

HT: 3 to 12 feet. LVS: winter deciduous. FLWS: dense, sometimes hanging racemes of several colors; early spring to late winter. SMR WTR: occasional deep watering. PROP: cuttings. EXP: full sun to light shade

Our native currants share many attributes: upright, multibranched habit; attractive maple-shaped, sticky, fragrant leaves (the fragrance reminiscent of sage); and chains of colorful flowers at winter's end. Some, like the chaparral currant (*R. malvaceum*), even flower during mild winters or in late autumn, a trait that enlivens the garden at a slow time.

The currants are among the easiest shrubs to grow; water them thoroughly initially, then taper off to occasional deep waterings, and they'll grow rapidly and look attractive through summer. They're easy to propagate from semihardwood cuttings in spring. Use them to advantage where the masses of colorful blooms will be appreciated at winter's end. This be could be as a backdrop to light up a woodland garden—they're especially fine around oaks because of their drought tolerance—or as a foundation shrub, specimen, or even informal hedge. Here are the best species:

R. *aureum*. Golden currant. For light shade. Unusual in its small, smooth green leaves and delicate racemes of bright yellow flowers, often centered red. Edible smooth, red berries follow. Rapid growth. Starts also from suckers.

R. *cereum*. Wax currant. Multiple branches from base of plant; handsome silvery-gray bark in winter; smallish dull to gray-green leaves; and tubular, pale pink flowers in early summer. Withstands very cold winters. Reddish berries have good flavor.

R. *indecorum*. White-flowered currant. Shrub to eight feet, from southern California; winter tender. Highly aromatic, sticky leaves and nearly pure white flowers in earliest spring. Full sun.

R. *malvaceum*. Chaparral currant. Highly drought-tolerant shrub, which will take full sun or light shade under oaks. Dull green leaves and pale pink to purple flowers, often in midwinter. Tough and durable.

R. nevadense. Sierra currant. Small shrub, often half-sprawling, with modest chains of pink-purple flowers, the petals barely flaring. Favors light shade in situations with occasional summer water. Good for mountain gardens; winter cold tolerant.

R. sanguineum. Flowering currant. The most widely used form is variety *gluti-nosum.* The main species has rose-red flowers, but the variety has pale pink to rose-purple flowers of great beauty at winter's end. Widely used for the edge of woodland gardens; responds to occasional summer water. Dull blue berries of questionable palatability.

R. viscosissimum. Sticky currant. A low, half-sprawling shrub from high montane forests. Sticky leaves; pale flowers that combine shades of yellow, green, and pink. Early summer bloomer. Best for mountain gardens.

Ribes bracteosum. Stink Currant. Gooseberry family (Grossulariaceae)

HT: 3 to 14 feet. LVS: winter deciduous. FLWS: in racemes, inconspicuous and greenish; through spring. SMR WTR: some deep watering. PROP: cuttings. EXP: shade

The unglamorous title of stink currant should not put off any gardener; actually the smell of the leaves here is no stronger than for most other currants, but the appearance is quite unlike that of the others. Stink currant favors moist coastal forests in the far north, where its broad branches carry large, bright green, maplelike leaves of great beauty. In fact, these are the main reason for growing this shrub; the inconspicuous greenish bronze flowers neither add to nor detract from its appearance, and the tight clusters of dark purple berries are incidental.

Use stink currant as a beautiful understory shrub in a moist forest, such as under redwoods, Sitka spruce, coast hemlock, or Douglas fir. Here it can form a backdrop or informal hedge. Its leaves blend well with vine maple (*Acer circinatum*) and thimbleberry (*Rubus parviflorus*) or complement those of rosebay rhododendron (*Rhododendron macrophyllum*), western azalea (*Rhododendron occidentale*), or spicebush (*Calycanthus occidentalis*).

Ribes viburnifolium. Evergreen Currant. Gooseberry family (Grossulariaceae)

HT: to 3 feet. LVS: evergreen. FLWS: small racemes of dark maroon flowers; early spring. SMR WTR: little or none. PROP: cuttings; layering. EXP: light shade

Evergreen currant is most unusual. It grows in canyons, often in the shade of taller shrubs or near oaks on California's Channel Islands. Unlike other currants, the stems are mostly horizontal, arching over gracefully and striking root as they touch the ground. Leaves are shiny, rounded to oval, lightly scalloped, fragrantly scented, and evergreen; the flowers are tiny, open saucers of maroon, more curious than beautiful.

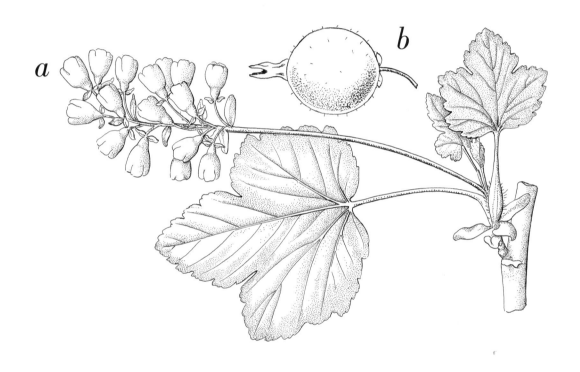

Sierra Currant (*Ribes nevadense*)
a. flowering branch   *b*. fruit detail

Pink Flowering Currant (*Ribes sanguineum glutinosum*)
Flowering branch with leaves

The main attributes are its low habit, making it useful as a woody ground cover in light shade—particularly suited to planting with oaks—and its handsome, deliciously fragrant leaves.

Use evergreen currant as a ground cover in light shade, or for a low informal barrier. It grows rapidly and needs little care, but it needs protection from heavy winter frosts.

Ribes spp. Gooseberries. Gooseberry family (Grossulariaceae)

HT: 2 to 9 feet. LVS: winter deciduous. FLWS: axillary, hanging under leaves, mostly red-purplish; early to mid-spring. SMR WTR: occasional deep watering. PROP: cuttings. EXP: shade

Even though usually assigned to the same genus, gooseberries differ in several particulars from currants: branches have stout nodal spines and sometimes additional soft bristly spines between; leaves are small and seldom scented; flowers are borne in axillary clusters under the leaves. Gooseberries favor canyon bottoms in light to moderate shade, from the oaks of foothills to the pine forests of mountains. They grow rapidly, are moderate in their use of water (they'll look much better with some summer water), and vary from winter tough to slightly tender according to origin. The spiny nature of the branches is compensated for by the spring floral display, if branches are placed so you can look up into them from beneath. The charming flowers are reminiscent of miniature fuchsias, and favored by hummingbirds. The red to purple fruits that follow are frequently spine covered and thus difficult to use for food, but are attractive to birds.

Gooseberries make a wonderful informal hedge in the shade, or they excel as shrubs for the backdrop of a wooded garden. At least one, the fuchsia-flowered gooseberry, is also decorative as a specimen plant. Here are the best species:

R. binominatum. Creeping gooseberry. A sprawling, crawling subshrub of high inner Coast Range mountains. Interesting (but not showy) green and white flowers in early summer. Cold tolerant.

R. californicum. California gooseberry. A five-foot shrub of low-elevation forests, spiny only at the nodes and with flowers red-purple and white. Easy to grow.

R. lobbii. Lobb's gooseberry. A low shrub to about two feet, with unusually attractive red-purple and pale yellowish flowers. Especially fine for mountain gardens; winter hardy.

R. menziesii. Canyon gooseberry. Similar to *R. californicum* but with bristly spines between the nodes in addition to the nodal spines.

R. montigenum. Mountain gooseberry. Small, half-sprawling shrub to three or four feet, from high mountain forests. The curious saucer-shaped, orange and red flowers are miniaturized marvels upon close inspection. A fitting shrub for mountain gardens.

R. roezlii. Sierra gooseberry. A rather small shrub, to three or four feet, with large red-purple flowers. Berries are especially spiny. Good for mountain gardens with cold winters.

R. speciosum. Fuchsia-flowered gooseberry. Outstanding for the long branches decked in bright red tubular flowers, loved by hummingbirds. Somewhat winter tender. Fantastic for an oak woodland. California's showiest gooseberry.

Romneya coulteri. Matilija Poppy. Poppy family (Papaveraceae)

HT: 4 to 8 feet. LVS: winter deciduous. FLWS: very large, solitary white poppies with golden centers; summer. SMR WTR: none. PROP: root cuttings; root divisions. EXP: full sun

Matilija poppy is one of California's crown jewels. Strictly speaking, it is not a shrub; rather it is a large perennial with woody base. Also unlike many shrubs, the roots wander far and wide, sending up stalks here and there in a helter-skelter fashion, so Matilija poppy must be afforded lots of room. A striking plant even out of flower—with bluish green, deeply slashed leaves on tall stalks—it is simply spectacular in flower, with a long succession in summer of huge, white saucers measuring several inches across. The petals, crinkled like crepe paper, surround dozens of bright golden stamens.

Matilija poppy is actually described as two species, although *R. trichocalyx* mainly differs in having hair-covered sepals. Both hail from the openings of summer-hot chaparral in southern California, where the roots quickly establish large colonies in areas that have been burned or otherwise disturbed. Although seeds may be set by the thousands, germination is uneven and unpredictable. To prepare seeds try igniting dry leaves above the soil, soaking the seeds in kerosene, or using long stratification. Matilija poppy is mainly propagated by root divisions; these should be potted up until strong growth and vigorous roots are made, since direct transplanting seldom works. Vigorously rooted new plants transfer well to the garden in winter.

Matilija poppy is best planted in a site devoted exclusively to it, and one with plenty of sun and warmth. Around the periphery complementary shrubs can be included: fremontias, ceanothuses, salvias, and bush poppy (*Dendromecon rigida*). Penstemons are excellent subjects for the foreground; their blue or purple flowers complement the white and gold theme of Matilija poppy. Once established, Matilija grows with vigor and enthusiasm, but to maintain health and good appearance clip off all branches to ground level at fall's end; this assures vigorous new growth the following spring and removes unsightly old branches in winter.

Rosa spp. Wild Roses. Rose family (Rosaceae)

HT: 1 to 9 feet. LVS: winter deciduous. FLWS: open single roses from white to deep rose, scented; mostly late spring to summer. SMR WTR: occasional deep watering. PROP: root divisions; cuttings; seeds (stratify). EXP: full sun to shade

California's several wild roses share more similarities than differences: multiple canes from wandering roots; stems lined with prickles; pinnately compound, serrated leaves; and small clusters of open, single rose flowers mostly in some shade of pink. These have a fine perfume at close range and bright red-orange "hips" for fruit. The hips, beloved by birds, are a good source of vitamin C and make excellent preserves and teas. Most wild roses favor forest edges from sea level to the subalpine and from moist coastal forests to the edges of high deserts, most often in canyon bottoms, frequently along dry stream banks. There they may form hedges through their wandering roots. Most favor light shade, although at least one species, *R. californica*, may thrive in full sun where there's some summer fog.

Wild roses grow readily from root divisions, have rapid growth once established, and make fine informal hedges or barriers, leafless in winter and laden with flowers in summer and brightly colored fruits in autumn. Like other plants with wanderlust they need to be alotted extra room, but otherwise they demand little. The low-growing kinds make excellent informal ground covers for shade. Trim back canes in late fall for extra vigor the following year. Here is a brief synopsis of species:

R. californica. California wild rose. One of the easiest to grow, with stout re-curved prickles, large flowers. Grows to nine feet. Will take full sun.

R. gymnocarpa. Wood rose. Dense shrub to six or more feet that takes deep shade (notably in redwood forests). Small, dark pink sweet-smelling roses and small, sepalless hips; stems with fine prickles.

R. nutkana. Nootka rose. A striking shrub to six feet with stout, straight prickles and large, handsome, deep pink flowers. Favors coastal forests with summer moisture.

R. pinetorum. Pine rose. A modest shrub to three feet from the pine belt, with slender prickles and modest flowers. Good for mountain gardens.

R. pisocarpa. Cluster rose. Similar to ground rose except the flowers are borne in clusters. Foothill to mountain gardens. Nice miniature form.

R. spithamnea. Ground rose. Miniature rose that forms low ground cover in shade. Charming for woodland garden.

R. woodsii. Wood's or Sierra rose. Shrub to nine feet with slender prickles and large, handsome flowers similar to California wild rose. Color may vary from white to pink, and plants can be trained low as ground covers. Excellent for dry areas with cold winters.

Rubus parviflorus. Thimbleberry. Rose family (Rosaceae)

HT: 3 to 6 feet. LVS: winter deciduous. FLWS: large white single roses; spring and early summer. SMR WTR: occasional deep watering. PROP: stem or root divisions; cuttings. EXP: shade

Thimbleberry is atypical of its genus, in which stems are usually spiny and plants frequently are viny. Instead, thimbleberry has multiple upright stems from widely traveling roots, the stems lined with long strips of brownish bark. The handsome large leaves are pale green, soft and velvety to the touch, and maplelike in shape. From stem ends come small clusters of pretty white, single-rose-like flowers followed by thimble-shaped, delicately flavored, deep red berries in midsummer. Thimbleberry slowly loses its leaves in fall: often they turn palest yellow just before they drop.

Since thimbleberry grows in many zones—wherever there are cool forest glades—it is adaptable to gardens at many elevations, given some shade and summer water. When happy the roots grow rapidly, sending up vigorous new shoots over wide areas; you can consider ways to contain thimbleberry or else give it carte blanche to roam widely. You can easily pull off new shoots where they occur in unwanted places, but this requires diligence.

Thimbleberry is an altogether attractive shrub with pretty leaves that are fragrant on hot days, pleasing flowers, and brightly colored berries. It is the essence of a shade shrub, where it can wander among ground covers such as redwood sorrel (*Oxalis oregana*), wild ginger (*Asarum caudatum*), redwood violet (*Viola sempervirens*), or woodland anemone (*Anemone deltoidea*). It is also pretty combined with various woodland ferns.

Rubus spectabilis. Salmonberry. Rose family (Rosaceae)

HT: 6 to 15 feet. LVS: winter deciduous. FLWS: small deep dark-pink single roses; spring. SMR WTR: occasional deep watering. PROP: stem divisions; cuttings. EXP: shade

Salmonberry is a sort of cross between the sprawling blackberries and the upright thimbleberry; its canes stand tall and straight for several feet, then arch over at their tips. Vigorous and fast growing, salmonberry soon establishes a hedge, which is dense and all but impenetrable. Its pretty leaves are divided into three ovate, textured, dark green leaflets, the stems lined with slender, weak prickles. The flowers are of the lovely deep color that "rose" denotes. The most striking feature, however, is the brilliant orange-red berries, which look like so many salmon eggs surrounded by a fringe

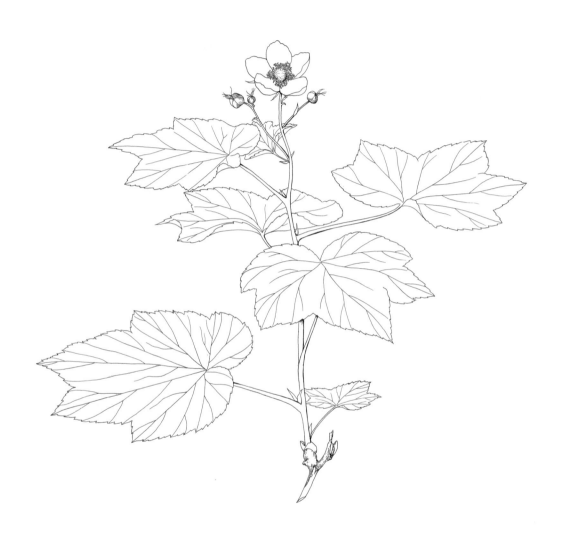

Thimbleberry (*Rubus parviflorus*)
leafy branches with flowers

of old stamens. These berries are relished by mammals and birds alike and are tasty to humans, but not as choice as blackberries or raspberries.

Because salmonberry grows so prolifically with summer water and shade, it is great for a barrier plant or informal hedge in the shade. There, its pretty blossoms and striking fruits are an added bonus. It does best where summers are cool and foggy, winters damp and rainy. One special use would be to create a "living tunnel" through a large stand, in the manner of several trails in the redwood country.

Salazaria mexicana. Paperbag bush. Mint family (Lamiaceae)

HT: 2 to 3 feet. LVS: summer deciduous. FLWS: in small spikes, two lips with a two-toned white and purple skein; through spring. SMR WTR: none. PROP: cuttings; seeds. EXP: full sun

Paperbag bush is a distinctive small shrub from California's warm deserts, where it often grows in gravelly soils. The plants are unusual even among the many small desert shrubs that lose their leaves in summer drought, for the bluish green branches stand stiffly at attention, then turn down at their spiny tips. This makes the shrub recognizable any time of the year, unlike so many of its natural companions. In spring, short spikes of curious two-lipped, snapdragonlike flowers put on their brief show with an attractive two-toned color scheme: pale purple to white on the upper half, rich purple below. Flowers are followed by "fruits" that look like miniature inflated paper bags, the kind kids love to pop, but actually they're inflated sepals, and the real fruits are hidden inside.

Because paperbag bush lives where it receives scant moisture with excellent drainage—in some of the hottest places in the state—it should be grown only in inland or desert gardens. There its unique appearance could create an eye-catching low, informal hedge. Or it could be combined with other small, spring-blooming shrubs for contrasting flower colors, such as apricot mallow (*Sphaeralcea ambigua*), desert senna (*Cassia armata*), and desert alyssum (*Lepidium fremontii*).

Salix spp. Willows. Willow family (Salicaceae)

HT: 3 inches to 50 feet. LVS: winter deciduous. FLWS: in catkins, male and female on separate plants, appearing before and with new leaves; spring. SMR WTR: moist soil. PROP: cuttings; layering; seeds. EXP: full sun to light shade

California's thirty-plus species of willow range the gamut from sprawling, miniature alpine shrubs to multistemmed trees, all favoring wet habitats: perennial streams and rivers, lake and marsh borders, and wet meadows. Because they grow rapidly and readily from cuttings, they have the ability to quickly colonize wet areas. Be aware, however, of certain liabilites: their rampant growth, brittle branches, thirsty roots, and messy fluff from the hair-covered seeds of female plants. Since they're

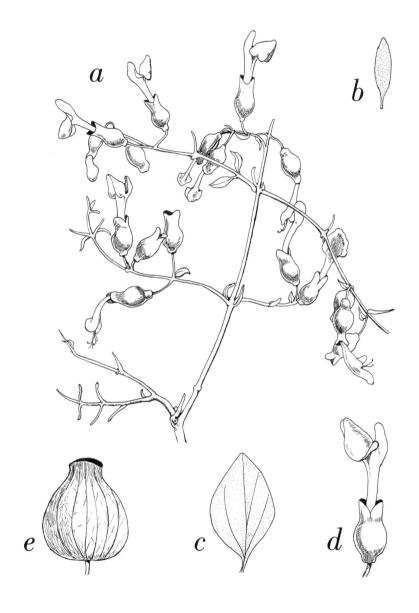

a

b

e   *c*   *d*

Paperbag Bush (*Salazaria mexicana*)
a. flowering branches   *b*. floral bract   *c*. leaf detail
d. flower detail   *e*. inflated sepals in fruit stage

dioecious—they have separate male and female plants—the selection of only the males is possible. The males' brief early-spring catkins bear pollen-laden stamens (hay-fever sufferers, be warned), but there's no mess from cottony seeds.

Willows also have virtues in large-scale gardens. For example, they quickly establish a screen of dense branches. Twigs are beautifully colored yellow, orange-brown, or red, a fine asset in winter. The "pussy willow"-stage catkins, covered in wooly bud scales before opening, are a pretty fixture in late winter and make excellent long-lasting dry bouquets.

Liabilities and assets aside, willows are unlikely to fulfill a role in most gardens, particularly those devoted to the wise use of water. Certainly the larger species, such as *S. lasiandra* (red willow) and *S. lasiolepis* (arroyo willow) can be summarily excluded from all but the largest-scale landscapes. Others, such as *S. lemmonii* and *S. drummondiana*, grow to less than fifteen feet tall and are pretty in a wet spot in mountain gardens.

The only willows likely to be candidates for the average garden are two alpines with low, sprawling branches half-buried in the soil. These charming alpines (*S. antiplasta anglorum*, alpine willow, and *S. nivalis*, snow willow) send up short side branches only inches tall. Both bear fuzzy catkins of great beauty on separate short branches, the former with the new leaves, the latter after the new leaves appear.

It's a shame that despite the lovely picture these two create in nature—tapestries over granite boulders, where they swirl around red heather (*Phyllodoce breweri*) and white heather (*Cassiope mertensiana*)—they're likely to fail or slowly waste away in lowland gardens. Better to leave dreams of such mountain scenes for the mountain gardens. If you're still determined, experiment with growing them from seeds. Sadly, neither of the "heathers" mentioned seems amenable to life in the lowlands either.

There are also two bushy willows with potential for wet places in large gardens. These are sandbar willow (*S. hindsiana*), a lover of gravelly streambeds where surface water may retreat in summer, and Del Norte willow (*S. delnortensis*), a rare endemic of bouldery stream banks in the far northern Siskiyou Mountains just next to the Oregon border. Both are unusual for willows in their possession of white to silvery, fur-covered leaves, sandbar with narrowly lance-shaped leaves and Del Norte with broadly elliptical leaves. Both are adapted to areas of hot summers and could provide a welcome addition as a leaf-color foil to the normally green-leafed shrubs of wet areas. For dramatic effect, try them along a dry stream border with azaleas and ninebark, or behind a pond where the silvery foliage is reflected.

One last noteworthy willow comes from subalpine meadows, where it lines streams carrying snowmelt. This is the Mono willow, *Salix orestera*, a compact, dwarf shrub seldom exceeding three feet, with crooked, deep-purple twigs and bark. If this little willow could be adapted to ponds in lowland gardens, its lovely bark would be a special focal point in winter.

Salvia spp. Sages. Mint family (Lamiaceae)

HT: 1 to 8 feet. LVS: evergreen (or partly summer deciduous). FLWS: mostly in whorls arranged in spikes, two-lipped and white, blue, or purple; spring to summer. SMR WTR: little or none. PROP: cuttings; seeds. EXP: full sun

California's several native sages have much in common with the culinary sage from the Mediterranean, *S. officinalis*: they're small shrubs with highly fragrant dull green to gray foliage and bear spikes of showy whorled, two-lipped flowers irresistible to honeybees. These salvias live in deserts or along the edge of sun-drenched chaparral in central to southern California. All are characterized by pairs of textured leaves and showy flower spikes from late spring through summer. All are well adapted to summer drought, demanding minimal maintenance except for the need to be sheared back after flowering and to have old growth cut back to encourage new growth in spring. The latter practice is important when cold, damp winter conditions have prevailed, for otherwise older growth would rot out.

Some species are frost tender; others live in high deserts where freezing is the rule. One other note: under prolonged drought and heat, sages lose their leaves temporarily; this may be avoided by judicious use of summer water (which unfortunately could shorten the overall life span; the native plant gardener is always faced with this dilemma of good looks versus shorter life span).

Sages are wonderful for the background in an herb garden, blending easily with such culinary herbs as cooking sage, savory (*Satureja* spp.), thymes (*Thymus* spp.), oregano and marjoram (*Origanum* spp.), and rosemary (*Rosmarinus officinalis*). They also complement larger chaparral shrubs, and extend the flowering period beyond that of taller, spring-blooming shrubs such as the ceanothuses, fremontias, manzanitas, and bush poppy (*Dendromecon rigida*). Their grayish leaves are a good foil for greener leaves, and their mostly bluish to purplish flowers complement the white and yellow Matilija poppy (*Romneya coulteri*). New plants can be easily established by cuttings in spring, or in quantity, from the prolific seeds. Here are several species to choose from:

S. apiana. White or bee sage. A closely clumped shrub with large, handsome, grayish white, strongly scented oval leaves. Tall flower spikes to seven or eight feet with a long succession of pale purple to white flowers. Loved by bees. Use as a dramatic specimen plant. Sensitive to winter cold and damp conditions.

S. clevelandii. Cleveland sage. One of the best small shrubs; crinkled, scalloped, narrowly elliptical leaves of dull gray-green with showy blue-purple flowers in summer.

S. dorrii and *S. pachyphylla*. Desert sages. A pair of similar low, spreading shrubs with spoon-shaped, gray, unwrinkled, smooth-margined leaves and showy spikes of blue-purple flowers complemented by purplish bracts. They withstand considerable winter cold.

S. eremostachya. Santa Rosa Mountain sage. A small, rather loosely branched shrub with lance-oblong, wrinkled, bright green leaves and flower spikes of delicate, pale blue-purple frilly flowers. Mid to late spring.

S. leucophylla. Purple sage. A medium-sized shrub with open habit in age; large, wrinkled, whitish leaves with fine scallops along their edges; and spikes of pale purple flowers in summer. Very drought tolerant. Susceptible to damp conditions.

S. mellifera. Black sage. Perhaps the least attractive; a compact shrub with dull green, wrinkled, scalloped, narrowly lanceolate to oblong leaves and modest spikes of pale purple to almost white flowers; strong scent. Excellent, however, for bees.

S. mohavensis. Mojave sage. A small shrub with wrinkled, scalloped, dull green, lance-oblong leaves and headlike spikes of pale blue to lavender flowers. Well adapted to very hot summers.

S. sonomensis. Sonoma sage. Low, creeping, woody ground cover with pale gray-green, wrinkled leaves and one-foot spikes of pale purple flowers. Excellent for containing dry embankments or rock walls.

S. vaseyi. Wand sage. A medium-sized shrub with handsome whitish, oblong-ovate leaves and long, graceful, wandlike branches of whitish flower spikes in late spring. Tolerant of high heat; great for rocky places.

Sambucus spp. Elderberries. Honeysuckle family (Caprifoliaceae)

HT: 2 to 25 feet. LVS: winter deciduous. FLWS: tiny creamy flowers densely packed into pyramid-shaped or flat-topped clusters; late spring to early summer. SMR WTR: occasional deep watering. PROP: suckers; cuttings; seeds (stratify). EXP: full sun to shade

California's elderberries range from low, mounded mountain shrubs to small trees along canyon bottoms in coastal forests. All grow rapidly, have thirsty, deeply delving roots, fluted bark on old trunks (old specimens develop trunks much like those of oak trees), and long, straight water shoots from the base or lower parts of the trunks (these should be pruned out unless specifically desired). Large, smelly, pinnately compound leaves are arranged in pairs along branches, and myriad tiny, creamy to greenish white flowers appear in dense clusters. The smell of the leaves, unpleasant and intense to some (but reminding others of peanut butter!), may be partially responsible

Black Sage (*Salvia mellifera*)   *a*. flowering spike   *b*. flowering detail
c. upper petal and stamen detail   *d*. stamen enlarged

for a reputed medicinal value; use crushed leaves to relieve the sting of nettles and bees. Flowers are followed by dull blue to bright red berries, which are colorful in themselves and tempting morsels to birds. These berries are good cooked (the blue ones only), making strong-flavored preserves, pies, or wine. The arching structure of the outer branches gives strong form to the plants in their winter leafless condition.

Elderberries may never win a contest for beauty of form, but they are a pleasant adjunct to a woodland garden for the background and are fine sources of colorful fruits and pretty spring flowers. A bonus in the blue elderberry is the powerful perfume that the flowers release in the early evening hours. Natural companions include California buckeye (*Aesculus californica*) and redbud (*Cercis occidentalis*) for blue elderberry, and western azalea (*Rhododendron occidentale*), western spicebush (*Calycanthus occidentalis*), and stink currant (*Ribes bracteosum*) for red. The few species are easy to sort out as follows:

> *S. caerulea* and *S. mexicana*. Blue elderberries. A very similar species pair; both are capable of making small trees in hot environments, and both have flat-topped clusters of flowers and dull blue, edible berries. The former has more leaflets per leaf and generally occurs in the pine belt. The latter is from lower elevations and more appropriate for lowland gardens.

> *S. callicarpa*. Red elderberry. A small tree; from moist coastal canyons, it needs light shade and more summer water than others. Pretty, pyramidal flower clusters in midspring and bright red but inedible berries in summer.

> *S. microbotrys*. Mountain elderberry. A low shrub to about two feet from granite scree, in openings of subalpine forest. Attractive pyramidal flower clusters in early summer and brilliant scarlet berries later. The showiest fruits of all, but inedible.

Senecio blochmanae and douglasii. Bush Senecios. Sunflower family (Asteraceae)

HT: 2 to 5 feet. LVS: sometimes summer deciduous. FLWS: yellow daisies in flat-topped clusters; late spring to fall. FLWS: yellow daisies in flat-topped clusters; late spring to fall. SMR WTR: little or none. PROP: cuttings (take half-ripe wood); seeds. EXP: full sun

California's two bush senecios are similar in appearance if not in habitat. Both are low, rounded bushes with an open appearance due to the very narrow leaves, which are pinnately divided into linear, feathery segments in *S. douglasii* and undivided in *S. blochmanae*. Both bear showy, flat-topped clusters of bright yellow daisies with rays and yellow centers (disc flowers). Both also flower over a long period, with *S. douglasii* continuing into the autumn months when little else gives color. Many find the fuzzy white seed heads unattractive, but a bush full of these can actually be quite beautiful in the proper setting.

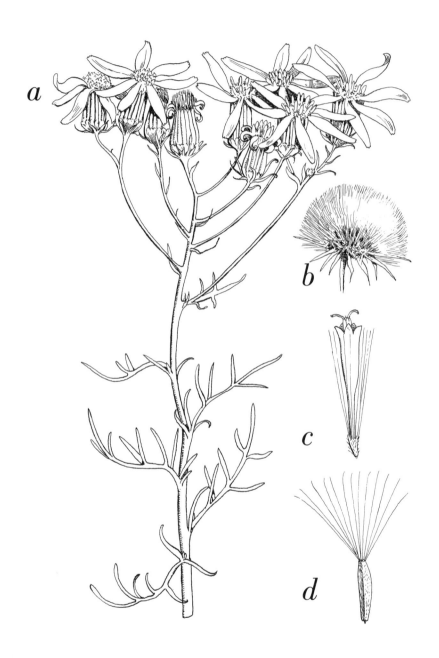

Douglas's Bush Senecio (*Senecio douglasii*)
a. flowering branches   *b*. fruiting head   *c*. disc floret detail   *d*. fruit detail

Because S. *douglasii* favors the margins of coastal sage and chaparral (also occurring in a varietal form on the desert), it needs plenty of sun, favors hot summers, and needs excellent drainage, preferably in rocky or sandy soil. It will flower more and lose fewer leaves when given supplemental summer water, but this also shortens the life span. Fortunately, shrubs are easy to replace from seeds, and usually each shrub furnishes more than enough future seeds. By contrast, S. *blochmanae* is a strictly coastal shrub on sand dunes: it requires cool summers and excellent drainage (again in sandy soils). Both species give cheerful color through the dry season, and so are welcome additions to a mixed border or in front of taller chaparral shrubs.

Sequoia sempervirens. Coast Redwood. Redwood family (Taxodiaceae)

HT: up to 360 feet. LVS: evergreen needles. FLWS: minute pollen cones in winter; small, woody seed cones ripen in fall. SMR WTR: some. PROP: suckers; seeds. EXP: light shade

You may well wonder what the world's tallest tree is doing in a shrub book. Were it not for the fact that occasional specimens behave like shrubs, it would not be here. Although the soaring spires of redwood create enormous trees, nature has pruned some individuals overlooking the Sonoma coast into broad, dense shrubberies no more than four to six feet high! Whether these particular individuals are genetically different no one has determined, for coast redwood seldom grows directly next to the ocean. Determination of whether normal-sized redwoods and this shrubby coastal form are genetically different would be confirmed only if both forms were to retain these differences in a common garden. There is potential to create a truly unusual and dramatic hedge for foggy coastal gardens. Shear it heavily as new growth appears each spring, and keep a steady eye on it all summer to make sure overzealous shoots don't overtake others.

Grown this way, the redwood has few rivals for its density as a natural hedge; gardenwise, it's similar to the popular English yew hedges common in eastern and English gardens. Unlike yew, however, coast redwood grows rapidly, and it is likely to prove superior for establishing a hedge in short order. Another imaginative use for coast redwood is containerizing it as a bonsai subject.

Coast redwood's liabilities should be noted: shallow, thirsty, wide-ranging roots (never plant it near water or sewage pipes); susceptibility to hot, dry summer conditions; and intolerance of long periods of freezing weather.

Shepherdia argentea. Buffalo Berry. Oleaster family (Elaeagnaceae)

HT: Up to 20 feet, but often less. LVS: winter deciduous. FLWS: tiny and brownish; males in small clusters, female single; April and May. SMR WTR: occasional deep watering. PROP: cuttings (use bottom heat); seeds (stratify). EXP: full sun to light shade

Buffalo berry is rare in California but common through the Great Basin and Range Province. It prefers stream sides, where it is to be found occasionally on the east side

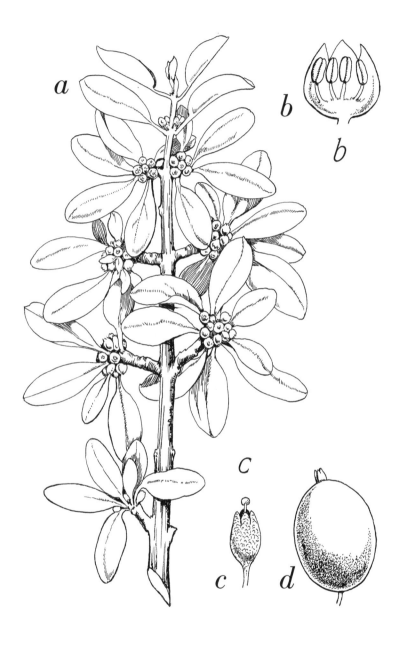

Buffalo Berry (*Shepherdia argentea*)
a. fruiting branches   *b.* male flower detail   *c.* female flower detail
d. fruit detail

of the Sierra Nevada, perhaps companion to water birch, wax currant, or service berry. This shrub stands out for its silvery scales on new twigs, on the backs of leaves, or even on the sour but edible berries. It is handsome in leaf or berry, but the flowers are tiny, dull, and insignificant.

Buffalo berry would thrive best where it receives hot summer sun but is watered deeply every three or four weeks. It should be considered as a choice for a dense shrubbery, where a leafy barrier is wanted in summer, or to plant toward the back of a rock garden with small, brightly flowered shrubs in front.

Simmondsia chinensis. Jojoba or Goat-nut. Boxwood family (Buxaceae)

HT: 3 to 7 feet. LVS: evergreen. FLWS: inconspicuous and greenish; male in short axillary clusters and female single; both in spring. SMR WTR: none. PROP: cuttings. EXP: full sun

Jojoba has gained fame in the last few years for its high-quality oil (from the nut), used as a lubricant and cosmetic ingredient and for food. It has seldom been indicated for the landscape, but it is not without potential: it's a tough (but slow growing) shrub with attractive manzanitalike, pale green to bluish-green, leathery evergreen leaves. It tolerates heat, needs no extra water, and favors slightly alkaline or salty soils. Flowerwise, jojoba wins few points; its male flowers are small greenish saucers with pale yellow stamens borne in small clumps in leaf axils; its nodding female flowers occur singly between leaves, with green sepals and a protruding green pistil that ripens into a nut. Because plants are either male or female, they should be propagated from cuttings; if production of nuts is important, be sure to include one male plant for pollination.

Jojoba is a good-looking shrub all year for the desert or hot inland garden; it can be pruned into an attractive hedge or provide a pleasing background to lower-growing, seasonally colorful shrubs.

Solanum spp. Native Nightshades or Blue Witch. Nightshade family (Solanaceae)

HT: 1 to 6 feet. LVS: mostly evergreen, sometimes summer deciduous. FLWS: in umbels, showy open blue to purple saucers with yellow centers; sporadically through the year. SMR WTR: little to none. PROP: layering; cuttings; seeds. EXP: full sun to light shade

The naming of our variable shrubby nightshades is confusing, and probably not worth pursuing in detail. All are small shrubs, often partially sprawling or with widely spreading branches and green bark, with wood only near the base. All have small, oval to rhombic-shaped, pale green leaves, which may be shed during long dry summers, and all bear umbellate clusters of jaunty saucer-shaped, pale blue to purplish flowers decorated with green nectar glands at their bases and complemented by shooting-star-like, central yellow stamens.

These shrubs grow along the borders of coastal scrub and chaparral or on the edge

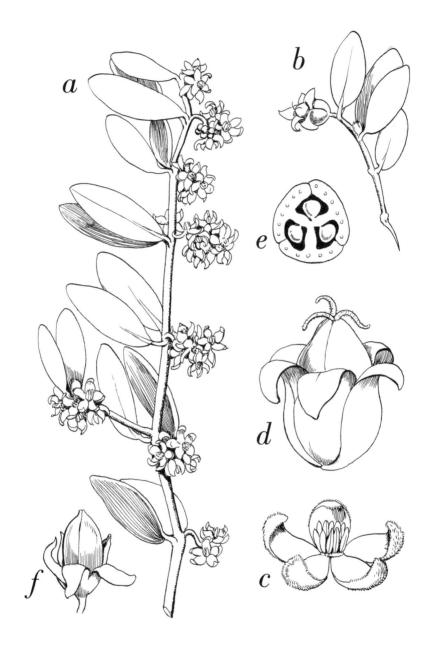

Jojoba (*Simmondsia chinensis*)
a. branch with male flowers   *b.* branch with female flower
c. male flower detail   *d.* female flower detail
e. cross section, ovary   *f.* fruit detail

of oak and mixed broadleaf forests. Material for starting the shrubs in the garden might best be selected from habitats closest to those of the gardener; coastal habitats for gardens with summer fog, hot chaparral habitats for gardens with hot, sunny summers, and forest edges for lightly shaded gardens. Although blue nightshades can bloom almost any month, they are often smothered in flowers in midspring. They are tolerant of some winter wet and cold, but a constant combination will eventually spell their death; better to offer excellent drainage and a site that gets winter sun.

The blue nightshades seldom grow in a neat and tidy way, and their straggly branches, often bereft of leaves in hot summers, make them unattractive then. But their beautiful flowers are worth the effort. A good use would be to highlight them in spring but interplant with shrubs of durable, all-year leaves—wooly blue curls and sages, for example. Or use them in a mixed border with a variety of other plants. Here are three species of note:

S. *umbelliferum*. A small shrub whose main difference from other species is its stems with branched hairs. Most common in northern and central California.

S. *wallacei* and varieties. Island nightshade. A shrub to six feet from forest edges of coastal islands; winter tender. Flowers are relatively larger than others, and stems are covered with long, sticky, tawny-colored hairs.

S. *xantii*. Similar to the first, but hairs unbranched. Mostly from southern California.

Sorbus spp. Mountain Ash. Rose family (Rosaceae)

HT: 3 to 15 feet. LVS: winter deciduous. FLWS: small white single roses in complex umbellike clusters; summer. SMR WTR: some summer water. PROP: cuttings; layering. EXP: light shade

Mountain ashes are small shrubs closely related to the cherished rowan trees of Europe. They're closely branched, clump-forming shrubs with pretty, deep purple new bark and silvery old bark. The leaves are ashlike, pinnately compound, the leaflets attractively saw-toothed and turning yellow with fall chill. Umbrellas of white, roselike flowers appear in summer, and bright red berries (actually pomes) by summer's end. They lend interest to the landscape all year.

Mountain ashes favor pockets between granite boulders where underground moisture may be tapped through summer, and they make attractive punctuations to openings in subalpine forests where lodgepole and western white pines join red firs and mountain hemlocks. Although they have a long winter rest, breaking dormancy only after snows melt in late spring to early summer, they adapt to lowland gardens—never, however, with quite the same vigor. Better to reserve a spot in a favored mountain garden. Use mountain ash with other rock garden shrubs: antelope brush

(*Purshia* spp.), bitter cherry (*Prunus emarginata*), or service berry (*Amelanchier pallida*) that has been pruned to grow low. The ashes' unusual leaf pattern allows them to complement these shrubs or make a pretty show in front of mountain maple (*Acer glabrum*), and their autumn display of colorful berries is a bonus in any mountain garden.

Sphaeralcea ambigua. Apricot Mallow. Mallow family (Malvaceae)

HT: 1 to 3 feet. LVS: partly summer deciduous. FLWS: bright apricot orange to red-orange in spikes; spring. SMR WTR: none. PROP: cuttings (take some wood); seeds. EXP: full sun

Apricot mallow is one of our most colorful desert subshrubs. Never fully woody, the numerous closely felted, wandlike branches have wooly, soft green, nearly round leaves, sometimes prettily lobed and scalloped. As with so many other summer-hot shrubs, leaves are sometimes sacrificed during particularly dry summers. Each stem carries a graceful spike of orange, hollyhock-type flowers in spring, a beautiful complement to such other desert shrubs as desert aster (*Machaeranthera tortifolia*), brittlebush (*Encelia farinosa*), and desert alyssum (*Lepidium fremontii*). Plant all in a grouping in a desert garden, for stunning and contrasting colors in spring. Later, the drab leaf colors and half-bare twigs create a muted theme appropriate to desert gardens.

Apricot mallow grows rapidly but is not long lived, especially with summer water, nor should it be given excessive winter moisture and chill. It is ideal in a desert setting, and it should be tried in inland gardens. Its special flower color makes it an ideal companion for shrubs with purple, yellow, or white blossoms.

Spiraea spp. Spiraea. Rose family (Rosaceae)

HT: 8 inches to 6 feet. LVS: winter deciduous. FLWS: pink-purple, tiny single roses in dense clusters; summer. SMR WTR: occasional deep watering. PROP: root divisions; suckers; layering; cuttings. EXP: full sun to light shade

Our two spiraeas are modest, pleasing shrubs with colorful summer flowers; one hails from the northern mountains and north coast, the other from high mountains on exposed granite. Both grow rapidly and easily under garden conditions, starting readily from cuttings or layering (or by root division for *S. douglasii*). Both have thin, pale green leaves with scattered saw-toothed edges, lax growth, and dense clusters of rose- or pink-purple flowers. Because they grow easily in well-drained sites and respond well to summer water, spiraeas are great for naturalizing along a woodland border, in the back of a rock garden, or as an integral part of a mixed border. Details of the two differ as follows:

S. densiflora. Mountain spiraea, rose spiraea. A low, neat-looking shrub to about three feet that can be pruned to make matlike mounds. Flat-topped clusters of flowers. Give plenty of light. Adapts well to rocky outcroppings; looks beautiful in granite rock. Combine with shrubby cinquefoil (*Potentilla fruticosa*) and mountain creambush (*Holodiscus boursieri*) for stunning effect.

S. douglasii. Steeple bush. A more open, sprawling shrub with wandering roots; grows to six feet. Partial to more moisture and light shade. Flowers are borne in pyramidal or steeple-shaped panicles over a long period. Allow it plenty of room to spread. Excellent with ocean spray (*Holodiscus discolor*) and mountain ash (*Sorbus californica*).

Staphylea bolanderi. Bladdernut. Bladdernut family (Staphyleaceae)

HT: 6 to 20 feet. LVS: winter deciduous. FLWS: white in drooping panicles; mid-spring. SMR WTR: some deep watering. PROP: cuttings. EXP: shade

This unusual shrub calls attention to itself twice: in mid-spring there are graceful panicles of small white blossoms hanging from leafy branches; in summer fruits ripen into curiously inflated three-sided, bladderlike, horn-tipped seed pods that split to shed seeds. Out of flower, this large shrub carries leaves divided into three broadly oval segments and delicately serrated along their edges. Bladdernut seeks the shade and high water table of protected canyons in the lower pine belt of the mountains. Thus it is not entirely drought tolerant, but occasional deep waterings should carry it through the summer.

Use bladdernut as an unusual shrub for the shade garden, behind a pond or against the shaded side of a house. Its seasonal interest and rare occurrence make it a conversation piece.

Styrax officinalis. Snowbell Bush or Storax. Storax family (Styracaceae)

HT: 3 to 14 feet. LVS: winter deciduous. FLWS: showy, pendant white bells; late spring. SMR WTR: occasional deep watering is best. PROP: cuttings (use bottom heat); seeds (stratify, and take precautions against damping-off). EXP: full sun to shade

Snowbell bush is one of California's little known yet highly ornamental shrubs, deserving a special place in lowland gardens. It is slow to mature, particularly in shade and with no summer water (occasional deep watering is best), but well worth the wait. It matures into a tall, graceful, multistemmed shrub with smooth, silver-gray bark—shown to advantage in winter—and horizontal twigs carrying nearly round dark green, smooth-edged leaves, heart shaped at their base. In May or early June, lines of white bells nod from under these twigs, carrying a subtle perfume and clusters of bright yellow stamens. As petals fall they give the impression of drifted snow, adding beauty to the soil beneath. One stunning natural arrangement includes sprawling mats of scarlet Indian pink (*Silene californica*) and common yellow-flowered stonecrop (*Sedum spathulifolium*) with a dusting of white petals from the styrax.

Steeple Bush (*Spiraea douglasii*)
a. flowering branch with leaves   *b*. flower detail   *c*. leaf detail   *d*. fruit detail

Snowbell bush can be easily started from seeds, but it is so prone to damping-off that special fungicides should be added to the potting medium to reduce seedling mortality. The shrubs form a fine backdrop to a woodland garden, or use them along a stream bank or as a foundation planting. They're handsome in company with natural woody companions such as mock orange (*Philadelphus lewisii*), western spicebush (*Calycanthus occidentalis*), or western redbud (*Cercis occidentalis*). There are two varieties: *californica* from central and northern California tolerates shade and has leaves smooth above but closely furred below, while variety *fulvescens* from southern California chaparral is an excellent candidate for full sun and heat, and has fuzzy leaves with tawny hairs beneath.

Symphoricarpos spp. Snowberries. Honeysuckle family (Caprifoliaceae)

HT: 3 inches to 6 feet. LVS: winter deciduous. FLWS: small white to pink bells or saucers, hanging under branches; spring to summer. SMR WTR: occasional deep watering is best. PROP: root divisions; cuttings; layering. EXP: full sun to shade

Snowberries are excellent subjects for large, informal gardens, where their spreading roots and stems can rapidly naturalize with graceful form. In small gardens or with more formal designs, snowberries are best containerized or omitted. The several species vary from low, creeping, woody ground covers to modest-sized, densely branched shrubs. Some are fine for rock gardens in sun, others for the dappled shade of a stream bank in a woodland. All have twigs of fine diameter, with fluted, peely brownish bark and pairs of pale green rounded leaves. The leaves can vary on the same plant as to details of lobing and teeth (often leaves look like someone has taken a bite out of one side!). Unpretentious, small, bell-shaped white to pink flowers hide under the leaves near branch tips. The showiest feature is the clusters of spongy white berries in late summer and fall, which are decorative but not edible.

For best effect, plant snowberries on a bank so that you can look up into the charming flowers in late spring or summer. Here are four species worthy of consideration:

S. longiflorus. Desert snowberry. From woodlands of high deserts: sprawling branches, bluish green leaves, and pretty flaring saucer-shaped flowers in summer. Drought tolerant.

S. mollis. Creeping snowberry. A rapid-growing, woody ground cover, favoring shade. Flowers are insignificant bells in spring. Excellent for retaining steep embankments in a hurry.

S. rivularis. Shrub snowberry. A tall multitwigged shrub—it has the best habit— that forms colonies in time. Grows well in shade. Modest, pale pink bells in late spring.

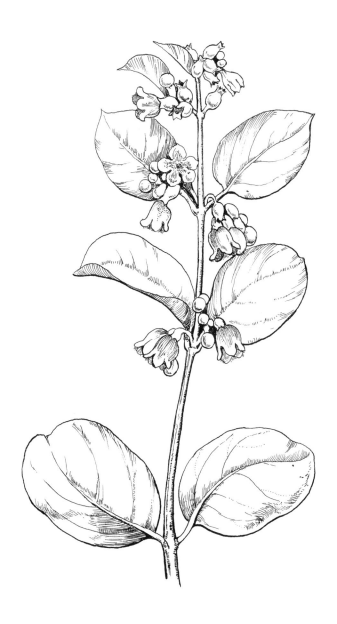

Shrub Snowberry (*Symphoricarpos rivularis*)
flowering branch

S. vaccinoides. Huckleberry-flowered snowberry. A pretty shrub to four feet from high mountains; it grows on granite in forest openings. Pretty, long, bell-shaped, pink huckleberrylike flowers in summer. Light shade to full sun.

Taxus brevifolia. Western Yew. Yew family (Taxaceae)

HT: to 20 feet. LVS: evergreen needles. FLWS: male with tiny cream-colored pollen cones; female with single seed surrounded by bright red cup (aril); spring. SMR WTR: occasional deep watering. PROP: cuttings (use bottom heat); layering. EXP: shade

Western yew is usually considered a tree, but within California's borders it behaves more as a large shrub, albeit sometimes with a single trunk. The handsome branches, arrayed in horizontal tiers, bear two rows of redwoodlike needles but lack the fragrance of most conifers. Yew is consistently an understory tree following watercourses and canyon bottoms of moist forests in northern California, often in company with flowering dogwood (*Cornus nuttallii*), alders (*Alnus* spp.), and western azalea (*Rhododendron occidentale*). It grows very slowly, seldom attaining great size within less than several decades, and so may be depended upon to retain its form indefinitely.

Perhaps the most unusual feature is that plants are dioecious. Males have tiny whitish pollen cones borne in axils of needles along branches with new growth. Females have berrylike "cones": single large seeds set in bright red, fleshy cups. Apart from these differences, male and female shrubs look alike.

Western yew makes a handsome understory shrub for deeply shaded forest aisles and stream sides, where its long-lived needles remain all year. It requires a minimum of maintenance and has few faults, but because of its ponderously slow growth it is likely to have limited garden use. The wood is especially strong and flexible, being used for bows. With the recent discovery of its cancer-curing properties, this conifer is likely to be in demand and in danger of being overharvested.

Tetracoccus dioicus. Coast Tetracoccus. Spurge family (Euphorbiaceae)

HT: 2 to 4 feet. LVS: evergreen. FLWS: small reddish male flowers in small clusters in leaf axils; female solitary, inconspicuous; in spring. SMR WTR: none. PROP: cuttings; perhaps seeds. EXP: full sun

Tetracoccus is a curious, seldom cultivated shrub from the chaparral of the far south. It has dense branches, the new twigs an attractive red color, and the narrow leaves a complementary green. Male and female flowers occur on separate plants and are not showy, although the male flowers are pretty at close range, with their reddish sepals surrounding the stamens. The main attribute here is the neat appearance all year with minimal fuss, and the tried-and-true drought tolerance.

Tetracoccus can be grown as a hedge or barrier shrub or as a low-key foundation

a

b

Western Yew (*Taxus brevifolia*)
a. fruiting branches   *b*. cut-away fruit detail

shrub, perhaps in combination with other shrubs of more colorful flowers and showy, seasonal personality.

Tetradymia spp. Cottonthorn. Sunflower family (Asteraceae)

HT: 2 to 4 feet. LVS: often summer deciduous. FLWS: small bright yellow heads without rays, in dense clusters; late spring and summer. SMR WTR: none. PROP: cuttings; seeds. EXP: full sun

Cottonthorns are low, densely branched shrubs that form a desert version of a bramble patch. The newer branches are densely felted in cottony white hairs, and their leaves are either modified into cottony spines or later become spiny. Greener leaves are borne in small clusters in the axils of these spines. In late spring to summer, large numbers of flowering heads, small individually but a showy golden yellow, transform the shrubs for a couple of weeks; flowers are later replaced by masses of whitish hairs covering seeds whose color matches the hairs protecting the branches. Cottonthorns are found in deserts or sometimes in the chaparral of southern California, where they are perfectly adapted to hot, droughty summers.

Cottonthorn is not for most gardens; many will find the appearance objectionable in summer and fall. They are, however, dependable, tough shrubs for the desert garden, and their unique spine and leaf design creates a barrier par excellence. Two species to consider are *T. comosa* from the chaparral and *T. axillaris* from eastern deserts.

Torreya californica. California Nutmeg. Yew family (Taxaceae)

HT: 15 to 60 feet. LVS: evergreen needles. FLWS: tiny male cones on male trees; fleshy purple "prunes" on female; fall. SMR WTR: none when well established. PROP: cuttings (use bottom heat); seeds (stratify or scarify). EXP: light shade

California nutmeg is among our oddest small trees. When you find it, scattered through the north Coast Ranges and Sierra foothills, it may be growing in small copses or mixed with other trees but then be missing from similar habitats in adjacent sites. Unusual features include the dagger-sharp, polished needle tips, the peculiar strong needle odor (some find it pleasant, others not), the bearing of male cones on separate trees from the female, and the large, fleshy, stone-fruit-like female "cone," whose fleshy outer wrapping turns wrinkled and purple when ripe. Inside is a seed about the size and shape of a nutmeg (hence the common name), which is not in any way related to the real thing.

Since California nutmeg never grows very large—and is slow to boot—it can serve in the garden as a miniature tree (in a large container) or, pruned when new shoots are just developing, as a hedge, interplanted with several individuals. The handsome glossy, dark green needles are both attractive all year and formidable barriers. Plant males, if all you want are tiny, cream-colored pollen cones; females, if you like the

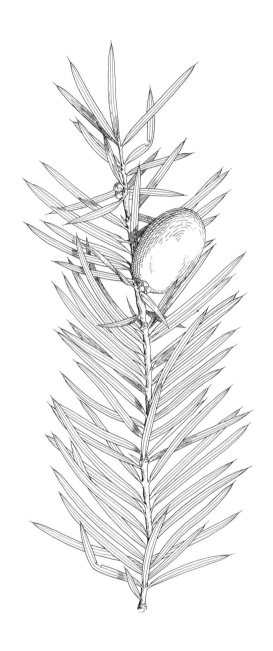

California Nutmeg (*Torreya californica*)
branch with needles and fruit

curious, prunelike "fruits." The only way to be sure of the sex of new plantings is, of course, to grow new plants from cuttings taken from already mature trees.

Trichostema lanatum. Wooly Blue Curls or Romero. Mint family (Lamiaceae)

HT: 3 to 5 feet. LVS: evergreen. FLWS: showy two-lipped with purple wool and blue petals in short spikes; late spring to summer. SMR WTR: none. PROP: cuttings; seeds. EXP: full sun

Wooly blue curls is a mint-sage relative of modest size, thriving on hot, dry, rocky slopes along the fringes of chaparral in central and southern California. Out of flower, the habit of the plant is less than ideal: branches are frequently weak and straggly. But tip pruning can improve overall shape and density. The narrow, pointed leaves are bright green above, curled along their edges and white wooly underneath, with a strong, sagelike aroma. The flowers are often produced in spurts throughout the year in mild climates, and they are ample reason to grow this shrub. Descriptions fail to portray the unique flower shape, adapted to hummingbird pollination: the sepals are encased in gorgeous purple wool around the longer two-lipped, gaping blue petals, the whole decorated by protruding curled blue stamens.

Wooly blue curls grows vigorously when given plenty of sun and good drainage, but it dislikes excessive winter rain. Frost tender, it thrives in southern coastal gardens and is amenable to sandy or rocky soils. Use it at the back of an herb garden, in combination with other, smaller shrubs (*Monardella* spp.; sunrose, *Helianthemum scoparium*; various salvias; and bush monkeyflowers, *Diplacus* spp.), or in a dry mixed border toward the back.

Trixis californica. Desert Trixis. Sunflower family (Asteraceae)

HT: to 3 feet. LVS: partly summer deciduous. FLWS: daisy heads of curious two-lipped golden flowers; late spring. SMR WTR: none. PROP: perhaps cuttings; seeds. EXP: full sun

Desert trixis is an out-of-the-ordinary small shrub related to other bush sunflowers and daisies (such as *Encelia*, *Gutierrezia*, *Acamtopappus*, and *Haplopappus*). The bushes grow fairly densely and look trim when watered, but it's really the flush of spring flower heads that draws attention. The flower heads are quite different at close range—instead of the typical strap-shaped, petallike rays along the edge and tiny star-shaped disc flowers in the center, trixis only has masses of small, golden, two-lipped flowers.

Since its cultural requirements are similar to a host of other desert shrubs', it could be planted to complement others with contrasting flower colors, such as desert aster, desert alyssum, apricot mallow, indigo bush, and desert mallow. It is likely to fade into the background in summer, when the leaves are partly shed to conserve water.

Umbellularia californica. California Bay Laurel or Pepperwood. Laurel family (Lauraceae)

HT: 4 to perhaps 10 feet (upper limit unknown). LVS: evergreen. FLWS: pale yellow in small umbels; through winter. SMR WTR: some deep watering initially. PROP: seeds. EXP: full sun to light shade

To the best of my knowledge, no book mentions this special form of California's familiar bay, nor has there been experimentation in the garden to see if the shrub form remains a shrub. But if you journey to the northwestern corner of the state you'll encounter this fine, compact shrub bay on hot chaparral slopes, where it accompanies shrub tan oak, coffee berry, boxleaf garrya, holly grapes, and others. In all other details—flowers, fruits, and leaves—it is identical to the tree form. As a shrub it grows into a dense rounded shape, and the new flush of leaves is a lovely red-bronze. As with bay trees, leaves are shiny, lance-shaped, dark green, and highly fragrant— overpowering, in fact, on hot days. The modest yellow, saucer-shaped flowers give extra beauty in winter (sometimes extending to early spring) and are one of the few nectar sources for bees at that time of the year. Fruits look like miniature avocadoes but turn deep purple when fully ripe, and the large, single seed inside makes propagation easy.

Shrub bay would be an asset in any garden receiving hot summer sun—it should be dependably drought tolerant once established— and could be grown as a specimen in a large container, trimmed as a hedge that stays attractive all year, or trained as a foundation shrub against a warm wall. It could also serve in the back of an herb garden, perhaps in company with the European bay *Laurus nobilis.*

Vaccinium spp. Huckleberry or Bilberry. Heather family (Ericaceae)

HT: 3 to 15 feet. LVS: deciduous or evergreen. FLWS: small white to pale pink bells under leafy branches; spring. SMR WTR: some deep watering. PROP: cuttings; seeds (stratify). EXP: shade

California's native huckleberries are close relatives to the eastern blueberries and cranberries; the high-mountain species are also known as bilberries. Although they vary from low, creeping ground covers to tall, openly branched shrubs, only two are discussed here as appropriate for gardens. (Most montane species require cold winters and wet summer conditions and are of questionable ornamental value, having tiny flowers and undistinguished foliage.) The two coastal species frequent moist forests in the north where they border lush redwoods or soaring spruces and firs; one is evergreen, the other deciduous. Both like acid soils that retain moisture in summer, and both bear delectable berries in fall or late summer. In other particulars, they differ as outlined below:

V. ovatum. Evergreen huckleberry. A relatively slow growing, handsome shrub with neat rows of small, shiny, leathery deep green leaves delicately serrated along their edges. In spring, the new leaves are at first flushed bronze, or an intense red in full sun. Leaves are long lasting and excellent for providing winter green in the garden or for complementing floral arrangements. Small, pale pink bells are produced underneath the leafy branches in spring; when laden with flowers and viewed from below, they are quite lovely. Deep black-purple to bluish berries follow in fall and are among the best-tasting wild fruits we have. Excellent for the shade of redwoods and other conifers, or for hedges and barriers.

V. parvifolium. Red huckleberry. This deciduous shrub prefers the wettest coastal forests, where it frequently germinates on old tree stumps or fallen logs, preferring soil high in humus. It grows much faster than evergreen huckleberry and has an open, airy branch pattern, with angular twigs, greenish bark, and small, pale green, scattered leaves. Flowers are small green urns, flushed pink, and hide under branches. Bright red, edible berries follow. Excellent subject to grow on old stumps and logs under conifers.

Viguiera spp. Desert Goldenbush. Sunflower family (Asteraceae)

HT: 1 to 5 feet. LVS: some summer deciduous. FLWS: gold daisies single or in flat-topped clusters; through spring. SMR WTR: none. PROP: seeds. EXP: full sun

Desert goldenbushes are unprepossessing small shrubs that tolerate hot summers with no water. Their attractive, ovate to triangular leaves vary from rough and greenish (*V. deltoides*) to downy white (*V. reticulata*), but they may shrivel or drop during the hottest, driest summers. As with so many desert shrubs, it's really the colorful yellow daisies that transform these shrubs in spring. Flowers are a bit deeper gold and somewhat smaller than those of the similar brittlebush (*Encelia farinosa*). The two may grow together, and they make a good coupling in the desert garden.

Like so many other desert shrubs, viguieras really belong in desert gardens designed for periods of drab color and little action in summer, but with great floral flourishes in spring.

Vitis californica. California Wild Grape. Vine family (Vitaceae)

HT: a woody vine growing many feet long. LVS: winter deciduous. FLWS: tiny, greenish, in hanging panicles; spring. SMR WTR: some deep watering. PROP: root divisions; cuttings; seeds. EXP: light shade

Athough really a tough woody vine, California wild grape deserves space in a shrub book for its great beauty. It lends a lush, tropical appearance to riparian woodlands

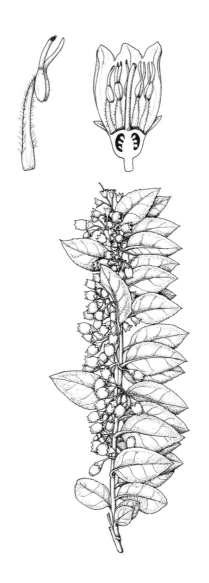

Evergreen Huckleberry (*Vaccinium ovatum*)
fruiting branch with leaves
upper left: detail of stamen
upper right: detail of flower

nearly throughout the state, where it creates great, leafy draperies over any support it can climb: willows, cottonwoods, alders, and many others. The nearly round leaves are much like those of cultivated vines but lack their deep lobes, being merely serrated along the edges. Leaves turn yellow, crimson, and flame red in late fall and are one of the true autumn glories of the foothills. The flowers are altogether insignificant (being dense compound clusters of minute green stars), but the grape fruits ripen to purple in fall and make excellent jams and jellies (though they are sour when eaten fresh).

Wild grape dies back to its woody old growth each winter, but it keeps increasing in size each year unless pruned in the manner of cultivated grapes. Pruning would be a mistake, however, for one of the chief charms is the vine's exuberant growth, appropriate for large trellises and as canopies over small trees. An archway under a canopy of vines would be spectacular and a cool adjunct in summer. Expect rapid growth, succeeding best with some summer water.

An alternative to the California wild grape is found in the desert grape, *V. girdiana*, from hot canyon oases in desert mountains; its leaves are covered with white, downy hairs, unlike the nearly hairless California wild grape.

Whipplea modesta. Modesty or Yerba de Selva. Saxifrage family (Saxifragaceae)

HT: to about 6 inches. LVS: winter deciduous. FLWS: tiny white saxifrage flowers in modest spikes; spring. SMR WTR: occasional deep watering is best. PROP: cuttings; layering. EXP: shade

Modesty is well named, for it's a plant without truly striking features. Still, it is one of the most effective ground covers or stabilizers of steep banks. It is a trailing woody plant, rooting as it grows, with neat, light green, fuzzy ovate leaves that are weakly toothed. In spring, tiny white flowers, much like those of herbaceous saxifrages, appear in small spikes. In winter, the leaves are shed and the plant becomes nearly invisible, with only the older woody growth intact. Modesty lives in the dappled shade of forest edges throughout northern California and is characteristic of steep, barren banks, where little else gains a roothold.

Modesty is ideal for an informal woody ground cover in the woodland garden and to hold steep embankments quickly, since it grows quite rampantly once established. Withholding summer water will keep it in bounds, although some summer water will encourage fast, healthy growth. Use it in combination with yerba buena (*Satureja douglasii*), redwood sorrel (*Oxalis oregana*), and vancouverias.

Xylococcus bicolor. Mission Manzanita. Heather family (Ericaceae)

HT: 5 to 15 feet. LVS: evergreen. FLWS: small panicles of white to pinkish urns; winter. SMR WTR: none. PROP: cuttings; seeds (stratify). EXP: full sun

Mission manzanita is a close relative of California's many fine true manzanitas (*Arctostaphylos* spp.). It differs in its tough, evergreen leaves curling under along their edges and having a close mat of white hairs underneath with deep green above (hence the name bicolor). The small clusters of flowers—in bloom in the winter—are exactly like those of manzanitas, with red sepals at the base of pale pink to white urn-shaped petals. The red-brown bark is especially attractive, peeling off in long strands or "shreds." The globular fruits are near black when fully ripe, and split into several sections. Mission manzanita comes from the coastal chaparral of far southern California or lives among Engelmann oaks (*Quercus engelmannii*). There it gets hot summer sun with no water.

Mission manzanita is a must for any moderate-sized, southern garden where sun and drought rule in summer. It is every bit as handsome in leaf as are true manzanitas, and it flowers when all other plants are dormant. Plant and prune it to show off the attractive bark—along a warm wall, with other chaparral shrubs, as a specimen, or as an informal hedge. The biggest difficulty will be in finding a commercial source of material.

Yucca spp. Yucca or Spanish Dagger. Agave family (Agavaceae)

HT: 1 to 14 feet. LVS: evergreen. FLWS: creamy bells in giant panicles; spring. SMR WTR: none. PROP: pups from around parent plant; seeds. EXP: full sun

Our yuccas are dramatic, unusual plants of deserts and dry chaparral. Their bold form sets them apart from anything else: large crowns of daggerlike, narrowly lance-shaped, green to silvery leaves. In flower they're even more dramatic, with giant panicles reaching three to ten feet. The numerous flowers are pendant, waxy, white to cream-colored bells of great beauty. Flowers depend upon pronuba moths for pollination, although all sorts of other visitors come for drinks of nectar or to chomp on the thick, fleshy petals.

Because yuccas grow in very hot, dry situations, they must have plenty of sun and warmth, coupled with excellent drainage. Once established they are long-enduring features in the garden. Use them as bold specimens in the middle of a desert garden, in large containers, in the back of a succulent garden, or with low-growing, gray-leafed ground covers and subshrubs for dramatic contrasts in leaf textures. Wherever they are placed, they are bound to draw the eye because of their size and shape. Here are the three species for gardens:

Y. baccata. Banana yucca. From California's eastern mid to high deserts, a dwarf yucca. It has dark blue-green rosettes of leaves close to the ground, no higher than three feet (often much less). The crown multiplies into additional rosettes. Flowering stalks to about three feet have creamy, waxy, bell-like flowers and fleshy seed pods, shaped like small bananas and used as food by Native Americans. Pretty in front of a desert garden, with assorted cacti.

Y. schidigera. Mojave yucca or Spanish dagger. From hot deserts, this kind slowly builds a solitary or few-branched trunk to twelve or more feet tall, carrying crowns of leaves there. Leaves are deep green and dagger sharp, with pretty curled filaments along the margins. Dense panicles of flowers are carried to three or more feet above the leaves and appear every year, but the plants have to live twelve or more years before they bloom. Best adapted to desert gardens.

Y. whipplei. Chaparral yucca or our lord's candle. From the chaparral of central and southern California. This yucca has no obvious stem; leaf rosettes are carried at ground level, growing larger in diameter each year. Leaves vary from light green to silvery. Flowers appear only once after ten to twenty years, and the huge panicles soar to eight or more feet, with hundreds of lovely creamy bells. Although the plant dies from the effort, it usually leaves behind a circle of new pups.

Zauschneria spp. Wild or Hummingbird Fuchsia. Evening primrose family. (Onagraceae)

HT: 1 to 3 feet. LVS: winter deciduous. FLWS: showy flared scarlet trumpets in spikes; late summer through fall. SMR WTR: none. PROP: root divisions; seeds. EXP: full sun

There are few subshrubs that are more beautiful for late color in the garden; from August on it has a long succession of scarlet trumpets with long, protruding stamens, produced up to the first autumn freeze. The flowers are not only valuable for their bright splashes of color at the end of the flowering season but are important nectar sources for hummingbirds. After the first serious freezing weather of fall, the stems die back to their widely wandering roots. Take advantage of nature's cue, and trim the unsightly old growth to the ground; vigorous new growth will appear the following spring. Leaves are narrow, almost linear, and pale green (Z. *californica*) or silvery white (Z. *cana*). The leafy stalks become a bit rangy before the first blossoms appear, and because the roots wander over wide areas, they earn for these plants an untidy reputation. Z. *cana* is the better choice in this respect, since its woody base sends out dense masses of leafy branches.

In the garden, hummingbird fuchsias are ideal for a natural planting among widely

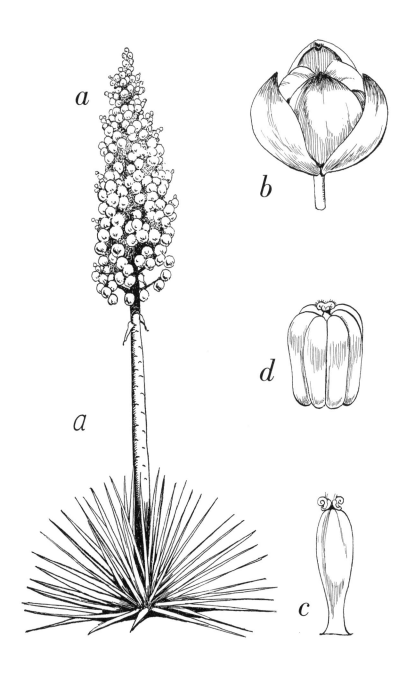

Chaparral Yucca (*Yucca whipplei*)

a. habit, flowering plant   *b.* flower detail   *c.* stamen detail   *d.* ovary detail

spaced bunchgrasses, in front of tall chaparral shrubs, along a stony watercourse, or with containment, in a dry mixed border. They are easy to propagate by root division or seeds (seeds are hair covered, and often produce volunteer seedlings) and extend their territories rapidly. Besides the usual scarlet-red forms, cultivars with pale pink and pure white flowers are now available; they make a striking combination with the usual flame-colored flowers. Other late bloomers that complement zauschnerias include the coyote mints (*Monardella*) and goldenrods (*Solidago* spp.), the latter drought-tolerant perennials.

PART THREE

APPENDICES

COMMERCIAL SOURCES OF NATIVE SHRUBS

PLANT SOURCES

Beecher's Nursery. 1218 N. Beecher Rd., Stockton, CA 95205

Blue Oak Nursery. 2731 Mountain Oak Lane, Rescue, CA 95672

Calaveras Nursery. 1622 Highway 12, Valley Springs, CA 95252

California Flora Nursery. P.O. Box 3, Fulton, CA 95439

Darling's Nursery. 7000 Petaluma Hill Rd., P.O. Box 570, Penngrove, CA 94951

Endangered Species. 12571 Red Hill, Tustin, CA 92680

Hortica Gardens. P.O. Box 308, Placerville, CA 95667

Las Pilitas Nursery. Star Route Box 23, Santa Margarita, CA 93453

Lawson Valley Nursery. 3616 Rudnick Dr., Jamul, CA 92035

Leonard Coates Nurseries, Inc. 400 Casserly Rd., Watsonville, CA 95076

Mayacama Botanicals. 2600 Eastside Rd./P.O. Box 689, Ukiah, CA 95482

Mendo-Natives Nursery. P.O. Box 351, Gualala, CA 95445

Mostly Natives Nursery. P.O. Box 258, Tomales, CA 94971

The Native Nursery. P.O. Box 1684, Big Bear City, CA 92314

Native Sons Wholesale Nursery. 379 West El Campo Rd., Arroyo Grande, CA 93420

Pecoff Bros. Nursery & Seed, Inc. Rt. 5, Box 215, Escondido, CA 92025

Redwood Nursery. 2800 El Rancho Dr., Santa Cruz, CA 95060

San Marcos Growers. 125 S. San Marcos Rd., P.O. Box 6827, Santa Barbara, CA 93111

San Simeon Nursery. Star Route, Villa Creek Rd., Cayucos, CA 93430

Saratoga Horticultural Foundation. 15185 Murphy Avenue, San Martin, CA 95046

Shooting Star Propagation. 9950 O'Connell Rd., Sebastopol, CA 95472

The Shop in the Sierra. Box 1, Midpines, CA 95345

Siskiyou Rare Plant Nursery. 2825 Cummings Rd., Medford, OR 97501

Skylark Wholesale Nursery. 6735 Sonoma Hwy., Santa Rosa, CA 95405

The Theodore Payne Foundation. 10459 Tuxford St., Sun Valley, CA 91352

U.C. Davis Arboretum. Davis, CA 95616

U.C. Santa Cruz Arboretum. Crown College, UCSC, Santa Cruz, CA 95064

Villager Nursery. P.O. Box 1273, Truckee, CA 95734

Western Hills Rare Plants. 16250 Coleman Valley Rd., Occidental, CA 95465

Wildwood Farm. 10300 Sonoma Hwy., Kenwood, CA 95452
Ya-Ka-Ama Nursery. 6215 Eastside Road, Forestville, CA 95436
Yerba Buena Nursery. 19500 Skyline Blvd., Woodside, CA 94062

SEED SOURCES

Abundant Life Seed Foundation. P.O. Box 772, Port Townsend, WA 98368
Carter Seeds. 475 Mar Vista Dr., Vista, CA 92083
Clyde Robin Seed Co., Inc. P.O. Box 2855, Castro Valley, CA 94546
Earthside Nature Center. c/o Mrs. John Connelly, 138 El Dorado St., Arcadia, CA
    91006
Larner Seeds. P.O. Box 11143, Palo Alto, CA 94306
Las Pilitas Nursery. Star Route Box 23, Santa Margarita, CA 93453
Mistletoe Sales. 910 Alphonse, Santa Barbara, CA 93103
Moon Mountain. P.O. Box 34, Morro Bay, CA 93442
Redwood City Seed Co. Craig Dremann, P.O. Box 361, Redwood City, CA 94064
Regional Parks Botanic Garden. Tilden Regional Park, Berkeley, CA 94708
S & S Seeds. 910 Alphonse, Santa Barbara, CA 93103
Santa Barbara Botanic Garden. 1212 Mission Canyon Rd., Santa Barbara, CA
    93105
Southwestern Native Seeds. Box 50503, Tucson, AZ 85703
Stover Seed Co. P.O. Box 21488, Los Angeles, CA 90021
The Theodore Payne Foundation. 10459 Tuxford St., Sun Valley, CA 91352
Twin Peaks Seeds. 12721 Ave. de Espuela, Poway, CA 92064
A World Seed Service. L. Hudson, Seedsman, P.O. Box 1058, Redwood City, CA
    94064

SOCIETIES AND GARDENS WITH SPECIAL PLANT SALES

California Native Plant Society. 909 12th St., Suite 116, Sacramento, CA 95814.
    (Each chapter has its own special time for a sale; after you have joined, inquire of
    your local chapter.)
Rancho Santa Ana Botanic Garden. 1500 N. College Ave., Claremont, CA 91711.
Regional Parks Botanical Garden. Tilden Regional Park, Berkeley, CA 94708.
Santa Barbara Botanic Garden. 1212 Mission Canyon Rd., Santa Barbara, CA
    93105.
Strybing Arboretum Society. 9th Ave. & Lincoln Way, San Francisco, CA 94122.
University of California Botanical Garden. Strawberry Canyon, U.C. campus,
    Berkeley, CA 94720.

REFERENCE BOOKS DEALING WITH NATIVE SHRUBS

Collins, Barbara J. *Key to Trees and Shrubs of the Deserts of Southern California.* 1976. California Lutheran College, Thousand Oaks, CA. A rather complete guide, with easier than average keys but rather sketchy line drawings.

Ferlatte, William J. *A Flora of the Trinity Alps of Northern California.* 1974. University of California Press, Berkeley. Fairly complete, with technical keys and descriptions. Several line drawings of good quality.

Hickman, James, editor. *The Jepson Manual: Higher Plants of California.* 1993. University of California Press, Berkeley. Supercedes the well-known *A Manual of the Flowering Plants of California* by Willis L. Jepson. The latter was the original fully described flora for California. Very complete and up to date, but technical. Amply illustrated with line drawings.

Howell, John Thomas. *Marin Flora.* 1949. University of California Press, Berkeley. A complete, technical flora of natives in Marin County. No drawings or photos in the main text. Technical keys.

Jepson, Willis L. *A Manual of the Flowering Plants of California.* 1909 to 1943. University of California Press, Berkeley. A large technical manual that was complete for its time but is now superceded by Munz (see below). Several fine illustrations; some people prefer the keys here. A number of names have been changed in newer works. *Important note:* Many of the illustrations for this book come from this source.

Lacey, Louise, editor and publisher. *Growing Native: The Newsletter of the Growing Native Research Institute.* A timely newsletter on native shrubbery published six times a year.

Lenz, Lee W., and John Dourley. *California Native Trees and Shrubs: for Garden and Environmental Use in Southern California and Adjacent Areas.* 1981. Rancho Santa Ana Botanic Garden, Claremont, CA. A complete guide to trees and shrubs for southern California but drily written and academically oriented, with many technical and scientific graphs and charts. Some good line drawings and average black-and-white and color photographs.

McMinn, Howard. *An Illustrated Manual of California Shrubs.* 1974. University of California Press, Berkeley. A very complete guide to California's shrubs, including technical keys and fine line drawings. One of the best features is comparisons of different species in large genera. The best reference source on this subject.

Munz, Philip, and David Keck. *A California Flora*. 1959 (with Supplement, 1968). University of California Press, Berkeley. Formerly the most complete technical work for the whole state. Few illustrations. Technical keys. Recommended for the advanced student only. *Important note:* Most of the names used in this book are derived from this source.

Smith, Clifton. *A Flora of the Santa Barbara Region, California*. 1976. Santa Barbara Museum of Natural History, Santa Barbara. A complete book for Santa Barbara County; no keys. Technical descriptions and some line drawings.

Thomas, John Hunter. *Flora of the Santa Cruz Mountains of California*. 1961. Stanford University Press, Stanford. Complete, technical flora of the Santa Cruz Mountains. Some line drawings. Technical keys.

Weeden, Norman. *Survival Handbook to Sierra Flora*. 1975. Distributed by Wilderness Press, Berkeley. Pocket-sized guide. Complete but with technical keys and rather poor line drawings. Useful for the experienced person.

GOOD SHRUB COMBINATIONS FOR THE GARDEN

Apache plume and fernbush
Apache plume and rabbitbrush
Azalea-flowered monkeyflower and
white-leaf bush lupine
Azalea-flowered monkeyflower and
scarlet bugler penstemon
Azalea-flowered monkeyflower and
snowbell bush
Bladderpod and desert senna
Bladderpod and desert sagebrush
Bladderpod and desert aster
Bladderpod and apricot mallow
Bladderpod and bush rue
Bush anemone and Sierra maple
Bush anemone and gooseberries
Bush anemone and currants
Bush anemone and fremontia
Bush anemone and western azalea
Bush lupines and bush monkeyflowers
Bush lupines and monardellas
Bush lupines and bush poppy
Bush mallow and fremontia
Bush mallow and blue witch
Bush mallow and rhuses
Bush mallow and salvias
Bush mallow and bush poppy
Bush monkeyflowers and low blue
ceanothuses
Bush monkeyflowers and coyote mints
Bush monkeyflowers and California
sagebrush
Bush monkeyflowers and coffee berry
Bush monkeyflowers and sunrose

Bush monkeyflowers and eriophyllums
Bush poppy and blue ceanothuses
Bush poppy and yerba santa
Bush poppy and fremontia
Bush poppy and chaparral pea
Bush poppy and prickly phlox
Bush rue and prostrate ceanothuses
Bush rue and California sagebrush
'Canyon Gray'
Bush rue and dwarf coyote bush
Bush rue and tree coreopsis
Bush sunflower and bush
monkeyflowers
Bush sunflower and coyote mints
Bush sunflower and white-leaf lupine
Bush sunflower and blue witch
California brickel bush and coffee berry
California brickel bush and rhuses
California brickel bush and dwarf
coyote bush
California brickel bush and medium-
sized ceanothuses
California buckeye and toyon
California buckeye and blue elderberry
California buckeye and hopbush
California hazelnut and western azalea
California hazelnut and flowering
dogwood
California hazelnut and vine maple
California hazelnut and thimbleberry
California holly grape and California
sagebrush
California holly grape and coffee berry

California holly grape and bush monkeyflowers

California juniper and scrub oaks

California juniper and yuccas

California juniper and redberry buckthorn (tall-growing form)

California pagoda bush and desert aster

California pagoda bush and paperbag bush

California sagebrush and coffee berry

California sagebrush and bush monkeyflowers

California sagebrush and dwarf coyote bush

California sagebrush and low ceanothuses

Ceanothuses (tall-growing form) and toyon

Ceanothuses (tall-growing form) and chamise

Ceanothuses (tall-growing form) and fremontia

Ceanothuses (tall-growing form) and chaparral pea

Ceanothuses (low-growing form) and sprawling form of chamise

Ceanothuses (low-growing form) and dwarf coyote bush

Ceanothuses (low-growing form) and California sagebrush 'Canyon Gray'

Chamise (low-growing form) and coffee berry (low-growing form)

Chamise and gray-leafed salvias

Chamise and sugar bush or lemonade berry

Chaparral mahogany and toyon

Chaparral mahogany and flowering currants

Chaparral mahogany and coffee berry

Chuparosa and blue witch

Chuparosa and bush snapdragon

Chuparosa and apricot mallow

Chuparosa and desert willow

Cliff rose and desert sagebrush

Cliff rose and apache plume

Cliff rose and antelope brush

Coast brittlebush and blue witch

Coast brittlebush and low-growing forms of coffee berry

Coast brittlebush and flat-top buckwheat

Coast brittlebush and bush monkeyflowers

Coast gumweed and dune sagebrush

Coast gumweed and California sagebrush 'Canyon Gray'

Coast gumweed and coyote mints

Coast gumweed and sprawling form of chamise

Creambush and service berry

Creambush and late-flowering blueblossom

Creambush and holly-leaf cherry

Creambush and coffee berry

Creek dogwood and willows

Creek dogwood and wild roses

Creek dogwood and native grape

Creek dogwood and western burning-bush

Creeping holly grape and dwarf coyote bush

Creeping holly grape and low-growing forms of sagebrush

Creeping holly grape and low-growing forms of manzanita

Deerbroom lotus and low-growing forms of California sagebrush

Deerbroom lotus and dune sagebrush

Deerbroom lotus and low-growing forms of coffee berry

Deerbroom lotus and bush monkeyflowers

Deerbroom lotus and blue witch

Deerbrush ceanothus and blue ceanothuses

Deerbrush ceanothus and mock orange

Deerbrush ceanothus and fremontia

Deerbrush ceanothus and snowbell bush

Desert agave and chaparral yucca

Desert agave and Mojave yucca

Desert agave and various large cacti *Echinocereus, Echinocactus,* and *Ferocactus*

Desert alyssum and desert aster

Desert alyssum and bladderpod

Desert alyssum and apricot mallow

Desert alyssum and incienso

Desert aster and chuparosa

Desert aster and apricot mallow

Desert aster and bladderpod

Desert holly and yuccas

Desert holly and various cacti

Desert holly grape and mountain mahogany

Desert lavender and chuparosa

Desert lavender and apricot mallow

Desert lavender and desert salvias

Desert olive and willows

Desert olive and desert willow

Desert olive and mesquite

Desert sagebrush and antelope brush

Desert sagebrush and desert peach

Desert sagebrush and rabbitbrush

Desert sagebrush and mountain creambush

Desert senna and desert aster

Desert senna and incienso

Desert senna and apricot mallow

Desert senna and chuparosa

Desert willow and mesquite

Desert willow and smoke tree

Dune sagebrush and low salvias

Dune sagebrush and zauschnerias

Dune sagebrush and low-growing forms of coffee berry

Dwarf coyote bush and low-growing forms of ceanothus

Dwarf coyote bush and low-growing forms of chamise

Dwarf coyote bush and low-growing forms of manzanita

Ephedras and incienso

Ephedra and big sagebrush

Ephedra and mountain mahogany

Fernbush and desert sagebrush

Fernbush and desert peach

Fernbush and mountain creambush

Flat-top buckwheat and St. Catherine's lace

Flat-top buckwheat and bush rue

Flat-top buckwheat and laurel sumac

Flat-top buckwheat and yerba santa

Flowering ash and willows

Flowering ash and creek dogwood

Flowering ash and snowbell bush

Flowering dogwood and western azalea

Flowering dogwood and creek dogwoods

Flowering dogwood and Sierra laurel

Flowering dogwood and spicebush

Flowering dogwood and Sierra maple

Flowering dogwood and bunchberry (*Cornus canadensis*) as ground cover

Fremontia and chaparral pea

Fremontia and salvias

Fremontia and Matilija poppy

Golden fleece and bush poppy

Golden fleece and blue penstemons

Golden fleece and chaparral pea

Incienso and paperbag bush

Incienso and apricot mallow

Incienso and desert aster

Incienso and desert senna

Island pitcher sage and bush poppy

Island pitcher sage and island
snapdragon

Island pitcher sage and blue ceanothuses

Island snapdragon and bush snapdragon

Island snapdragon and bush
monkeyflowers

Island snapdragon and coyote mints

Jamesia and spiraeas

Jamesia and low-growing forms of
service berry

Jamesia and pinemat manzanita

Labrador tea and western azalea

Labrador tea and salal

Labrador tea and cascara sagrada

Labrador tea and steeple bush

Malva rosa and Santa Cruz Island
ironwood

Malva rosa and gray-leafed salvias

Malva rosa and coffee berry

Manzanitas (tall-growing forms) and
tall-growing ceanothuses

Manzanitas (tall-growing forms) and
fremontia

Manzanitas (tall-growing forms) and
holly-leaf cherry

Manzanitas and bush poppy

Manzanitas (low-growing forms) and
low-growing ceanothuses

Manzanitas (low-growing forms) and
dwarf coyote bush

Manzanitas (tall-growing forms) of two
different leaf colors

Mock heather and beach lupine

Mock heather and dune sagebrush

Mock heather and low-growing forms of
coffee berry

Mountain alder and Sierra maple

Mountain alder and high-mountain
willows

Mountain alder and water birch

Mountain chinquapin and bitter cherry

Mountain chinquapin and snowbrush
ceanothus

Mountain chinquapin and huckleberry
oak

Mountain laurel and red heather

Mountain laurel and white heather

Mountain laurel and Labrador tea

Mountain mahogany and desert
sagebrush

Mountain mahogany and antelope
brush

Mountain mahogany and mountain
creambush

Mountain and dwarf willows

Native hawthorn and western azalea

Native hawthorn and wild roses

Ocotillo and various large cacti

Ocotillo and yuccas

Ocotillo and incienso

Oregon boxwood and kinnikinnick

Oregon boxwood and Oregon grape

Oregon boxwood and ground rose

Oregon grape and evergreen
huckleberry

Oregon grape and cascara sagrada

Oregon grape and thimbleberry
Oregon grape and western azalea
Oso berry and Sierra maple
Oso berry and ninebark
Oso berry and flowering currants or
  gooseberries
Palo verde and ocotillo
Palo verde and desert willow
Palo verde and smoke tree
Palo verde and mesquite
Prickly phlox and bush poppy
Prickly phlox and California sagebrush
Prickly phlox and low-growing forms of
  blue ceanothus
Prickly phlox and fremontia
Rabbitbrush and desert sagebrush
Rabbitbrush and Palmer's penstemon
Rabbitbrush and greenleaf manzanita
Red shanks and toyon
Red shanks and scrub oaks
Red shanks and holly-leaf cherry
St. Catherine's lace and zauschnerias
St. Catherine's lace and goldenrods
  (*Solidago* spp.)
St. Catherine's lace and coffee berry
Salal and evergreen huckleberry
Salal and Labrador tea
Salal and Columbia or Fort Bragg
  manzanita
Salal and western azalea
Salal and Nootka rose
Salal and rosebay rhododendron
Santa Cruz Island ironwood and holly-
  leaf cherry
Santa Cruz Island ironwood and toyon
Santa Cruz Island ironwood and rhuses
Santa Cruz Island ironwood and
  climbing penstemon

Service berry and bitter cherry
Service berry and mountain
  creambush
Service berry and Sierra maple
Service berry and mountain ash
Shrub chinquapin and evergreen
  huckleberry
Shrub chinquapin and Columbia
  manzanita
Shrub chinquapin and Fort Bragg
  manzanita
Shrub chinquapin and glorymat
  ceanothus
Shrub tan oak and silk tassel bush
Shrub tan oak and rosebay
  rhododendron
Shrub tan oak and Sadler oak
Sierra laurel and Labrador tea
Sierra laurel and salal
Sierra laurel and rosebay rhododendron
Sierra laurel and flowering dogwood
Sierra laurel and steeple bush
Sierra maple and mountain chinquapin
Sierra maple and snowbrush ceanothus
Sierra maple and bitter cherry
Sierra maple and twin honeysuckle
Silk-tassel bush and blueblossom
  ceanothus
Silk-tassel bush and dwarf coyote bush
Silk-tassel bush and various early-
  flowering manzanitas
Silk-tassel bush and shrub tan oak
Summer holly and holly-leaf cherry
Summer holly and rhuses
Summer holly and fremontia
Summer holly and blue ceanothuses
Toyon and holly-leaf cherry
Toyon and snowbell bush

Toyon and large blue-flowered
  ceanothuses
Toyon and fremontia
Tree coreopsis and salvias
Tree coreopsis and bush monkeyflowers
Tree coreopsis and haplopappuses
Twinberry honeysuckle and flowering
  currants
Twinberry honeysuckle and western
  azalea
Twinberry honeysuckle and ninebark
Vine maple and rosebay rhododendron
Vine maple and cascara sagrada
Vine maple and flowering dogwood
Vine maple and spicebush
Vine maple and western azalea
Water birch and willows
Water birch and aspen
Water birch and western azalea
Western burning-bush and Sierra maple
Western burning-bush and stink currant
Western burning-bush and western
  azalea
Western button bush and elderberries
Western button bush and wild roses
Western button bush and hopbush
Western leatherwood and coffee berry

Western leatherwood and oso berry
Western leatherwood and evergreen
  huckleberry
Western leatherwood and early-
  flowering manzanitas
Western redbud and fremontia
Western redbud and blue ceanothuses
Western redbud and snowbell bush
Western redbud and deerbrush
  ceanothus
Western spicebush and western azalea
Western spicebush and snowbell bush
Western spicebush and mock orange
Western spicebush and dogwoods
White heather and red heather
White heather and Labrador tea
White heather and prostrate willows
White heather and Sierra primrose
White-leaf and bush lupine (yellow)
Wooly yerba santa and coffee berry
Wooly yerba santa and blue
  ceanothuses
Wooly yerba santa and bush poppy
Yerba santa and chaparral pea
Yerba santa and bush poppy
Yerba santa and chamise
Yerba santa and gray-leaf manzanitas

POPULAR CULTIVARS OF NATIVE SHRUBS

For the first-time gardener as well as the experienced old-timer, the question of cultivars becomes important in selecting native shrubs. Here, a clarification of what cultivars are and what advantages they might have is followed by a selected and annotated list.

Definition and Origin of Cultivars

"Cultivar" stands for cultivated variety. Such varieties are often specific selections made from the variations seen in cultivated garden material or in wild species. So, for example, if a certain ceanothus plant out of hundreds of the same species should stand out in some way, it is a potential candidate for being singled out, named, and propagated as a distinct cultivar. Cultivars can also include outstanding plants selected directly from naturally occurring shrubs. Finally, cultivars are often selections from deliberate crossbreeding of two botanical species or varieties. Cultivars are often selected on the basis of superior vigor, disease resistance, rapid growth, pleasing shape, tolerance of heavy soils or extra summer water, attractive year-round foliage, foliage that changes color with the season, abundant flowering, unusual flower color or size, an extended period of flowering, and attractive fruits.

Cultivars Compared to Varieties

Cultivars and varieties differ from each other, as well as from the species they arise from, in distinguishable ways. Most botanical varieties show a "suite" of differences from the species per se, whereas cultivars may vary by only small differences, caused by few genes. Whereas botanical names—including varieties—are Latin or words converted to a Latin form, cultivar names are most often given (for our purposes) in English and enclosed in single quotation marks. (Also botanical names, being Latin, are italicized, as cultivar names are not.)

Propagation of Cultivars

Because cultivars are specific genetic selections within the broader variation of a species, they seldom "come true" from seeds. Since the process of making seeds results in variation in the offspring, this result is easily predictable. The point for you the gardener is that, to propagate a special cultivar exactly, you need to use *vegetative* means of reproduction: cuttings, layering, or rooted suckers from the base of the parent shrub.

The Merits of Cultivars

Many cultivars have been established through naming in the most popular groups: ceanothuses, manzanitas, fremontias, and such. Although some of the earliest-named remain among the best, many of the cultivars listed below are old and have largely been abandoned in favor of newer ones. Any list of cultivars will cite some decidedly superior strains and some that are marginally better or not better than the run-of-the-mill plants of the given species or cross between species. In the list below, the best selections are indicated by asterisks. Don't expect most native plant nurseries to carry the most venerable or more than a few in each group; generally they have hit upon a combination of what sells best and what they feel is superior.

As to the question of whether you will want to give serious consideration to cultivars, that is a difficult matter to decide. The difficulty lies in the fact that for groups such as the ceanothuses and manzanitas, the numerous cultivars are hard to sort through; you may find as you read species descriptions in the Encyclopedia that the typical species are equally or more appealing than the cultivars themselves. In smaller groups, or where cultivars are limited in number (such as for fremontias or garryas), the choices are more straightforward. Also the choice depends upon the needs of your situation, the availability of alternative material (i.e., wild species), and your sense of adventure. There are many fine species that are seldom seen in gardens, and the potential there is still great. On the other hand, if you want more predictable results based on garden experience by horticulturists and nursery people, cultivars may be your best answer.

CULTIVARS OF NATIVE SHRUBS

No attempt has been made to list all currently available native-shrub cultivars. What follows is merely a guide to some well-known ones:

Arctostaphylos bakeri. 'Louis Edmunds'
Upright shrub to about 6 feet, with gray-green leaves and pink flowers.

A. densiflora. 'Harmony'
Grows to 8 feet tall. Bright green leaves tinged pink. Similar to A. 'Sentinel'
  *'Howard McMinn'
Dark green leaves on a low, mounded shrub to 2 feet high, with lots of rose-pink flowers in early spring.
  *'James West'
Similar to 'Howard McMinn,' but low spreading, with small, pink flowers in late winter.
  'Sentinel'
Taller; 6 to 10 feet, with large clusters of pink flowers in late winter to early spring. Vigorous. Trainable as a tree.

Arctostaphylos. 'Dr. Hurd'
Large shrub, to 12 to 15 feet high and quite broad. Pure white flowers in large clusters in March; mahogany bark, red berries.

*Arctostaphylos. 'Emerald Carpet' = A. *uva-ursi* × A. *nummularia.*
Mounding ground cover to slightly over a foot high, increasing height with age; dark green leaves, and pink flowers in March and April.

Arctostaphylos. 'Festival'
Grows to 2½ feet tall. Foliage changes color: in autumn leaves are gold, russet, or bronze. New growth in spring is scarlet. Not easy to grow.

Arctostaphylos. 'Greenbay'
Low growing—to 2 feet tall—and widespreading. Dull, deep green leaves; pink flowers. Heavy shearing is recommended.

Arctostaphylos. 'Greensphere'
At first grows as a dense sphere, with flowers produced on inside branches. Later grows 4 to 6 feet tall and opens up, with flowers better displayed. Slow growing.

*Arctostaphylos. 'Havensneck'
Low growing with trailing red stems. Bright green leaves. Fast growing and heat tolerant.

Arctostaphylos hookeri. 'Monterey Carpet'
  Compact growth to a foot tall, with branches that root as they grow.
    'Wayside'
  Tall—3 to 12 feet—with glossy dark green leaves. White flowers in late winter to
  early spring.

Arctostaphylos hookeri × A. *pajaroensis.* 'Sunset'
  Grows into a rounded shrub to 6 feet tall, with coppery new leaves and pink flowers in midspring.

Arctostaphylos. 'Indian Hill'
  Low growing—to 1 foot high—and wide spreading. Leaves gray-green; flowers
  white tinged pink. Moderately fast grower.

Arctostaphylos. 'Lester Rowntree'
  Tall, spreading shrub to 10 feet. Leaves blue- or gray-green; new stems red; flowers white flushed pink; fruits shiny red to carmine.

Arctostaphylos. 'Ophio-viridis'
  Ground cover to 1½ feet tall, with long stems. Bright green, closely spaced leaves
  overlapping in a spiral pattern (scalelike appearance). Unique form.

Arctostaphylos. 'Sandsprite'
  Low-growing shrub to 1¼ feet tall, wide spreading. Leaves light green; rose-
  colored flowers in March; mahogany-red fruits. New leaves bright red. Unusual.

Arctostaphylos. 'Sea Spray'
  Low-growing shrub to 2 feet tall; dense. Leaves dark green, leathery; flowers
  white, flushed pink.

Arctostaphylos stanfordiana. 'Trinity'
  Very beautiful: open and spreading shape. Flowers red-purple instead of pink as
  for regular species. May be short lived, but choice.

Arctostaphylos uva-ursi. 'Massachusetts'
  Small leaves and very flat stems, with good resistance to leaf spot and galls.
    *'Point Reyes'
  Dark green, closely placed leaves, with greater tolerance of heat and drought than
  'Radiant.'
    *'Radiant'
  Shiny leaves; persistent red berries; white, pink-edged flowers in late winter to
  early or midspring.

*_Arctostaphylos._ 'Winterglow'
Low shrub to 2 feet tall. Pale green leaves hidden by masses of pale pink flowers in March; bright red fruits in June. New growth coppery red. Moderately fast grower.

*_Artemisia californica._ 'Canyon Gray'
Low, mounding, graceful form; seems to flow over its surroundings.

Baccharis pilularis pilularis. 'Pigeon Point'
Has relatively large light green leaves, and is a very fast grower.
    *'Twin Peaks'
Has small, dark green leaves and is a moderate-paced grower.

Ceanothus arboreus. 'Theodore Payne' × _C. cyaneus_ 'Gentian Plume'
Tall shrub, to 14 or more feet, with open plumes of dark, gentian-blue flowers in early to mid-spring.

Ceanothus. 'Blue Cascade'
Erect shrub to 8 feet tall, with broad spread. Leaves shiny and bright green; flower cluster long and narrow, flowers medium blue, in April.

*_Ceanothus._ 'Blue Jeans'
Erect shrub to 6 feet tall; branches spread outward and upward. Leaves dark and shiny; flower clusters small, borne on side spurs, lavender. Fast growing and vigorous; good for heavy soils.

Ceanothus. 'Blue Wisp'
Erect shrub to 8 feet tall, with equal spread. Leaves pale green in small spiralled rosettes, pleasantly scented; flowers ice blue in 3-inch clusters, in April.

*_Ceanothus._ 'Concha'
Shrub to 7 feet tall, with equal spread. Dense, dark green leaves; flowers red in bud, opening dark blue in April. Fine choice.

Ceanothus. 'Consuelo'
Similar to 'Concha,' but buds are not red. Flowers in April.

Ceanothus. 'Fallen Skies'
Prostrate to 14 inches tall, wide spreading. Leaves dark green, leathery; flowers pale blue and produced in abundance in March. Fast grower. Needs good drainage.

*_Ceanothus._ 'Frosty Blue'
Shrub to 8 or 10 feet tall. Leaves dark green, deeply furrowed; long flower clusters, with sky blue flowers having a frosted look, in April. Good for heavy soils. Excellent choice.

Ceanothus gloriosus. 'Anchor Bay'
Compact shrub to about 1½ feet with tight leaves and deeper blue flowers than the usual form.

Ceanothus gloriosus exaltatus. 'Emily Brown'
At least 3 feet tall, with dark green hollylike leaves and dark violet flowers. Does well in coastal situations.

Ceanothus griseus. 'Louis Edmunds'
Five- to 10-foot height; large clusters of sea blue flowers in April and May. Tolerates heavy soil and summer water. Reliable.
    'Ray Hartman'
Tall shrub, to 18 feet; compound clusters of bluebird-blue flowers in early spring. An early selection but still good.
    'Santa Ana'
Medium shrub to 8 feet tall; flowers in short clusters of rich, pure blue from late winter to mid-spring. Needs pruning to look its best.

Ceanothus griseus horizontalis. 'Hurricane Point'
Compact, sprawling shrub to 3 feet tall, with pale blue flowers; grows rapidly but may become rank.
    *'Yankee Point'
Taller but densely branched shrub to 5 feet tall, with medium blue flowers. Better growth habit than 'Hurricane Point.' Flowers April and May.

Ceanothus impressus. 'Puget Blue'
Shrub to 6 feet tall, with small dark green leaves and 1-inch clusters of deep blue flowers. Heavy soils.

Ceanothus. 'Joyce Coulter'
Shrub to 5 feet tall but spreading to 12 feet, often forming mounds. Leaves are medium green. Flower clusters are 3 to 5 inches long, flowers medium blue, in April.

Ceanothus. 'Mountain Haze'
Shrub to 8 feet tall, with smallish round glossy leaves and spikes of medium blue-gray flowers in April. Less striking than some.

*Ceanothus oliganthus×C. spinosus. 'Blue Buttons'
Tall shrub, to 17 or more feet, growing into a vase shape; flowers in rounded clusters of intense blue in late winter to early spring.

Ceanothus. 'Owlswood Blue'
Sprawling and untidy habit of growth to 10 feet tall, and with equal spread. Leaves dark green; flower clusters 4 to 6 inches long, flowers dark blue in March.

Ceanothus papillosus roweanus. 'Joyce Coulter'
Low ground cover to about 1 foot tall with dark green, wrinkled leaves, and a profusion of dark blue flowers from spring to early summer.

*Ceanothus papillosus roweanus×*C. impressus*. 'Julia Phelps'
Shrub to at least 8 feet (often described as shorter), with dark green furrowed
leaves and dense rounded clusters of deep cobalt blue flowers in midspring.
   'Dark Star'
Similar to 'Julia Phelps' but with very small leaves, and is said to be deer proof.

Ceanothus. 'Puget Blue'
Open-patterned shrub to 6 feet tall. Leaves dark green, deeply furrowed; flower
clusters small but in dense groups, with reddish buds opening deep blue in
March or April. Good choice.

*Ceanothus rigidus. 'Snowball'
Dense, mounded shrub to 6 feet maximum in height; short glossy dark green
leaves and dense balls of pure white flowers.

Ceanothus. 'Sierra Blue'
Shrub to 20 feet tall with equal spread. Leaves glossy, medium green; flower clusters 6 to 8 inches long, the flowers medium blue. Fast grower. Makes large trunks
and is long lived.

Ceanothus thyrsiflorus. 'Millerton Point'
Tall shrub, to 12 or more feet, with narrow, 2-inch leaves and 3-inch spikes of
white flowers.
   *'Snow flurry'
Tall shrub, to over 15 feet, with 2-inch leaves and a profusion of snowy white
flowers.

*Fremontodendron mexicanum×*F. californicum*. 'California Glory'
Very prolific bloomer with deep golden flowers.
   'Pacific Sunset'
Dark yellow flowers; better disease resistance than many.
   'San Gabriel'
Similar to 'California Glory,' but leaves are deeply lobed and maplelike.

*Mahonia. 'Golden Abundance'
Dense, intricate shrub to 8 feet tall. Nearly flat dark green leaves up to 10 inches
long and 5 inches wide, with 7 to 9 leaflets of round to ovate shape and with 6 to
10 slender spines on each side. Flowers in large, dense clusters; fruit deep purple
with whitish bloom.

Rhamnus californica. *'Eve Case'
   Compact dense growth to 6 feet or so; abundant berries.
      *'Sea View'
   Dense, low-creeping growth by pinching out upright stems. Can be kept to about
   1½ feet high.

Salvia clevelandii × *S. leucophylla.* 'Allen Chickering'
   Good form with clear blue-purple flowers.

**Salvia leucophylla.* 'Pt. Sal'
   More compact form of the shrub.

GLOSSARY

ACHENE. A one-seeded fruit; its seed is dispersed from the plant while contained inside the walls of the fruit (as with, for example, unshelled sunflower "seeds").

ACID. In soil, describes a measure of pH less than 7 (neutral). Acid soils are typical of cool wet climates and are particularly common in coniferous forests.

ADVENTITIOUS. Describes roots that grow from stems rather than as part of the main root system.

AERATION. The flow of air (oxygen) through water or soil. Particularly important for maintaining health in most roots.

ALKALINE. In soil, describes a measure of pH above 7 (neutral). Alkaline soils are typical of dry, desert climates.

ALPINE. Describes plants that live above the natural timberline in the mountains. Alpine conditions are very harsh with short, intense growing seasons.

ALTERNATE. Describes the arrangement of leaves where there is a single leaf attached at any one place (node) on the stem.

ARIL. A fleshy clump of tissue attached to a seed, often brightly colored. Attracts animals, which nibble off the aril, in the process discarding the seed.

AXIL (AXILLARY). The angle between the leaf and the stem where it's attached. Axillary flowers are borne in the axil of the leaves.

BANNER. The uppermost petal of a pea-type flower.

BERRY. A fleshy, multiseeded fruit, often brightly colored.

BRACT. Any modified leaf associated with flowers. Some bracts are merely small versions of ordinary leaves; others are highly colored or modified in various ways.

BURL. An enlarged root crown, with dormant buds. The burl is important in regeneration of some shrubs after fire, such as certain species of manzanita.

BURR. Sharp, hooked spines surrounding a small fruit. Designed to catch on animal fur or human clothing for transport.

CANE. One of the main, upright stems on berry bushes and roses.

CAPSULE. A seed pod that has two or more compartments inside, *and* opens to shed its seeds.

CATKIN. A long, chainlike cluster of tiny, petalless flowers, adapted for wind pollination. Sometimes catkins resemble cones.

CHANNEL ISLANDS. Eight islands off the southern California coast, with several endemic plants.

CHAPARRAL. A kind of dense evergreen shrubs occurring on hot, rocky slopes. Such vegetation is typical of the Mediterranean climate.

CIRCUMBOREAL. Describes a distribution around the northern hemisphere. A number of plants are circumboreal, occurring in North America, northern Europe, and northern Asia.

COASTAL SAGE (SCRUB). A plant community of coastal southern California that is an open form of chaparral with soft-leaved shrubs, often with heavy sage odor. By contrast, "hard" chaparral is dense, with stiff-textured leaves.

COLORADO DESERT. California's southernmost desert, between the Peninsular Ranges of San Diego County and the Colorado River along the Arizona state line.

COMPOUND. Describes a leaf that consists of two or more discrete, separate leaflets (rather than a single blade). A compound leaf may be distinguished by the fact that the axillary bud is at the base of the whole leaf (not of the leaflets), and, when stipules are present, they too are at the base of the whole leaf.

CONE. A woody structure in which seeds are borne on flat or umbrella-shaped scales, as are produced by pines, redwoods, firs, and other conifers.

CONIFER (CONIFEROUS). A plant, usually a tree, bearing cones rather than flowers. Coniferous forests are dominated by such trees (including pines, firs, and spruces).

COPSE. A small grove of trees.

CRENATE. Describes a leaf with scalloped edges.

CULTIVAR. An abbreviated word for cultivated variety. Cultivars are propagated vegetatively so that their peculiar genetic traits do not change. Most cultivars are mutants or odd variants, as crop up occasionally in a population of more ordinary plants; if a mutant is considered superior, it might then be named and propagated as a special cultivar.

CYME. Describes (generally, as it commonly is applied) flat-topped clusters of flowers.

DAMPING-OFF. A fungal disease that attacks new seedlings as they first emerge from the soil. The condition is indicated by the top of the seedling suddenly wilting or leaning over.

DECIDUOUS. Describes a plant that loses all of its leaves at one time, typically in the fall.

DECUMBENT. Describes a plant that tends to grow near the ground, the ends of the branches only gradually turning up.

DEFOLIATE. Losing leaves, deciduous.

DESERT. An area receiving less than ten inches of rain per year, usually with very hot summers.

DIGITATE. Said of leaves that are divided into fingerlike segments.

DIOECIOUS. Having male flowers borne on separate plants from female flowers.

DISC FLOWER. One of the small central flowers found in most members of the sunflower or composite family. Under magnification, the individual disc flowers show five starlike petals.

DISSECTED. Deeply divided—in the case of leaves, lobes divided almost deeply enough to separate them into different leaflets.

DORMANT. Describes a plant or seed in a resting state. During dormancy plants grow little, or they may die back to specialized buds or underground parts.

DRUPE. A stone fruit, such as a plum, in which the fleshy ovary covers a single large seed, often with an inner shell or pit around the seed as well.

ECOSYSTEM. An entire unit of living organisms within a given framework. Technically, ecosystems include not only all of the organisms but their complex interactions.

ENDEMIC. Restricted to a specific area. In California many species are endemic to highly specialized environments, such as serpentine soils.

ENTIRE. A leaf or petal with no lobes or teeth.

ESPALIER. To train a shrub (or tree) to have branches flattened in one plane, usually against a wall. Also the trained shrub or tree.

EVERGREEN. Describes a plant that does not lose all its leaves at one time. This does not mean, however, that evergreens keep their leaves permanently; they simply retain some leaves while also shedding older leaves, throughout the year.

FAMILY. A typically large grouping of species (although some families are so small they have a single species) that are linked together by common traits (usually based on flower and fruit characteristics). When attempting to identify a new flower, the first step is to find its family. Family names usually end in -aceae: Rosaceae (rose family), Ericaceae (heather family), Asteraceae (sunflower family).

FLORIFEROUS. Full of flowers or producing many flowers.

FOLLICLE. A kind of seed pod that has one chamber and opens by one lengthwise slit (such as ninebark and milkweed pods).

FRUIT. Botanically, the ripe container in which flowering plants produce their seeds. Some fruits are pods that split open; others become fleshy and are dispersed as a unit with the seeds inside.

GENUS (PL. GENERA). The next category under family. Most families consist of several genera. Example: wild plums, hawthorn, crabapple, ninebark, and mountain ash are genera belonging to the rose family, Rosaceae. The technical genus name always begins with a capital and is italicized, and it is the first of the two names given when the scientific name is requested. (See also *species*.)

GLAND. A sticky, often rounded structure that exudes a sticky substance on leaves or on hairs attached to various parts of the plant; or in flowers, the area that secretes nectar.

GLAUCOUS. A bluish or grayish green color.

GRANITE. A rock type common in the Sierra Nevada and other mountains. It is recognized by its gray color and up close is revealed to be mottled by several kinds of embedded crystals, such as mica and feldspar.

GREAT BASIN AND RANGE PROVINCE. The vast desert valleys and ranges between the Sierra Nevada in California and the Rocky Mountains. Includes most of Nevada and Utah and parts of northern Arizona and New Mexico.

GREEN-WOODY. Describes a plant whose oldest branches feel firm and woody but lack a brown, gray, or black bark, having instead a green skin.

GYMNOSPERM. A large, varied group of plants that reproduce by seeds, but without flowers. Seeds are often but not always borne in cones.

HABIT. The overall form of a plant (low shrub, tree, vine). Don't confuse with *habitat*.

HABITAT. The kind of home in which a plant lives—its soil, slope, plant community, and other factors. Don't confuse with *habit*.

HALF-RIPE. Describes the part of the stem where wood and bark are just beginning to form and have not yet become fully hard.

HARDY. Usually applied in horticulture to plants that tolerate freezing temperatures. Often the degree of hardiness is stated as the minimum temperature at which a given species will survive.

HEAD. Where many flowers are tightly clustered together at the end of a single stem. The head is the typical arrangement of flowers throughout the composite or sunflower family.

HIP. The fleshy "fruit" of the rose. The bright orange hip is actually a sepal cup surrounding the several hard, dry achenes (the latter are the true fruits).

HOOD. Cup-shaped structures in milkweed flowers, which produce the nectar. Hoods are often colored and appear to be extra petals inside the true petals.

HUMMOCK. A raised area in a bog where conditions may be somewhat less soggy.

HUMUS. Decayed or decaying leaves and twigs.

INFLORESCENCE. The general term for a clustering or arrangement of flowers. There are many kinds of inflorescences: heads, umbels, and racemes, for example.

LANCEOLATE. Lance shaped.

LATERAL. Pertaining to the side of something.

LENTICEL. Tiny openings in the bark that allow it to breathe. Lenticels often look like tiny dots of contrasting color.

LINEAR. Describes leaves that are very narrow, with the sides nearly parallel.

LOBED. Describes a leaf or petal that consists of several rounded sections separated by deep gashes.

MIXED BORDER. A type of garden design in which different sorts of plants edge or border a path or lawn. The mixture can contain perennials, annuals, shrubs, and bulbs, for example.

MOJAVE DESERT. The relatively low desert between the Transverse Ranges of southern California and southwestern Nevada and northwestern Arizona.

MYCORRHIZA (PL. MYCORRHIZAE). Special fungi living in the upper layers of soil that form a special bond with shrub or tree roots. The fungus breaks down leaf litter into its component parts and passes some of these nutrients to the tree root; the tree root in return passes some of the sugars made by its leaves to the fungus.

NODE. The place on a stem or branch where a leaf is attached.

NODULE. Tiny swellings on roots in which special nitrogen-fixing bacteria live. These bacteria make nitrogen available in a form usable by the roots; the roots in return provide sugars for the bacteria to feed on.

NUT. A fruit with a hard outer shell and large inner, usually edible, seed.

NUTLET. A hard, one-seeded fruit that is shed as a unit (rather than its seed falling out). Generally much smaller than nuts. Nutlets are typical of members of the mint family.

OBLANCEOLATE. A lance shape turned upside down.

OBLIQUE. Describes the angle of a leaf to the sun when it is neither horizontal nor vertical. Prevents the leaf from drying out so rapidly.

OBOVATE. An ovate shape turned upside down.

OPPOSITE. Describes leaves arranged two to a node or two at the same level on the stem (paired).

OVARY. The swollen base of the pistil of a flower. The ovary contains the seeds and matures into the fruit when the seeds have ripened.

OVATE. Describes the shape of a leaf that is broad and rounded at the base, then tapers gradually to a point at the end.

PH. The measure of hydrogen and hydroxyl ions in the soil. When these are in balance, the pH is said to be neutral; more hydrogen ions makes an acid condition, and more hydroxyl ions creates an alkaline situation. The measure of pH is important in the kinds of plants that will grow in a soil; most plants do best near a pH of 7.

PALMATE. Describes leaves that are divided, veined, or lobed in a pattern like the fingers on a hand (for example, most maple leaves are palmately lobed).

PANICLE. A compound raceme of flowers. That is, a main long stem that carries many side branches, themselves rebranched.

PAPPUS. The hairs or scaly structures (often nearly microscopic) attached to the fruits in members of the sunflower or composite family. A good example is the hairy parachutes attached to dandelion fruits that allow them to float on breezes.

PEA. In flowers describes a shape characteristic of members of the pea family, Fabaceae. The flower consists of an upper petal (the banner and two side petals), wings, and two fused boat-shaped petals (the keel, located between the two wings).

PETAL. Usually the showy, colored parts of a flower (although sometimes sepals or bracts take over this role). Typically the petals are the second layer of a flower (the sepals being the outermost layer).

PETIOLE. The stalklike portion of a leaf; some leaves consist of only a thin blade, without a stalk.

PINNATE. Describes lobes, leaflets, or veins arranged like the whiskers of a feather.

PIONEER. A plant that quickly moves into and grows in a newly cleared area, such as a garden, pasture, field, or road cut.

PISTIL. The female and usually central part of a flower. The pistil typically consists of three parts: a top knob or section (the stigma), the slender tube below that (the style), and a swollen ovary at the base in which the seeds are produced.

POLLEN. The fine dustlike powder made by the stamens (most often colored yellow) that contains the male portion. (See *pollination*.)

POLLINATION. The process of moving the pollen from its source (the stamen) to the top of the pistil (the stigma). From there, the individual pollen grains send out long tubes that eventually reach the preformed seeds inside the ovary (where fertilization then takes place).

POME. A fleshy fruit similar to a berry except that the ovary is the papery inner layer around the seeds, and the fleshy layer results from the outgrowth of the receptacle, as in an apple.

PRICKLE. Spines borne along stems or twigs but between nodes (and thus not the equivalent of leaves).

PROSTRATE. Growing flat along the ground.

PUP. A miniature plantlet; typically several are produced in a circle around the parent plant.

RACE. A genetically different strain of a species, with a corresponding ecological or geographical distribution of its own.

RACEME. A flower arrangement in which a number of side branches are arrayed or attached along a main stem. Generally, the flowers open from the bottom up.

RAY FLOWER. The outer flowers of a composite or sunflower or daisy. Each ray resembles a petal, although the ray itself consists of five petals fused together into a single strap- or tongue-shaped structure.

RECEPTACLE. The end of the stem to which all parts of the flower are attached. In some cases, the shape of the receptacle is important in recognizing a particular flower (for example, three-sided receptacles that hold the seed pods of *Ceanothus*).

ROOT CROWN. The top of the root where it joins the stem. This is often the part most vulnerable to fungal attack and rot.

ROSETTE. A circular arrangement of leaves, usually at or near ground level.

SAMARA. A one-seeded fruit with a wing attached (as in maples and ashes).

SCAPE. A naked, leafless flowering stalk.

SCARIFICATION. Treating seeds by scratching, rubbing, or fraying the seed coat so that water can penetrate more easily for germination.

SCREE. Loose rocks, often on steep slopes.

SCRUB. A general term for shrubby vegetation.

SERPENTINE. A slick, bluish or greenish rock found in California's foothills and mountains. The soil derived from the breakdown of this rock is low in nutrients, particularly calcium, and has toxic amounts of magnesium and some metals.

SERRATE. Describes sawlike teeth along the edge of a leaf (the teeth pointing toward the leaf tip).

SHRUB. A woody plant with multiple branches from the base, or at least lacking a prominent trunk.

SIERRA NEVADA. The main mountain range to the east of California's Central Valley, running north and south several hundred miles.

SIMPLE. Describes a leaf whose blade is in one piece, not compound (although such a leaf may be lobed).

SPECIES. Often the smallest unit of classification, the specific kind of plant. For example, in the pine genus (*Pinus*) the many species include sugar pine (*Pinus lambertiana*), digger pine (*Pinus sabiniana*), and yellow pine (*Pinus ponderosa*). Notice that when the scientific name is cited both the genus name (the first word) and the species name (the second word) are given. Species names start with lower-case letters and are italicized.

SPHAGNUM. A special kind of moss that is very spongy and acid and has the ability to absorb large amounts of water. Sphagnum bogs are wet areas dominated by these mosses, and because the conditions there are highly specialized, only a few plants are capable of living in them.

SPIKE. A clustering of flowers in which the flowers are attached directly to a single long stalk (there are no side branches).

SPUR. Usually a long, hollow, tapered part of the petals or sepals that contains the nectar. Spurred flowers are most often pollinated only by special pollinators, such as butterflies, moths, and hummingbirds.

STAMEN. The male parts of a flower, generally occurring in a row between the petals and pistil. Each stamen consists of a stalk (the filament) and a saclike part at the end (the anther), where the pollen is produced.

STAMINODE. A sterile stamen, or stamen without the anther.

STIGMA. The top portion of the pistil, often enlarged, knoblike, or divided into lobes and sticky or fuzzy. This is where the pollen needs to be placed in order for pollination to be successful.

STIPE. A stalk that carries the ovary above the rest of the parts of the flower. (Don't confuse the stipe with the stalk to which the other flower parts are attached.)

STIPULE. Pairs of leaflike structures at the side or base of an ordinary leaf, differing from leaves in being relatively small and not prominent. Stipules sometimes appear in modified form as spines or glands, or in many cases they are absent.

STRATIFICATION. The process of wetting and chilling seeds before planting. Usually, seeds are wrapped in damp sphagnum moss or perlite and put in a refrigerator.

SUBALPINE. Describes the zone in the mountains just below timberline where there is still some tree growth. Typically the subalpine in California mountains is characterized by western juniper, mountain hemlock, whitebark pine, and lodgepole pine.

SUBSHRUB. A shrub that is half-woody, or woody only at the base, and generally low growing.

SUBSPECIES. Occurs where a species has two or more recognizable races that have their own separate geographic ranges. Subspecies are capable of forming hybrids where they overlap.

SUBWOODY. A term sometimes used to describe the degree of woodiness in the tissues of a subshrub. Also describes growth in shrubs or trees that is halfway between soft, green new growth and hard, woody mature growth.

SUCCULENT. Any plant in which part of the roots, stems, or leaves are modified to store water.

SUCKER. Sprout or shoot that appears around the base of a shrub or tree.

SUFFRUTESCENT. Subwoody or half-woody.

TALUS. Loose rocks on a steep slope. Much like scree.

TAPROOT. A single thick, deeply penetrating root (such as a carrot).

TENDER. In horticulture, describes plants that are intolerant of frost or freezing conditions.

TENDRIL. A coiled, stalklike extension of branches or leaves that helps support vines as they climb.

TEPAL. A flower structure in which the sepals and petals are colored and shaped similarly. Most members of the amaryllis and lily families have tepals.

TERMINAL. At the end or top.

TERNATE. Divided into threes.

TOMENTUM. A close, woollike covering of hairs on leaves or stems.

TOPIARY. A carefully pruned, shaped shrub or tree. Often shapes are evocative of some animal.

TREE. A woody plant with one or a few trunks (the trunk is clearly more massive than the side branches).

TRIFOLIATE. Describes leaves divided into threes.

TWO-LIPPED. Describes flower petals arranged in two distinct liplike portions with the entrance to the floral tube between. Typical of flowers in the snapdragon and mint families.

UMBEL. Formed by flowers arranged at the ends of spokelike stalks that radiate from the end of a single larger stem, umbrella like.

UNISEXUAL. Describes flowers that have either only stamens or only pistils.

VARIETY. Loosely, a subunit of the species. The term is often applied when there is variation within a species, such as different flower color, or greater or lesser size of the plant. Unfortunately, the term is so imprecise that it is often meaningless.

VEGETATIVE. Refers to the leaves, stems, and roots of the plant as contrasted with the reproductive parts, such as flowers or cones. Vegetative reproduction involves making new plants directly from the leaves, stems, and roots.

VERTICAL. Describes leaves arranged so that their edges receive the sun but their flat surfaces are at right angles to it. (In hot-summer plants, this minimizes the impact of the sun.)

WHITE MOUNTAINS. A tall desert range, straddling the California-Nevada state line on the east side of the Owens Valley and opposite the high southern Sierra Nevada.

WHORL. An arrangement of three or more leaves attached at the same level of the stem.

XERISCAPE. A landscape using little water, with plants well adapted to droughty conditions.

INDEX

Page numbers in bold type indicate locations in the Encyclopedia section; numbers in parentheses indicate illustration pages.